PRAISE FOR DAVID HEWITT AND *ON THE ROAD: RECORDING THE STARS IN A GOLDEN ERA OF LIVE MUSIC*

"My first major live recording was a very complex, worldwide television broadcast at the United Nations General assembly in New York. With dozens of stars, actors, and world leaders, I was amazed at how David Hewitt and his crew made order out of the chaos. Virtually every live recording I produced after that I booked Hewitt to run the remote trucks. I knew everything would work with no drama or excuses, no matter where it was. We recorded everything from The Eagles in Melbourne, Australia, to Eric Clapton's Crossroads Guitar Festivals and many other stars you will read about in this book."

—**Elliot Scheiner,** engineer, producer, and designer

"Roy Cicala told me Record Plant NYC had bought a remote recording truck and he wanted to make sure we engineers and assistants were ready to pull together and do the hard work of making it successful.

However, it was going to take more than a bunch of us who lived in a studio bubble to make it happen.

This is the way Roy operated at Record Plant. He relied on a gut feeling for how each of us should be designated. For example, he assigned Greg Calbi, who was an assistant, to the Master Cutting room and taught him how to master records. As usual, it was a good call. He put Shelly Yakus behind the board as well as Jimmy Iovine and myself, and many other successful engineers or producers after he had trained us all personally.

David Hewitt had just arrived at the studio. From Pennsylvania, I think. I seem to recall that he was recommended by Frank Hubach who I had played in bands with and brought into the studio. David turned out to be smart and talented in many fields. Good with a hammer or a soldering gun, a screwdriver and wiring, good with his ears. Plus, he could drive a truck. Roy knew this was his man. Soon he was running the whole deal, accompanied by Frank Hubach. David turned remote recording into an art and along the way, he has defined the way it is done. I and a good many of my compadres have been very fortunate to have shared the box with David."

—**Jack Douglas**, record producer

"In 1974, I was hired at the Record Plant Studios, NYC. Two weeks later I was let go due to cutbacks. It was a Friday, and I thought my world had ended. When I was hired back on the following Monday to work on the Record Plant remote truck with Dave Hewitt, I had no idea that it would change my life. Dave's reputation was already immense. Tall and intimidating, when he strode into the room with a booming low voice everyone listened. Going on the road with Dave prepared me in so many ways. As road warriors, not only did we have to battle weather and road conditions, but each venue had its own fortress to penetrate, and each sound company had its crew to convince and overcome. We would usually come to record in the middle of a tour, so those entrenched with the band defended their turf.

Dave was respected by all and considered the King of the Road because he could navigate through any problem. Loved and tough, he made things happen. There was only one shot, and his job was to make it work. Learning the art of problem solving from Dave under the ever-present pressure of a live performance was extremely helpful to me throughout my career. I later became a recording engineer and record producer, but always had the extra respect and invaluable knowledge for being part of Dave Hewitt's remote crew."

—**Thom Panunzio,** engineer/producer,
senior VP/A&R head, Geffen Records

"David Hewitt created and perfected the art and technique of modern remote multi-track recording with Record Plant Remote and Remote Recording Services.

His mobile recording studios not only were the facilities of choice for virtually every great artist of every genre, but, and perhaps more importantly, served as a classroom and welcoming home for countless engineers and producers.

Both as a mentor and a dear friend, David's contributions to my life have been invaluable.

David addressed the chaos of remote recording with a thoughtfully, and practically, designed facility, and calm, knowledgeable staff.

David's interactions with decades worth of entertainment royalty are fascinating reading."

—**Daryl Bornstein**, producer/engineer, road manager for Lou Reed, Leonard Bernstein, and PBS's *Great Performances*

"For decades Dave Hewitt and Remote Recording Services were our partners in the art of recording music. Whether it was a symphony at Carnegie Hall, a ballet in Lincoln Center, a show on Broadway, or a rock concert at the Cotton Bowl, Remote Recording Services was there with us and paved the way for how it got done. We will always be thankful for our collaborations in capturing truly *Great Performances*."

—**Mitch Owgang**, supervising producer on public television's
Great Performances series

"Recording in a studio was safe. The goal was to make everyone feel like they were on stage in their comfort zone. We tried to make the recording process invisible. On the other hand, with remote recordings, you never knew what would happen.

I had the honor of working with David Hewitt on many occasions. The Modern Jazz Quartet (MJQ)'s *The Complete Last Concert* remote recording, from New York's Lincoln Center, was a unique experience I will never forget. The MJQ was like recording a mini symphony, and as usual, they performed brilliantly. Our job was to stay out of the way and capture the music and magic in the room. David and his crew did just that! A seamless recording.

After mixing the project at Atlantic Recording Studios in New York, the band and label executive producer Nesuhi Ertegun and others were very pleased with the results.

I had the chance to share my experience with engineer/producers Arif Mardin and Tom Dowd, who agreed with the results.

There's nothing like the magic of a live recording: musicians blending themselves, natural leakage, and room sound . . . what a concept.

As my Dad Les Paul would say, 'Technology Doesn't Make Music.'

Thanks for the memories."

—**Gene Paul**, G&J audio

"It was an amazing time, socially and politically, and in the middle of it all was the music. No, not in the middle, leading it. Whether you thought it started with Dylan or the Beatles or the Airplane or the Dead or the Who, live music brought us all together. And it just kept going Jimi, Janis, Bruce, U2. I created *The King Biscuit Flower Hour* to bring this to everyone. The center for me was the Record Plant. Dave Hewitt and Carmine Rubino made it all happen. Dave Hewitt witnessed and recorded more of this magic than anyone. There are great stories to be told by those lucky enough to have witnessed it firsthand!"

—**Bob Meyrowitz**, founder of *The King Biscuit Flower* radio show

"There's a couple of sayings (maybe they should be called aphorisms) when it comes to a live recording: One is—the show should start on time, end on time, and, if you're lucky, no one gets hurt and the second adage is that a live recording consists of three elements: (1) the gig, (2) the location, and (3) the money, and you're only granted two out of the three. Now, with David Hewitt in the chair, the gig always started on time, ended on time (unless there were encores) and no one (at least on the crew) got hurt. Now, about the second pearl of wisdom, I'm sure David got not two out of three, but three out of three! To make sure, you'll have to read the book!"

—**Jim Anderson**, professor, Clive Davis Institute of Recorded Music, Tisch School of the Arts, New York University

"I'd imagine a large percentage of the general public don't think there's much to recording a music concert or even give it much thought at all. It's one of those things that just happens, which is all they really *need* to think. They need not have any particular awareness of someone like David Hewitt, one of the very top behind-the-scenes professional recording engineers who not only pioneered recording all sorts of concerts from the New York Philharmonic Orchestra to The Rolling Stones but turned the live recording process into an art form in itself.

When David approached me to write this blurb, I was delighted. I've known David for 40 years . . . yes, we're that old! After recording live rock shows for that long, you can imagine the stories he has. First, I'd like to explain what it takes to be a live recording engineer. For a start, nerves of steel, second knowing your equipment and crew in and out, then having A, B, and C plans . . . then, when all hell breaks loose, a recovery plan.

Over the years, I've had the absolute pleasure to have worked with David and his crew on a number of projects, actually starting and ending with The Stones. From parking and leveling his huge recording truck to negotiating with the various front-of-house and stage monitor mixers about mic choices and grounding problems to the local labor unions and police, it always seemed like there was so much to go wrong yet, once the show started, it always went smoothly, start to finish. That first recording of The Stones at Giants Stadium in New Jersey David and I did was one of the most exciting events of my career and I couldn't have shared it with a better partner.

This book is a treasure chest of fascinating and extremely fun and entertaining stories. I know you will enjoy exploring the incredible journey of the man who defined recording the biggest music shows on the planet."

—**Bob Clearmountain**, engineer, producer, and designer

"I met Dave Hewitt in 1972 when I lived in London Terrace Towers in Chelsea, NYC.

I had recently bought a vintage Ferrari which was a bit ropey, but I loved it.

I took Dave for a ride up the West Side Highway at probably close to 100mph—he really dug it and we bonded over the love of great sports cars and racing!

My first taste of recording with Dave was with the Record Plant mobile unit, which he was running. We recorded the band Foghat in the magnificent old Woolworth Mansion on Long Island, NY.

Dave always had the most amazingly even keeled demeanor, even when all about us things were coming apart or mics and cables were malfunctioning, Dave always had an answer and was calm as could be under fire!!

I loved to record bands in unusual spaces like old mansions and there was quite a laundry list of the oddest buildings I found that on the surface one would say 'You gotta be kidding—it will never work out!'. . . way too reverberant etc. But Dave was always there for the adventure and the gung-ho attitude of 'Let's try it!!'

A great example was Ace Frehley's solo album for KISS. I found the Colgate mansion in Connecticut with fabulous different sounding acoustics for each room. Ace's amps in the main living room, bass in the parlor, and the drums on the first landing of a massive staircase! Oh, and plenty of ghosts to keep everyone unhappy at night!!

What great sounds we got with you, Dave. You are the king of remote sound recording!"

—**EHK** (Eddie Kramer), engineer, producer, and designer

ON THE ROAD

ON THE ROAD

Recording the Stars in
a Golden Era of Live Music

David W. Hewitt

Backbeat
Books

Guilford, Connecticut

Backbeat Books
An imprint of Globe Pequot, the trade division of The Rowman & Littlefield
Publishing Group, Inc.
4501 Forbes Blvd., Ste. 200
Lanham, MD 20706
BackbeatBooks.com

Distributed by NATIONAL BOOK NETWORK

Grateful acknowledgment is made to the following for permission to use their writings:

Daryl Bornstein, Taxi Briell, David DB Brown, Eddie Kramer, and Joel Spector.

Unless otherwise noted, all photographs are from the author's personal collection.

British Library Cataloguing in Publication Information available

Library of Congress Cataloging-in-Publication Data

Names: Hewitt, David W., author.
Title: On the road : recording the stars in a golden era of live music /
    David W. Hewitt.
Description: Guilford, Connecticut : Backbeat Books, 2021. | Includes
    index.
Identifiers: LCCN 2021009839 (print) | LCCN 2021009840 (ebook) | ISBN
    9781493056170 (cloth) | ISBN 9781493056187 (epub)
Subjects: LCSH: Hewitt, David W. | Sound engineers—United
    States—Biography. | Live sound recordings—History—20th century.
Classification: LCC ML429.H46 A3 2021 (print) | LCC ML429.H46 (ebook) |
    DDC 781.49/092 [B]—dc23
LC record available at https://lccn.loc.gov/2021009839
LC ebook record available at https://lccn.loc.gov/2021009840

To my nuclear family:
The Colonel and Mrs. W. W. Hewitt (USAF) who brought life, love, and meaning to a bunch of unruly Air Force brats: me (David), brother Gary, and the twins, Lynn and Laurel Hewitt. Proud of you all.

To the loves of my life:
Sherrie Hill who brought her love, her music, and a recording career to my life. I couldn't play guitar well enough to be in her band, but I learned how to press the record button. I still listen to my muse.

Lynne Rosenberg who brought the joy of family life with our three wonderful civilian brats, Ryan, Allison, and Nathaniel. They in turn brought more wonders, Eva Skye and Benjamin Hewitt. I am so proud of them all!

And Kate Draper, who brought her many arts, love, and a New York City life back to me just in time. Saved my sanity and taught me so much.

I will always be grateful for having you all in my life.

To my sports car racing heroes, Bob Holbert and Roger Penske, for early lessons on when to go fast and when to turn left.

To my music recording heroes who allowed me to turn left: Bob Liftin, Joel Fein, and Chris Bond at Regent Sound Studios; Chris Stone and Roy Cicala of Record Plant Studios in New York; Frank Hubach who hired me on the Record Plant Remote Truck and all the many "Planters" who were fortunate to work there from 1968 to 1987. See the Rogues list. They are family to this day.

To Phil Gitomer, who joined me on the Record Plant Remote Truck in 1978 and never left until the last truck did in 2016. Phil undertook every responsibility in that demanding live recording business and perfected it. From the complex stage craft of Rock Tours, driving and maintaining the big Peterbilts, mastering all the recording technology from analog to digital, and finally, for being a Mensch and my greatest friend for all those years. Cheers Phil!

CONTENTS

FOREWORD

Like most boys, I always thought that my dad was the best. It wasn't until I started working with him and joining him on the road at age thirteen that it was first confirmed. As I sit writing an introduction to a book full of his stories, I still believe that he is the best.

Very few people ever get to work with one rock star, let alone the stars of nearly every musical genre ever invented. Everyone from Aerosmith to Frank Zappa, Miles Davis to Frank Sinatra, and from Ozzy to Pavarotti flowed through his fingers on the faders. His discography is simply mind-bending, but to him, it was just a day at the office—wherever that office might be parked that day.

Over the last year or so, when we were discussing the stories that he would include in this book, so many were left on the cutting room floor that it blew my mind just how much music my father has had his hands on. He's always been a humble man, not thinking that his role was particularly important, yet he was incredibly demanding of himself and his crew to make sure everything went perfectly. He was as committed to getting the job done right as anyone I've ever seen and is directly responsible for instilling that work ethic in me as well.

My father excelled in that and, most importantly, not missing any of those details. I've seen his notes from when he was a tape-op at the beginning of his career, and they were impeccable. He would revise input lists and track sheets incessantly. He always made sure his gain structure was perfect for the recording. He nearly always deferred to the band's engineer to choose microphones that the band was used to working with and would only raise an issue if something was unworkable. But he could always make things workable. It is in his nature to take what he's given and make it shine. Even when his role was backing up another engineer, he planned and executed the job with the same level of attention as if he were completely in charge.

His dedication to the job of capturing a live performance made him one of the most in-demand live engineers in the world. His professionalism earned him the respect and friendship of the most discerning and talented artists, producers, and engineers. Neil Young refused to do an *MTV Unplugged* show unless my father and his truck were there. Ed Cherney demanded his presence at any live event he recorded, even if the event couldn't be on our truck. After years in retirement, and more than 30 years after making *Live Bullet* together, Bob Seger brought dad in on his last tour and made a point of visiting the truck to say hello.

One of my earliest memories of actually working with dad on a gig was a tribute show of some kind at the Capitol Center in Washington, DC. I must have been thirteen years old and sitting on the couch in the Black Truck working on some task. David Crosby walked into the truck looking for my dad. Of course, I knew who he was from all the music that my father shared with me, but the idea that a rock legend was looking for *my* father didn't quite hit home at the time. He would always explain to me that it was just part of the job. Then there was the time that Keith Richards called the house looking for him, and my aunt, who was babysitting us at the time, innocently answered the phone. Another time I wound up at a meet-and-greet at an Aerosmith show when I was in high school, and I boldly asked Steven Tyler if he remembered my dad from their time working together on *Rocks*, *Draw the Line*, and many live shows. He lit up and boomed "David Hewitt from Record Plant? Hell yeah! How's he doing? Who are you??" Joe Perry turned around and asked the same. My dad is *indeed* cool.

The stories in this book are just the highlights and, maybe, some more revealing pet project moments in the career of David Hewitt. I'm overjoyed that he has shared them, so the world might know who the guy behind some of the greatest live recordings is. I'm so excited for this private, humble, and honorable man to open up and share his experiences, and I'm so proud of the body of work that he has created in the musical universe and now in the literary space. I hope that you enjoy these stories as much as I enjoyed growing up with them.

Ryan Jonathan Hewitt

PREFACE

Every story has to start somewhere . . .

Music was not my first love . . . first there was flying. My father was an Air Force pilot and flew B-17 bombers in World War II. When he returned home to Montana, it was to start a civilian aircraft dealership. He took me flying when I was 18 months old, and I loved it! There was music at home. Mom and Dad loved their Big Band 78s, and I even had a little kid record player. Listening to Tex Ritter singing "I've Been Everywhere" may have started me dreaming of a life on the road. In the late 1940s, we did'nt have a TV set, but the radio provided all the entertainment we needed: *Sky King*, *The Lone Ranger*, and of course, *Abbott and Costello* kept us entertained.

My father was called up with the start of the Korean conflict, and he flew Douglas C-47s, airlifting military supplies, personnel, and combat medical evacuations. He stayed in the Air Force, and in 1953 we were stationed in Mobile, Alabama. Many Air Force bases supported a civilian Aero Club with a few light planes that pilots could fly to stay current. My father was busy developing the new Convair C-131s, but he would take me flying on weekends whenever he could. I began to dream of becoming a fighter pilot.

In the 1950s' South, country and rockabilly music was on the radio, and my aunt blasted it. I liked Gene Vincent, Carl Perkins, and even Elvis. It was still the Jim Crow South in those days, which was hard for me to understand, but my parents, who grew up hardscrabble in the Great Depression, taught us that a person's worth is not determined by the color of their skin. Those lessons stayed with me for life.

My father's next deployment was San Antonio, Texas, and they had a great Aero Club at Stinson Field, which was probably the oldest civilian airfield in the country. I was now old enough to hang out there, sweeping out the hanger, and cleaning the airplanes in exchange for rides and informal lessons. There was no question in my mind that I was headed for the Air Force Academy. But there were other distractions now; music was becoming more important because of those blossoming young girls. Now Elvis made a bit more sense because the girls loved him, but I really liked Link Wray, The Coasters, and Bill Justis's "Raunchy." I had one of the first Japanese portable transistor radios plugged in my ear and earned enough money at my history teacher's chicken ranch to buy a black leather jacket. I was now a "juvenile delinquent." My interest in the mechanics of aircraft started to turn toward hot rods and drag racing.

In 1960, we rotated to France, where my father started with the C-130 Hercules program. We lived in a beautiful chateau in the little village of Conches for a year before being transferred to Wiesbaden, Germany. There was an Aero Club and I continued flying, but a US plane had been shot down over East Germany and because it was during the Cold War, all civilian flights were grounded. That ended my chance for a solo flight. But my love for automobiles had turned to European sports car racing, which was enjoying a postwar golden era. I traveled around Europe to the great race tracks, the Nürburgring, Spa-Francorchamps, and Le Mans. I was now dedicated to building race cars. Music was still all-important to my social life and girlfriends. We had the great US hits playing in the US teen club jukebox in addition to all the British bands on Radio Luxembourg. The Beatles were now playing in Germany at Hamburg's Indra club and would soon take over the world. Later on, I foolishly turned down a trip to see them in London because there was a race at the Nürburgring that weekend.

We rotated back Stateside in 1964 just in time for the World's Fair in New York. The United States had changed a lot in four years, and the culture shock was intense. Listening to manic New York AM radio disc jockeys was quite different from the European stations. I seriously studied auto mechanics and did an internship at my racing hero Bob Holbert's Porsche dealership. He was kind enough to give me a recommendation to Roger Penske's first Chevrolet Dealership in Philadelphia. I managed to get to the 1966 Watkins Glen Can-Am race with one of the pit crew, just in time for Mark Donohue to crash the Lola T-70. I then managed a small shop for a British chap who raced a Lotus 23B and had promised me an old Porsche

356 to campaign—yeah, right . . . the first of many lessons in business. My next gig was at an MG and Jaguar dealership that also featured a pretty young receptionist. She introduced me to the local music scene that was thriving in Philadelphia. It was another golden era! FM "underground" radio now played a wide variety of music and inspired me to pick up a guitar again. I saw Gabor Szabo at the Jazz Showboat Theater, Bonnie Raitt at The Main Point, and Cream at the Electric Factory. There were so many incredible guitar players appearing everywhere around Philly.

Then I met this lovely singer/songwriter who really taught me the true love of music. As her music evolved, I couldn't keep pace as a guitar player, but I figured out how to press the record button. Gradually those race cars faded in the distance and music recording became my life—yet another golden era.

ACKNOWLEDGMENTS

My sincere thanks to fellow recording engineer Dirk Devlin, who encouraged me to write this book, and his wife, Anne G. Devlin of Max Gartenberg Literary Agency, who found a home for it here with Backbeat Books.

To the many musicians, engineers, producers, and all who became friends and clients over the last 50 years, I hope this book will bring some good memories of that golden age of live music.

I especially want to remember the late Ed Cherney and his frequent partner in crime, Elliot Scheiner, or the "Ed and Els Show" as they were known. They were funny enough in everyday life, but when they would take the podium at AES or other functions, it would really get hilarious. Like the time they did a last minute save at the TEC Awards. I was to be inducted to the TEC Hall of Fame by Neil Young, who had a problem on the way and couldn't make it. Ed and Els stepped up to the podium and ad-libbed a bit of a roast for me; it was great fun. They saved my moment in the spotlight!

That spirit would continue on some of the major shows we would record together, like the Eric Clapton Crossroads Guitar Festivals and Woodstock '94, or Mud-Stock, as it became known. On one of the late-night Raves, the vocals were droning along, so we hooked up a mic in the remote truck so Ed could sing along; it was hysterical.

Ed passed on October 22, 2019, and a celebration of Ed Cherney's life was held at Village Recorders on December 7, 2019. It was a gathering of family more real than any industry trade or award show could ever create. Ed was an LA guy, but his friends came from around the world. In my retirement, I no longer work on all those LA shows, but I had to go out for Ed and Rose. It was the most heartwarming gathering imaginable. The Mourner's Kaddish given by Cherney's rabbi and joined by many voices, was so powerful with the overflowing crowd of friends. Many speakers and much music followed. It was a fitting farewell to a special friend. A salute to you, Ed.

A special thanks to Record Plant Studios in New York 1968–1989.

The rogues list of those who helped keep the remote trucks rolling: the Boss: Roy Cicala, Penn Stevens, Paul Prestopino, Michael Guthrie, Jack Douglas, Jay Messina, Carmine Rubino, Jim Reeves, Frank Hubach, Shelly Yakus, Rod O'Brien, Thom Panunzio, Jimmy Iovine, Paul Sloman, Phil Gitomer, Kooster McAllister, David DB Brown, Norman Mershon, Lila Wassenaar, Randi Mitchell, Patti Joblon, Fred Ridder, Fritz Lang, John Venable, Dave Roberts, Taxi Briell, Steve Barash, Jim Falconer, Neil Steingart, J. B. Matteotti, Doug Tourtelot, and all the other Record Planters who lent their support and encouragement.

The Remote Recording Services years, 1984–2002

Paul Wolff for the API; Jim Falconer, Designer; Glenn Bostock, Cabinet Maker; Brian Skinner, Fabricator; Ron Lorman, Speaker Consultant; and Sean McClintock, Stage Manager, Fabricator, and Digital Engineer.

Special thanks to my legal mensch, Fredric Rubin Esq.

The Brinton Services, Inc. years, 2003–2009

Thanks to the Brinton Family: Karen, James, and Lorraine Brinton. Special thanks to Sam Berkow for his brilliant designs. A whole other book.

SST and IIWII Studios, 2012–2014

Thanks to John Hanti for surviving me; Hurricane Sandy, rebuilding the flooded studios; and for the Rolling Stones secret sessions.

And finally, many thanks to my oldest son, Ryan Hewitt, who has supported my remote recording adventures from his first gig with me at the age of fourteen, pulling cables on a rock 'n' roll stage and helping build the remote trucks. His career as a recording engineer and producer has long exceeded mine, and he has become my trusted advisor to this day. Love ya, Ry!

❶

INTO THE STUDIO
AND OUT ON THE ROAD!

Early Hall & Oates, Bruce Springsteen, and the Rise of Rock 'n' Roll Radio

FIRST THE STUDIO

As a frustrated musician looking for a gig in a recording studio, I had no qualifications other than loving music and wanting to learn. There were no schools for recording back then, but there was the "indentured servitude" approach. I had been to several studios with my singer/songwriter girlfriend to cut demos and I saw my future. One of those studios was Regent Sound Studios in Philadelphia. Chief engineer Joel Fein was kind enough to let me apprentice for some months gratis until I became worth $50 a week. I loved every minute of it. We were definitely number two behind Joe Tarsia's famous Sigma Sound Studios, home to Gamble & Huff, producers of all those great "Philly Soul" records. But we did manage to work with Stevie Wonder; jazz great Chico Hamilton; and a young folk duo, Daryl Hall and John Oates. In fact, I ended up going up to New York with them and guitarist Christopher Bond to meet Tommy Mottola, who had just started with Chappell Music Publishing. Tommy became their manager and got them signed to Atlantic Records with the master arranger Arif Mardin producing their first record. I would work with John and Daryl many times over the years as they became international stars, and also with Tommy on his way to becoming CEO of Sony Music Global. There are many stories there, not the least of which is Tommy discovering Mariah Carey.

In the predigital era of live recording, you needed to lug a lot of gear around to the musician's location. Unlike all those great live jazz and classical records recorded in mono or stereo, clients now wanted multitrack recording. My first "remote" involved schlepping a new 650-pound Ampex MM-1000 16-track recorder and way too much gear in cardboard boxes to record a demo for what would become the feature film, *The Buddy Holly Story*. It was a steep learning curve; film production is a whole different universe in which music is just a small part. When Regent Sound got a booking to record a big live TV pilot at the Academy of Music, it was time to call for help. The show featured a 26-piece Richie Rome Orchestra, an electric rhythm section, and lots of vocalists. I knew the Record Plant Studios in New York had recorded former Beatle George Harrison's The Concert for Bangladesh with their remote recording truck. I called the studio, and they connected me to co-owner Chris Stone. Chris and Gary Kellgren founded the Record Plant in 1968 and were at the top of their game. Chris was all high energy and enthusiasm: "No problem; we'll take care of everything! I'll send my best crew and gear." As promised, the remote truck and crew were there bright and early, with crew chief Frank Hubach managing all the details, and veteran engineer Carmine Rubino, fresh from recording a live album for the British band Yes, which became *Yessongs.*

I was amazed at how fast and efficiently the Record Plant crew set up and solved the many problems of a one-off complex live recording. There were so many things that you never have to deal with in studio life: union stage crews, sound reinforcement interface, television producers, orchestra and artist camera blocking (your microphones are in my shot!), and if you are lucky, a few minutes for a sound check. Then the adrenaline rush of the live show opening with a packed house cheering the emcee, "Ladies and gentlemen, please welcome . . ." and the two Ampex MM-1000s are recording huge reels of 16-track tape in staggered record for total backup. No one dares miss a second of a live show because there is no going back. It's controlled chaos for hours and then suddenly it's over and the applause winds down with the faders. It's time to stop tape and check the playback—all good? Great; that's a wrap, get the truck packed up, and on the road.

The next day in the studio, I was thinking, "You know, that was kind of like the sports car racing business I used to do, only instead of a race car, I'm hauling a recording studio around. It's not quite as dangerous as racing, but damn near as loud!" Then I'd travel to some other theater and record a different band. And I found that I liked the idea.

OUT ON THE ROAD

Regent Sound had been sold to the entrepreneur Anthony A. Martino, founder of the AAMCO Transmissions chain. Tony was a great hands-off owner who let Joel and I run the studios and even allowed me to rebuild the old Cameo Parkway Studio B, which was better suited for rock bands. I had previously commissioned Everything Audio in LA to do a new studio design for Regent Sound when it looked like we had a big client commitment. That didn't materialize, but I learned a lot and was able to help design the updates. It was a great experience and sounded pretty good but was limited to the 8-track Liftin console and Scully 280 8-track recorder. There just weren't enough bookings to keep the studio busy and Tony had just opened his new MAACO auto painting franchise business. Last time I looked, they made $500 million per year.

I decided to try my luck on the West Coast. Record Plant LA was building a new studio in Sausalito, just outside of San Francisco. I drove out to California with my girlfriend Dusty in a 1969 VW camper and met with Record Plant cofounder Gary Kellgren. He was receptive, but the studio was not yet operational, and he had already brought engineer Thom Flye out from New York. So, I headed down to Record Plant LA and stopped in to see Chris Stone. He had sold the New York studios and was concentrating on the West Coast operations. Chris was nice, but there were already guys waiting in line for any open positions. Ditto with the other studios I visited. We were low on money, so we headed back East. We stayed with friends on a farm in Pennsylvania until I could find a studio gig.

I visited Record Plant in New York early in January 1973 to see about work. Frank Hubach was now the director of remote operation, and when he saw me in the hallway, literally hijacked me to go on a remote. Record Plant was always short on qualified assistant engineers that had any road experience. Well, I had plenty of that and had even driven trucks in the military—plus I knew how to run the Ampex MM-1000 recorders. We went to Buffalo in the dead of winter. This was the first recording for a new Record Plant client, D.I.R. Radio Network and the *King Biscuit Flower Hour*. The name was derived from an early blues radio program, and they were building a new syndicated live radio show that would become hugely successful. They were quite eclectic in their programing, and the band we were recording was a fiery fusion group, the Mahavishnu Orchestra. They were led by English guitarist, John McLaughlin and drummer Billy Cobham (who met while recording Miles Davis's *Bitches Brew*) and included keyboardist Jan Hammer, bass player Rick Laird, and violinist Jerry Goodman. They were electrifying, and this original lineup would soon change, making this a classic recording. This show would be paired with other bands as D.I.R.'s debut on national FM radio. Veteran engineer Jim Reeves would be at the board for this important beginning.

There was also an up-and-coming rock band opening for them called Aerosmith. I would see a lot of those guys in the years to come, but for now I had to concentrate on the headliner.

From Buffalo we drove directly to Boston to record the Boston Pops Symphony Orchestra conducted by Arthur Fiedler for RCA Red Seal Records. The RCA engineers insisted on taking the console and recorders out of the remote truck and moving them upstairs into the concert hall. The client is always right and thankfully Frank had come prepared with a B-3 organ dolly from the studio, so we turned the DeMedio console on end and moved it upstairs. It was a fantastic learning experience for me. As I placed the microphones, directed by the veteran RCA engineers, I was able to walk among the orchestra musicians while they were rehearsing. Listening to musicians of that caliber up close was a classic epiphany, although the music wasn't classical. It was the Boston Pops Orchestra and the album was to be titled *Greatest Hits of the 70s*. The sessions went well, and as without an audience, Fiedler was able to get as many takes as he needed. The album was issued in the Quadradisc format and discreet four-channel vinyl. Try finding a phono cartridge for that now.

After moving the console and machines back downstairs, we found that the truck lift gate battery was dead! It was freezing cold and getting dark and there was no way even the strongest stagehands could lift those monsters into the truck. Frank spotted a construction site down the street and bribed a forklift operator to come and load the gear up onto the truck—yet another lesson in creative problem-solving on the road.

We only had one travel day, so it was a mad dash for New York City to record a little-known artist named Bruce Springsteen at Max's Kansas City. Max's was a hip hangout for notable artists like Andy Warhol, Allen Ginsberg, and Lou Reed. Bruce would be the opening act for the singer Biff Rose. Springsteen had just released his first album, *Greetings from Asbury Park*. The original E Street Band was backing him up, and they smoked through two amazing sets. According to Bruce's biography, he was still sleeping on the floor of a friend's apartment in New Jersey and busing to New York. He would make the rounds in the Village, where he met Jackson Browne at The Bitter End folk club, and opened for Dave Van Ronk and other artists at Max's to keep paying those obligatory dues.

Bruce's show would be combined with the Mahavishnu Orchestra gig and a Blood, Sweat & Tears recording to become the first *King Biscuit Flower Hour* live radio show on February 19, 1973. D.I.R.'s *King Biscuit Flower Hour* was founded by visionary producers Bob Meyrowitz and Peter Kauff and would become a huge live recording client for Record Plant in the years to come.

It's hard to imagine today, but back then radio was about the only way to hear new music. Television was just beginning to air live rock shows, and of course, there was no Internet. The cassette had not yet arrived, so there was no way to make copies of music unless you owned an expensive reel-to-reel tape recorder. So, every Sunday night at 8:00 p.m. more than 300 FM radio stations around the United States would air the latest *King Biscuit* show with great live bands and interviews that you couldn't hear on playlist radio. It was hugely successful and aired until 2007, but you can still find those shows on the Internet.

I would see a lot of Bruce Springsteen in the next few years because he spent endless hours recording his albums *Born to Run* and *Darkness on the Edge of Town* at Record Plant in New York. I think he still holds the record for the number of two-inch master tapes recorded. Record Plant veteran Thom Panunzio, who worked on many of those sessions, told me the number was more than 500. The lesson being: never stop tape; you might miss the magic take!

Thus, began the rise of a guy named Jimmy Iovine from lowly assistant to Bruce's engineer, then on to star producer of Tom Petty and Stevie Nicks, and finally, to music mogul. He was a cofounder of Interscope, Geffen A&M Records, then with Dr. Dre, Beats, and the $3 billion deal with Apple Music. Back then at Record Plant, he was just "Jimmy Shoes" to us, sort of a Brooklyn honorific after his footwear fashion sense and nicknamed like in the gangster movies.

Every success story starts somewhere; Jimmy had been working at Phil Ramone's A&R Studios before he came to Record Plant. I know that because he ran right into me as I was coming out of Studio A. Without an apology, he demanded "Where's Roy Cicala!!" and I pointed him to the right door. He had just been let go at A&R, but Phil sent him over to Roy, who had also worked at A&R. In fact, about half of Record Plant's staff had once worked at A&R.

Anyway, after that frantic week on the road, I needed to go back home to my forest retreat at the Delaware Water Gap in Pennsylvania and at least get a change of clothes. In the days before cell phones, I had to call in to Record Plant to see if they needed me for any last-minute shows. I had just missed a Stevie Wonder gig at Carnegie Hall, but there was another Steve, Stephen Stills and his band Manassas were playing the Academy of Music in New York and then ABC television's new *In Concert* rock show at a Brooklyn venue, Bananafish Gardens, which was named after the J. D. Salinger short story. The show was a bit complicated because not only did they have Stills's large band, the Mahavishnu Orchestra again, but also Randy Newman and the Dr. Hook Band. They all shuffled through the narrow stage of the magnificent old 1927 Loews Theater. Sadly, it was later demolished, but it continued my lifelong interest in those wonderful classic theaters.

I was continuing my education in live television with Record Plant engineer Jay Messina, there to assist the ABC union engineer, who was not used to dealing with large numbers of rock-and-roll musicians. Rehearsals were moving right along until a strange thing happened. I ran out to the stage for a set change, but when I opened the stage door, it was pitch black and totally silent. Then complete chaos erupted! There had been a massive electrical failure for most of Brooklyn, and we were out of business until Con Ed could get us back online. The upside was that it gave me time to visit with the video crew and learn more about their technology. They were recording on the huge Ampex VR-2000 Quad 2-inch videotape recorders. It was the same transport that our MM-1000 2-inch audiotape recorders were based on. Those video trucks were a whole different world with minimal audio capability. They were used to recording sports and talk show entertainment and not these loud hippy rock bands—and some of the older TV guys were not happy about it. We did eventually get our power back and ended up with a great show. I was always a fan of Stills's guitar playing and would often get to record him in the years to come. This was groundbreaking television back in the day, and some of the classic ABC *In Concert* episodes can still be found on the Internet.

I was still living at a mountain retreat near the Appalachian Trail in Pennsylvania and commuting to Record Plant gigs . . . that couldn't last. Hubach managed to get me a part-time tech gig aligning tape machines in the studio so we could almost afford a New York apartment and not miss any remotes. Record Plant had many great engineers available, but they were short on tech staff. However, they did have a gentle genius heading the tech department, Pendleton Stevens. Pen was a Princeton grad and Army Signal Corp vet who was an old school chief electrical engineer.

In this digital age of instantly obsolete software and cheap throw-away hardware, it's hard to imagine designing, building, and modifying the analog audio equipment needed to run three studios, a mix room, duplication, and mastering rooms running around the clock every day. Pen, Paul "Presto" Prestopino, and many others kept Record Plant studios and remote trucks at the top of their game for decades.

The wonderful thing about the studios of that era and Record Plant New York, in particular, was the sense of camaraderie and adventure. If you wanted an entry-level job and were lucky enough to be in the right place at the right time with the right attitude, the door might open a crack. Then you had to survive the grueling work schedule and the freshman initiation, which might include fire extinguisher fights, being gaffer-taped to a chair and rolled out on 44th Street at three o'clock in the morning, or something less harmful, like being ordered to go empty out the tape hiss from the Dolby racks.

Maybe after cleaning toilets, logging tapes in the library, and learning how to set up sessions, anything from vocal overdubs to full-blown orchestras, you might become an assistant engineer and be allowed in the control room. In a couple of years, maybe you'd get a break and be thrown into a session as the engineer. Rough as it sounds, there were always the "adults on duty" watching over you to make sure you learned your studio craft and culture. Chief engineer Roy Cicala was now the owner of Record Plant New York, and along with senior engineers Shelly Yakus and Jay Messina, you would be guided up to your solo flight.

Many talented people graduated from Record Plant New York to become the legends of the record business. Jack Douglas produced Aerosmith, John Lennon, and many more. Jimmy Iovine produced Tom Petty, U2, Dr. Dre, and Billions for Beats. Thom Panunzio worked with Ozzie Osbourne, Joan Jett, Alice Cooper, and headed Interscope Studios for Iovine. Paul Sloman was the studio manager then and went on to head Atlantic Records Studios, A&M Studios, and Sony's Studio Complex in New York. Greg Calbi graduated from Record Plant's cutting room to senior mastering engineer at Sterling Sound. He has mastered about 7,500 records!

And just a few records were made at Record Plant New York . . .

Jimi Hendrix: *Electric Ladyland* (his studio was not finished yet)
John Lennon: *Imagine, Double Fantasy*
George Harrison: *The Concert for Bangladesh* (live recording)
Woodstock: *Music from the Original Soundtrack*
Aerosmith: *Toys in the Attic, Rocks, Draw the Line, Live Albums*
Bruce Springsteen: *Born to Run, Darkness at the Edge of Town, Live 1975–1985*

David Bowie: *Lodger, David Live 1974,* and *Station-to-Station Live Nassau Coliseum*

Don McLean: *American Pie*

Cheap Trick: *Cheap Trick*

Blue Oyster Cult: *Don't Fear the Reaper* (famous *Saturday Night Live* more cowbell skit)

Rolling Stones: *Still Life* (live), *Let's Spend the Night Together* (film), etc.

Chuck Berry: *Hail! Hail! Rock 'n' Roll* feature film

And hundreds more.

2

THE LONG AND WINDING ROAD

Record Plant Studios, John Lennon,
and Later, Paul, George, and Ringo

In the early 1960s, my Air Force family was stationed in France and Germany. Dad was a pilot, flying C-130 Hercules to the "garden spots" of Africa and the Middle East. It was the Cold War. He couldn't talk about it, and we kids were too busy exploring Europe to ask. Many years later his stories were incredible.

Yes, there was Beatlemania in Germany and certainly among all of us military and diplomatic brats attending US high schools in Europe. I first heard the Beatles' records in English over Radio Luxembourg in 1962 and would later hear them singing in German over local radio stations in Wiesbaden Bierstubes. I still remember one instance where I was standing at the bar (drinking age was not an issue in Germany) and the jukebox was playing a Beatles song in English. The guy next to me, dressed in jeans and a leather jacket, was singing along with a perfect accent and had a pack of Marlboro's by his ashtray. I had my Lucky Strike cigarette, but no match, so assuming he was a US soldier, I asked him for a light. He looked puzzled at me and shook his head, "Nicht sprechen English." Americans always assume every European speaks some English. I would learn that most Europeans speak at least two or three languages but would not admit it, if I didn't try to speak something in their language. So, I learned how to talk about cars and beer.

I started my sports car racing days in Germany and a friend who imported British cars invited some of us to London for a Beatles show in 1963. I didn't go because there was a race at the famed Nürburgring course I wanted to see—big mistake. I would attend many more races, but I would never again have a chance to see the Beatles perform as a group.

Fast forward to New York City in 1973, where I had just started working at Record Plant. One day I walked in just as John Lennon and Yoko Ono were walking out! I had no idea they were recording there. I thought that perhaps I could make up for missing the Beatles in London! John Lennon was there recording his album *Mind Games* with Roy Cicala, now the owner of Record Plant New York, and engineer Jack Douglas, who would go on to produce many of John's later albums.

His next album, *Walls and Bridges*, would also be recorded at Record Plant in 1974. Roy Cicala had been mentoring a young engineer named Jimmy Iovine and allowed him to record overdubs with Lennon. Jimmy's career really started to take off at this point. His name may sound more familiar these days as Dr. Dre's partner selling Beats to Apple for $3 billion. Back then he was known as "Jimmy Shoes."

John Lennon and Yoko Ono had become part of the Record Plant family; I would often see them when I returned from a late-night recording gig on the remote truck. We recorded many shows in New York City and the entire East Coast. As the remote business grew, we would go west to Detroit and Chicago and south to Nashville, Atlanta, and Miami. Later on, as I built the bigger diesel remote trucks, we would range farther out to the West Coast from Los Angeles and San Francisco to Seattle. We managed to cross the border into Canada as well.

One summer day I was out working on the remote truck, which was parked across the street from the studio. The lift gate was halfway down and the big rear doors were open, exposing the studio interior. John Lennon happened to come outside, noticed the truck and walked over. We sat on the lift gate and just talked about random stuff: cabbages and kings, nuts and bolts. I think he was just glad to be an ordinary New Yorker for a few minutes. Then he smiled and became John Lennon and went back to work in the studio.

John Lennon's final live performance was for a television special, *A Salute to Sir Lew Grade: The Master Showman*. Sir Lew was a major business owner and producer in British television. He also had interests in music publishing, as I would soon find out.

Record Plant's remote truck was called for the recording, at John's request, no doubt. Fortunately, another master, Phil Ramone, was producing and engineering the audio for the TV show. Phil was experienced at television work, which can be different from studio recording. Music often takes a back seat to all the drama on camera, even if it was John Lennon. There was an all-star cast of movie stars, like Julie Andrews, Kirk Douglas, Shirley MacLaine, and Peter Sellers . . . not to mention a live orchestra backing up other guest singers like Tom Jones.

Many thought it odd that he would participate in a salute to Sir Lew, who had gained control of John's music publishing and would not sell it back. We soon found out that John had payback in mind that would prove frustrating. The band that would be backing for the show was known as BOMF. They were a great bunch of young musicians that John also used for Yoko's projects. There were several versions of what BOMF stood for; Band of Mother Fuckers was the most popular.

During the show rehearsal, I was having trouble with the SMPTE time code feed from the video truck and had to trace the cable back to its source. As I entered the video control room and looked up at the screens, I saw John in a red jumpsuit with the band in blue suits, but they all had "life masks" on the back of their heads, making them look like something out of a sci-fi horror movie. It was a rather obvious insinuation about Sir Lew's double-faced dealing with John's music rights! Check out the video online; it is well worth watching.

Producer Phil Ramone had decided that they would use prerecorded band tracks with John singing live. In rehearsal, one song ran so long that Phil edited the playback tape to fit. That would prove to be disastrous in the show.

During the live show, I was standing behind Phil, operating the two Ampex MM-1000 16-track recorders while he played back the stereo tape and mixed in Lennon's live vocal. I was getting nervous as the leader tape marking the edit approached, but Phil had his hand on the faders and I didn't dare second-guess him . . . big mistake! Phil forgot his edit and the tape ran out, leaving John's live vocal hanging in midair with no band music playing! John recovered with his usual humor and the audience, being mostly show business stars themselves, graciously took it in stride and laughed it off. I learned a lesson on trusting my own judgment and speaking out.

That performance would turn out to be John Lennon's last live show. He retired from performing but would later return to Record Plant, working with producer Jack Douglas on the *Double Fantasy* album. As he returned home from the studio on December 8, 1980, he was shot dead by a religious zealot for his perceived disrespect of Christianity. His killer wanted to be more famous than John.

David DB Brown was my Record Plant remote tech on the evening of John Lennon's death. The remote truck had just returned from a trip to Washington, DC. I asked him to recall that fateful night.

A REMEMBRANCE OF JOHN LENNON

Thirty-nine years ago, on December 8, 1980, we had just gotten back to the Record Plant Studios from a remote gig [Kennedy Center Honors] and were unloading the remote truck when we heard there was a party up in the mix room for the couple who had been working there and over at the Hit Factory on a double album. Phil and I decided to go up and say "hi" and grab a couple of free beers; John Lennon (with his cowboy hat on) was sitting in the corner by the upright piano and Yoko Ono was sitting on his lap.

We went back downstairs and finished putting the gear away and as I was leaving work to go home, I saw the limo sitting in front of our remote truck in the "No Parking/NYP Plate only" zone with the engine running and thought "they must be about to head up to the Dakota," and I got on the E-Train to go home to Queens.

When I got home and turned on the TV to catch the late news there was a special report on saying John Lennon had been shot and killed. I stood in my living room trying to argue with the TV that it couldn't be true because I had just seen him.

Thirty-nine years later and we still don't have the will to do anything about unstable people and gun violence. I don't think Mr. Lennon would approve.

—David DB Brown

When I heard of John's horrible death, I hate to say it, but one of my first thoughts was "They finally assassinated a rock star, and now that flood gate has opened." I had just finished working on the Kennedy Center Honors, a live television show in Washington, DC, celebrating all the best of US culture. It all seemed to pale with this horrific murder of a brilliant British artist.

From then on when I visited friends at the Dakota Apartments, where John and Yoko had lived, I would have to walk up the driveway where he was murdered. Along with the memories of John Lennon's memorial at the Imagine Circle in Central Park, I will always remember him and wonder what could have been.

RIP John Winston Lennon, October 9, 1940–December 8, 1980.

Recommended Recordings

Mind Games
Apple Records 1973

Walls and Bridges
Apple Records 1974

A Salute to Sir Lew Grade: The Master Showman
Video 1975 on YouTube

Double Fantasy
Geffen Records 1980

John Lennon
Anthology Capitol Records 1998 C2 7243 8 3061426

JOHN, PAUL, GEORGE, AND RINGO: THE MOST FAMOUS FOURSOME IN MUSIC HISTORY

The Paul McCartney Recordings

I had always hoped to work with Paul McCartney someday, but I didn't expect it be on a concert honoring more victims of religious fanatics, eerily like John Lennon's murder.

On that infamous date, 9/11/2001, the World Trade Center towers in New York were burned to the ground by suicide airliner hijackers.

On that very morning, Paul McCartney and his wife Heather were sitting on the runway at New York's JFK airport, waiting to take off for London. Their flight, along with every other flight, was immediately grounded. From their airplane window, they could see the twin towers billowing with smoke. Soon they would learn how disastrous it was.

Paul was well-known for his work with charitable causes, and he was instrumental in organizing the largest event honoring the 2,996 people that perished in the attack and recognizing the first responders that courageously tried to save them. It would be known as The Concert for New York City and took place on October 20, 2001, at Madison Square Garden, barely a month after the attack.

Sony Music organized the recording of the concert, it was produced by their veteran A&R chief Don DeVito, along with Chuck Plotkin, Bob Clearmountain, and Thom Cadley. Remote Recording Services, the company I founded, brought in our Silver Truck and were joined by the MTV TNN remote truck with veteran engineer Marc Repp. We were there to mix the live music broadcast and record it for later sale to raise money for the Robin Hood Relief Fund. That fund helped the many people affected by the attack and was unique in that its board of directors underwrote all expenses so that 100 percent of the money went to aid the victims!

Many of McCartney's fellow British stars joined to honor an embattled United States that had once welcomed them as foreigners: David Bowie, the Rolling Stones' Mick Jagger and Keith Richards, Eric Clapton, and The Who. Paul had written a song, shortly after the catastrophic collapse, that would become the anthem for The Concert for New York City.

Words cannot describe the power of the music that was made that night. I would ask the reader to find and play the audio or video recordings of this incredible testimony to the human spirit. They are listed here, but especially listen to Paul McCartney's heartfelt performance of his songs:

"I'm Down"
"Yesterday"

Paul spoke to all the firefighters and first responders and then started the song he wrote for them:

"Freedom": "Fight for the right to live in freedom"

It was a rousing performance, energizing the crowd of 18,000 to sing along with the choruses of "Freedom," while Eric Clapton played a soaring solo. "Let It Be" brought a beautiful coda to the concert, but Paul's reprise of "Freedom," accompanied by all the stars of the concert with solos by Billy Joel and Eric, playing out the finale to a grateful audience.

The post produced video shows with the testimonies by the firefighters:

"The concert was a special way to remember the 343 firefighters who were lost. On behalf of my brother firefighters, a heartfelt thank you to everyone who was involved in the performance."

—Firefighter Bobby Fraumeni, Ladder Company 147

"No one who attended the concert on Saturday could doubt the healing power of music."

—Lieutenant Brenda Berkman, Ladder Company 12

Recommended Recordings

The Concert for New York City
Columbia Records 2001
Paul McCartney's songs Disc 2 #13–16

The Concert for New York City
Sony DVD and VHS 2002
Available on YouTube in full

The George Harrison Recordings

The 1971 Concert for Bangladesh

The performance that really brought me around to live rock concert recording was George Harrison's The Concert for Bangladesh. It was recorded by Gary Kellgren on the Record Plant White Truck. Not only was it an incredible live performance by a diverse group of star musicians, but it would also begin a humanitarian trend among musicians to promote philanthropy with their large-scale concerts. Despite the costs of the recording and filming, they did make huge donations for the cause.

Think of the many concerts that followed George Harrison's example.

In 1979 the United Nations' Music for UNICEF concert raised funds for world hunger and was broadcast around the world from the United Nations General Assembly in New York. Many stars of the day contributed their performances: ABBA, the Bee Gees, Rod Stewart, and Donna Summer, among others. Recorded by the Record Plant Black Truck with Elliot Scheiner and myself and the Wally Heider remote trucks with Ed Greene.

The 1985 Live Aid concerts were created to raise funds for the terrible famine in Ethiopia. They were held primarily in Philadelphia and London but also simultaneously in other countries around the world, including Canada, Japan, Australia, the Soviet Union, and West Germany. An estimated audience of almost two billion people viewed the concerts. The

Philadelphia concert audio was mixed by Record Plant Black and White Trucks, and Le Mobile, and were organized by me.

The 1985 Farm Aid concerts were directly inspired by Live Aid to rescue US farmers in dire financial distress. They were successful and continue to this day. They feature a mix of country and rock music with a much-needed political message.

Eric Clapton's Crossroads Guitar Festivals were created to support the Crossroads Center for drug treatment in Antigua. Started in 1999, they became hugely successful and continue to this day. The shows also bring many great older players back to the stage for long overdue recognition. I recommend binge watching!

The Concert for New York City, previously detailed, commemorating the victims of 9/11 was also one of these.

I am proud to have provided engineering and recording on most all of those events. It's a better world for having shared the caring via music.

The original Record Plant Studios in New York entered the live recording business by leasing one of Wally Heider's California remote trucks. Wally pioneered the modern remote truck. Record Plant cofounder Gary Kellgren used it to record George Harrison's Concert for Bangladesh. Because of that recording, I called Record Plant New York to book that truck for a live TV concert. I was then an engineer at Regent Sound in Philadelphia, where I had done some remotes with portable gear, but this was too complex for that.

Working on that show in the Record Plant remote truck started my career in live recording.

After Bob Dylan's appearance at The Concert for Bangladesh, George Harrison returned the favor to Dylan and performed at his *30th Anniversary Concert Celebration.*

George Harrison took lead vocals and guitar on Dylan's rarely recorded 1966 song, "Absolutely Sweet Marie." On "My Back Pages," George shared vocals and guitar solos with Roger McGuinn, Tom Petty, Neil Young, Eric Clapton, and Bob himself. They also sang "Knockin' on Heaven's Door" for the finale.

For the grand finale, Clapton opened with a solo; as a live mixer you could always count on Clapton to step forward and save the mob of guitar players—not to mention the video director—and it sounds like Harrison got his licks in, too.

Recommended Recordings

Bob Dylan: The 30th Anniversary Concert Celebration

Ringo Starr's All-Starr Band Recordings
PINE KNOB THEATER IN CLARKSTON, MICHIGAN, MAY 30, 1997
RINGO STARR'S ALL-STARR BAND: GARY BROOKER, JACK BRUCE,
PETER FRAMPTON, SIMON KIRKE, AND MARK RIVERA

In the many years after the Beatles broke up, Ringo would occasionally pop up, like his cartoon character in the movie *Yellow Submarine*. I was always glad to see what he was up to: movies, talk shows, and even at a Formula 1 racetrack. He always seemed to have that relaxed smile, like he knew the inside joke that everybody else was missing. It took many years before the critics would recognize how important he was in making all those Beatles records. The real musicians knew and would see how much, when Ringo started up Ringo Starr & His All-Starr Band in 1989 and went on tour. At last count, he has played with 14 different versions of this band and is still going strong.

I came in on the fourth version in 1997 when I got a call from producer David Fishof, who wanted to capture this group of guest musicians playing with Ringo. Fishof knew us from our many recordings at Lincoln Center, among them were the Hebrew Academy for Special Children (HASC) benefit concerts that he produced.

I caught up with the tour at one of the Detroit area's favorite rock venues, the semi-outdoor "shed," Pine Knob Theater. There are many a great show in my log book from there. I knew most all the local and touring crews and had recorded a few of Ringo's band members before, especially my friend, Mark Rivera, a great reed player. Rehearsal went smoothly, and Ringo came out to the remote truck for a playback and a few words. Ever the humorous English gentleman, he seemed happy with the recording and flashed his famous peace sign and grin on the way out. The other band members were over in the catering area for dinner with the crew; this was a relaxed rock tour with no superstar posing. I ended up in line behind Jack Bruce and had a few words. Would he be playing "Never Tell Your Mother She's out of Tune"? He looked askance and shook his head. He did play "I Feel Free" and "White Room." Jack wrote many of those songs that were hits for Cream; he sang most of them, too.

Recommended Recordings

Ringo Starr and His All-Starr Band: The Anthology So Far
Eagle Records/Eagle Rock

Yoko Ono Recordings

Star Peace Tour behind the Iron Curtain

In 1986 Yoko Ono set out on a goodwill world tour for Starpeace, mostly visiting Eastern European countries that she felt were in need of her message of peace. Ono refused to tour with a corporate sponsor and personally financed the endeavor herself. The media were largely unfair in their coverage of the tour, accusing Ono of "ego-tripping" and ridiculing her for underselling venues. In one case, a photo of Ono rehearsing to an empty hall before the show was printed as if nobody had come to the actual concert. A German DJ was also encouraging people to turn up and throw glass bottles at her.

However, the fans loved the shows, critics widely praised her for her performances, and she filled a venue of 15,000 in Budapest. I recorded the shows with a remote truck from Austria, and they were a great success in a country still under Russian control. Yoko had a wonderful dinner for the band and crew to celebrate her son Sean's birthday. That took place in a 400-year-old castle after a local concert of Cuban players.

Recommended Recordings

Rykodisc 1997
CD reissues of Ono's albums made available live versions of "Imagine" and "Now or Never" from the tour.

3

DAVID BOWIE LIVE

The 1974 Live Album on through to
Opening The Concert for New York City, 9/11

David Bowie's first live album, simply called *David Live*, was recorded on July 11–12, 1974, at the Tower Theater in Upper Darby, just outside of Philadelphia, Pennsylvania.

Bowie, ever the enigma and always changing, was playing music from the new *Diamond Dogs* album on this tour and dressed in a stark white, padded shoulder suit with a reddish coiffure. The previous identity, Ziggy Stardust, was "done and dusted" as the Brits say; he now had a new persona.

Michael Kamen, a Julliard-trained pianist, was directing a great new band of rock and jazz musicians. Michael would go on to write string arrangements for many rock stars and film scores like *Mr. Holland's Opus*, and the *Die Hard* series, many of which we would record on location with remote trucks.

There were more than a few issues for the Showco touring sound crew to deal with on this show. It was a tight squeeze, trying to pack an arena-sized Bowie show into the 1920s' Tower Theater with 3,000 seats. It was worth the effort because Bowie loved the "Philly Sound" of all those great R&B records, and Philadelphia loved him back, selling out his shows and buying his records. He would also record most of his next album, *Young Americans*, at the famous Sigma Sound Studios. There were also some band issues when several musicians found out the shows were to be recorded and refused to play without certain concessions. Thankfully, it was resolved in time for me to hit the record button.

As often happened in those days, I had no advance information on who would engineer the recording, so I just set everything up the way I normally did. We were into the sound check when Bowie's Olympic Studios engineer, Keith Harwood, showed up and took command. He was great, just dove right in and got a mix going, as I expected from the man who engineered for the Rolling Stones and Led Zeppelin. Thankfully, all the political, financial, and technical issues on stage were resolved and the show went on.

The opening song started with Kamen's *Twilight Zone* riff, into Bowie's 1984 rendition, followed by "Rebel Rebel." When Bowie sang his big hit "Space Oddity," he was raised above the audience on a crane, but on one of the shows it became stuck, leaving David literally in space! I could see it on our original black-and-white video monitor (we didn't get a color camera for a few years) and hear the stage crew on the intercom trying to fix it. But the show must go on; Bowie didn't panic, he just sang another song until they got him down. By 1974 Bowie already had enough hits to make a great show, "Changes," "All the Young Dudes" (a song he gave to Mott the Hoople)—plus covers like "Knock on Wood." The live album finished with "Rock 'n' Roll Suicide," a rather dark way to go out, but the audience loved it and Bowie loved Philadelphia. He would record his next album, *Young Americans* at Sigma Sound Studios in Philadelphia, where he and producer Tony Visconti would be inspired by the masters of Philly Sound.

These live recordings have been mixed, overdubbed, remixed, and reissued a number of times; pick one and enjoy a great time in the Bowie evolution. The original LP album went Gold in November 1974 and was reissued many times on CD and then again on LP as vinyl made a comeback.

Recommended Recordings

David Live at the Tower Theater in Philadelphia, 1974
RCA 2 × LP, Rykodisc reissue, EMI remaster, *Who Can I Be Now?* box
  set edition

Mott The Hopple Live
CBS Records 1974 (contains their version of "All the Young Dudes,"
  which revived their career). We recorded this album two months before recording *David Live*.

LIVE NASSAU COLISEUM '76
BOWIE ISOLAR TOUR

Concert tours were often designed to support a record album; in this case it was Bowie's latest, *Station to Station*; so our clients were RCA Records and the *King Biscuit* Radio Network, who would mix selections of the show for their radio series. It was a success on nationwide radio, but it was not released as a recording on CD until 2017.

This tour became known as The Thin White Duke Tour, and I saw why as Bowie stepped out of the tour bus, which was parked close to the remote recording truck. It was yet another character change to a darker persona; he was dressed in almost 1930s' cabaret style and rumored to be living on cocaine and milk.

One chilling memory of this show was from the opening film, a 1928 Salvador Dali surrealist black-and-white classic with the infamous scene of a woman's eyeball sliced by a razor! I've never forgotten that scene.

Bowie recalls those times as very dark, including rumors of fascist flirtations and salutes, which he later denied. All I remember is recording some great Bowie songs like "Fame," which he had recently written with John Lennon at Record Plant, where I was working. His version of Lou Reed's "Waiting for the Man" seemed appropriate for this tour. So did the hallucinogenic "TVC 15." I didn't find out until later that it was about Iggy Pop's acid trip, where his girlfriend is being absorbed by the TV set. "Rebel Rebel" and "The Jean Genie" now seemed normal by comparison. The *King Biscuit* radio show producers were great clients for us in that era, and founder Bob Meyrowitz was happy with the show, as was I.

Judge for yourself.

Recommended Recordings

Parlophone Records Ltd CD, Vinyl, DD
Numerous online sources

TIN MACHINE LIVE AT RADIO CITY MUSIC HALL
THE GQ AWARDS

The British comedy group Monty Python had an ongoing intro on their television show: "And now for something completely different. . . ."

When I got the call to record David Bowie in his new persona as a member of the band Tin Machine, that was most welcome, but I was a bit surprised that it was for *GQ*, a men's fashion magazine, usually associated with old-money trust-fund types. But it was always great, recording shows at the magnificent Radio City Music Hall. If you are not familiar with this 1930s' art deco music hall, look it up; it's a treasure. Radio City was better suited to big shows like the *Grammys* and *MTV Music Awards*, but I've also recorded everyone from Aretha Franklin to Jay-Z with an orchestra in sold-out shows.

It was very interesting to witness Bowie acting as a member of a creative group with other extremely talented musicians. Reeves Gabrels on guitar, Zachary Alford playing drums, Mike Garson on keys, and Gail Ann Dorsey playing an amazing performance of "Pressure," singing and playing bass. This being New York, Lou Reed's "Waiting for the Man" was appropriate and played up-tempo was interesting. Of course, Bowie would do his hit song "Fashion" for this show, flavored with some wild guitar sounds. Being Bowie, he threw in one spooky piece: "My Death." It's very powerful and sad to know now that he is. Truly one of the giant talents of our time. "The Man Who Sold the World" is always relevant as is "Always Crashing in the Same Car." Who needed an award show when it was a Bowie show!

It is well worth watching a few of these performances online.

Recommended Recordings

YouTube: David Bowie Live at the *GQ* Awards
Radio City Music Hall in New York City, October 15, 1997

THE CONCERT FOR NEW YORK CITY
HONORING THE 9/11 FIRST RESPONDERS
LIVE FROM RADIO CITY MUSIC HALL IN NEW YORK CITY ON OCTOBER 20, 2001

This concert took place a little over a month after the terrorist attacks on the World Trade Center and emotions in New York were running high. It was dedicated to the first responders of the attack, and the audience was full of survivors and families of those who were lost.

Radio City has 6,000 seats and huge stages. It was perfect for hosting all the many artists who volunteered for this commemorative fundraiser. Here I focus on David Bowie's performance at the beginning of the concert.

I have engineered many a show going out live to the world but waiting for this opening act was the most highly charged I have ever felt. We did not do a rehearsal for David Bowie's opening song, and my hands were on the audio faders waiting to see what he would do. I don't recall who did the introduction, but as the huge opening applause died down, a lone spotlight shone on Bowie, sitting cross-legged on the lip of the stage. The audience was quietly mystified by the bare solo setting. He started by playing a simple intro on a little keyboard, almost a calliope sound, and then began gently singing Simon and Garfunkel's "America." When he got to "Walk off to look for America," it brought a swell of emotional response, as the audience realized where this was going. Of course, in the next verse is "I've come to look for America." Such a brilliant, understated but perfect statement, coming from a British immigrant to the United States. The repeated chorus of "they've all come to look for America" brought the house down. He then paid tribute to his local Ladder Company. "My fellow New Yorkers. . . . it's an act of privilege to play for you tonight."

Just as "America" was a brilliant selection for the opening song, Bowie launched into his song "Heroes" for the coda. It was the perfect tribute to the first responders on 9/11, played at full volume with his electric band . . . "Heroes Just for One Day."

If you can find the recording, turn it up loud for Bowie's performance of "Heroes." You can find a more complete story of The Concert for New York City in chapter 21.

Recommended Recordings

The Concert for New York City (to benefit The Robin Hood Relief Fund) Columbia C2K 86270

4

E. C. WAS HERE

The Eric Clapton Recordings from
Comeback to *Crossroads* to Cream

Clapton, a legendary guitarist, has probably toured longer and played more guest appearances than any other rock star. I was fortunate to have recorded Eric at salient points along the arc of his career. All the way from the comeback tours after his drug years, to the many Crossroads Guitar Festivals that support his drug and alcohol rehabilitation centers.

I recently heard a radio show host apologize for playing a live version of a rare classic rock song because he felt it wasn't the same perfect version he was used to hearing. Well, sometimes the live performance itself or the recording quality isn't that great, but I always loved being there in the moment, hearing great artists perform their art live and never to be played exactly the same again.

I first experienced Eric Clapton's live playing with Cream in 1968 at the original Electric Factory in Philadelphia. Up close and way too loud, surrounded by freaking fans—it was indeed electrifying and a whole new reality from the studio recordings played on the radio. *Disraeli Gears* were changing faster and louder.

I went home to my guitar and bass and sighed. I had to concede, I would never be good enough to play in my girlfriend Sherrie's band. She was an established singer/songwriter when we met, and she introduced me to the recording studio world in New York and Philadelphia. One of those studios was Regent Sound in Philadelphia, where I met chief engineer Joel Fein. It was a pivotal moment in my life, and I would never look back. If I couldn't play, I would learn how to punch the big red "record" button!

As you read in previous chapters, Joel did hire me and the long and winding road led to Record Plant in New York, where I landed in the driver's seat of the White Truck.

THE LIVE ALBUM: *E. C. WAS HERE*
CIVIC CENTER, PROVIDENCE, RHODE ISLAND, JULY 25, 1975, AND NASSAU COLISEUM, LONG ISLAND, JULY 28, 1975

I finally got my chance to record Eric Clapton with Ralph Moss engineering on the 1975 US tour, following the *Eric Clapton 461 Ocean Boulevard* album release. It was a great band with George Terry on guitar, Carl Radle on bass, and Jamie Oldaker on drums. You can hear some of our recordings on the *E. C. Was Here* live album. Ralph did a great job engineering, despite a near-disaster at the Nassau Coliseum show. Shortly after the show started, the recording truck dramatically lost power, blacking us out with a bang! I raced outside to check that our circuit breakers were OK and then ran back to the under-rated electrical panel the coliseum had given us. The fuses were blown, there were no spares, and no electrician could be found; so I pulled the load wires out of another small electrical panel and hooked us up. I cautiously turned the truck on and thankfully everything survived. We managed to get through the show and only lost a song or two. Later I found out I had taken out power to the concession stands upstairs. But people could get their beer on the next floor up because the show must go on.

The *E. C. Was Here* live album did well and has been reissued many times. RSO Records also used it to promote the release of the studio album *No Reason to Cry*.

ERIC CLAPTON'S 1978 *SLOWHAND* TOUR
CIVIC CENTER IN SPRINGFIELD, MASSACHUSETTS, APRIL 5, 1978

For the 1978 US Tour, RSO Records again booked the Record Plant New York remote truck. I was now officially the director of remote recording and would be engineering these shows. We were extremely busy, designing and building the new state-of-the-art Black Truck, while keeping up with a full calendar of live recordings. I had been engineering *King Biscuit* radio shows, including the Ramones and Santana, while starting Bob Seger's live album. With producer Jack Douglas and engineer Jay Messina, we recorded six straight Aerosmith shows (see chapter 6), leaving me one day to get to Clapton's first date.

We were able to send all the Aerosmith tapes and outboard gear back to New York and load in fresh tape and gear for Clapton's gig just in time for the show in Springfield, Massachusetts. I think it was Showco PA system then, so we got all our interfacing done by sound check. Thanks to their help, everything worked and sounded good. It's a great band, that included George Terry, who had worked with Clapton on the *461 Ocean Boulevard* album and wrote songs for Eric, like "Lay Down Sally."

After the show, I remember Eric's manager taking me into the dressing room to meet Eric and tell him about the recording. Turns out he had not told Eric we were recording. When he introduced me and told him the recording news, Eric just smiled and said, "Yeah, when I spotted the shotgun mic over the snare drum, I figured you were up to no good!" No PA company puts up Neumann U-87s and a Sennheiser shotgun mic up high. We had a brief chat before the room got crowded, so I eased out the door and back to wrapping up the remote truck. Everyone had to prepare for our next recording in Montreal, Canada: passports, customs carnets, air travel, etc.—all the fun stuff.

But I would not be going to Montreal with them. When I got back to the hotel, there was an urgent message from Record Plant to call my home. In the days before cell phones, it could be difficult to find us on the road. When I did call I found out that my mother had suddenly passed away after a long illness. My father and family were stationed near Salt Lake City, Utah, at the time because the most advanced kidney dialysis machines that she needed were close by. Those early machines extended her life for many years, but they could not save her. It was heartbreaking to have missed being there for Mom in her final hours.

The greatest thing about the Record Plant New York was the sense of family when the going got tough. I was able to call on my friend Rod O'Brien, a veteran studio engineer with remote experience, who immediately flew to Canada and took over the recording without a hitch. I also had a pretty stable crew by then, with Phil Gitomer as stage manager; I stole him from Daryl Hall and John Oates, where he had been their monitor mixer. I also had been poaching David DB Brown from the studio to handle tech and tape recorders. This excellent Record Plant studio crew went on to record a tour with the Atlanta Rhythm Section, for star engineer/producer Eddie Kramer.

I was finally able to get back to Record Plant in time to return the favor by helping studio chief engineer Jay Messina record a live promo film for the Rolling Stones. We set up a recording control room in a film studio over on the East Side of New York, where Jay could play back a prerecorded track and they would film Mick Jagger singing live. As usual, Mick kept adding musicians and I had to call Record Plant and get the remote truck sent over with more gear. When it arrived, the assistant driving it looked upset. When I asked him what the matter was, he just pointed up to the roof of the truck. The whole front section was smashed in! He had been directed to drive through Central Park, not knowing the 1850s' stone bridges were too low.

But there was no time to make major repairs to the truck's crumpled roof because it was booked to record jazz guitarist Al Di Meola at the Palladium Theater and then drive out to Michigan to meet Alice Cooper's concert film crew. Because there were rainstorms on the way, we gaffer-taped a big tarp over the roof and the remote truck made the 1,400-mile round trip.

Then the remote truck drove back to Record Plant, unloaded the master tapes and gear, loaded fresh tape and gear, and drove downtown late that night to the Bottom Line Theater. The next day I went to get the truck studio ready to record back-to-back Garland Jeffries and Lou Reed recordings. I opened the side door to a surreal nightmare: It was raining inside the studio! Water was running down the inside of the slanted hardwood ceiling (just missing the console) and soaking the 1960s' shag carpet. All the Midwest rainstorms had been filling up the 18-foot-long ceiling panels through the crashed front end. Amazingly enough, none of the electronic gear was wet, except for condensation. Try walking on a waterlogged shag carpet sometime. Needless to say, we bought lots of hair dryers.

I was also able to return the favor to my friend Rod O'Brien, who came in to engineer Lou Reed's show (Reed was his client). The studio gear was dry by then. Those shows would become the album *Lou Reed Live: Take No Prisoners.*

ERIC CLAPTON'S 1987 TOUR
CIVIC CENTER IN PROVIDENCE, RHODE ISLAND, APRIL 26, 1987, AND MADISON SQUARE GARDEN IN NEW YORK, APRIL 27, 1987

I finally caught up with Eric again, and this time with the newer Black Truck. This tour featured drummer Phil Collins, formerly of the band *Genesis* and now a solo star in his own right. Bassist Nathan East and Greg

Phillinganes on keyboards made the foursome a powerful arena presence. Madison Square Garden's 20,000 seats can be a lot of space to fill, but these four managed just fine. There were lots of blues and more recent hits as well. Another blues great, Robert Cray, joined in for the encore.

Something rarely discussed about these big concerts is the venue box office. Even in the age of credit cards, there is still a lot of cash flowing through the box office. When I presented my bill for the remote truck, tape, crew, and all the expenses, management asked if I could take cash, like in the old club days. After they settled with the box office, I was presented with a paper bag stuffed full of hundred-dollar bills. It always makes me nervous to be holding that much cash. I always pay attention to who is in the room and who else might know you have it. It's New York City, and mugging is a favorite sport. I delivered it to Record Plant the next day, but we agreed to not take cash anymore because counterfeit hundreds were starting to show up from the Middle East and we couldn't chance it.

BABYFACE *MTV UNPLUGGED*, SEPTEMBER 24–26, 1997

Eric Clapton has made guest appearances with many of the artists that he admired, so it's hard to pick a favorite. But for me it's got to be the show he played with Babyface, the incredibly soulful singer and songwriter. Eric added a new dimension to Babyface's many hits, opening with a beautiful guitar intro to "Change the World," then adding a long solo behind Babyface's vocal vamping, and finishing with an extended outro with his usual flourish. Next came "Talk To Me," in which Babyface credits Eric with adding to the neck bone, grits, and greens. You sure can hear it in the choruses and solos. They make a great duo. Eric was really enjoying that show; you should give it a listen sometime.

ERIC CLAPTON SESSIONS FOR ROBERT J
DALLAS, TEXAS, JUNE 2–3, 2004

In 2004, I was happy to get the call to record a series of dates for Clapton using Remote Recording's Silver Truck. The main event would be Eric's huge Crossroads Guitar Festival, but the first recordings would be the *Sessions for Robert J.* album. These sessions were produced by Clapton and longtime partner Simon Climie, with engineer Alan Douglas. Happily, this turned out to be a heartfelt testimony to blues legend Robert Johnson, who had been Clapton's inspiration from the beginning of his career. There would be two different locations for us, first in the Las Colinas rehearsal studio with Clapton's touring band and then in a decrepit building that Robert Johnson himself had once recorded in.

The amplified band was classic Clapton: great musicians all, Steve Gadd on drums, Nathan East on bass, Billy Preston on B3, Chris Stainton on piano, and Doyle Bramhall on guitar. Always glad to see Gadd: I ran out of superlatives years ago because there's been so many great recordings! In 2003, Steve Gadd was awarded the American Drummers Achievement Award at the Berklee College of Music, with a star-studded audience, including a performance by James Taylor and his band. Steve had played many tours with James, and would again at the Crossroads Guitar Festival.

The songs with the electric band were classic Clapton blues, masterfully played by these stellar musicians. My favorite, especially in these days, is "I Wish I Had Possession over Judgement Day." All the amplified tracks are worthy, but the real gems are the acoustic tracks with just Eric and Doyle Bramhall playing in that old rundown room where Robert Johnson had once recorded "I ain't superstitious," as the song goes, but there was a real feeling of spirit in that room. The DVD is the best way to experience their performance of Johnson's legacy. My favorite was "Me and the Devil Blues," with Bramhall on slide guitar.

It is unique scenes like these that make all my miles on the road worthwhile.

ERIC CLAPTON'S CROSSROADS GUITAR FESTIVAL 2004
THE COTTON BOWL IN DALLAS, TEXAS, APRIL 6, 2004

It was just a short drive over to the famed Cotton Bowl Stadium in Dallas, Texas. The outdoor field, dating to 1930, was once the home of the NFL Dallas Cowboys, but it has hosted many concerts as well. I first went there to record Aerosmith and a few of the other bands at the first Texxas Jam. It set a record for the 80,000 fans that sweltered through that July day 1978. The air conditioner failed in the old Record Plant White Truck while we were recording. Was it only 120 degrees? Turn down the lights and never stop tape!

This 2004 Crossroads concert was the first official Crossroads Guitar Festival, although there was an earlier benefit for the Crossroads Center at Antigua. It's important to understand that this festival supports a number of programs for drug and alcohol addiction at the Crossroads Center at Antigua. Clapton founded this nonprofit center to help the many on the island and elsewhere that suffer from addiction. You can read a letter from Clapton at crossroadsantigua.org to get a better understanding.

I believe everyone involved in this festival was chosen not only for their talents and history, but their understanding and support of these programs.

The concert film was produced by friend Mitch Owgang of WNET/13, the flagship PBS TV station in New York City. I have worked on hundreds of theatrical and concert shows with Mitch, and he is always the consummate professional. We would alternate recording the bands as they appeared on stage between Remote Recording's Silver Truck and the MTV remote truck. There was also a second stage that featured bands playing between the main acts. That stage would be recorded by Kooster McAllister, our old friend, on his Record Plant remote truck—a later version of the same truck I brought to Dallas in 1978 for the first Texxas Jam.

There was a great cast of characters for this gig. Producing the audio recording was star engineer Elliot Scheiner in Remote Recording's Silver Truck and Ed Cherney onboard the MTV remote truck. They are two of the best mixers I have ever worked with, and I heard that verified by the legendary guitarist/writer J. J. Cale, when he met these two gentlemen backstage. You might even remember one of his songs, "After Midnight"— Clapton certainly does.

The talent lineup of more than 40 acts plus guest performers was selected by Eric Clapton himself to suit the Crossroads mission of support for the treatment center in Antigua. There were veteran blues artists like Hubert Sumlin and David "Honey Boy" Edwards to B. B. King and Buddy Guy. Jazz great John McLaughlin and the unique Latin soul of Carlos Santana, rockers Joe Walsh and ZZ Top, and acoustic guitarist James Taylor.

Everybody had their favorite performances, Elliot remembers standout performances by James Taylor with Steve Gadd on drums playing with Jerry Douglas and Joe Walsh. I loved John McLaughlin's "Tones for Elvin Jones "and Clapton playing with Cale on "After Midnight." There were so many great solo and shared performances that I recommend looking up the recordings to appreciate the incredible talents that played that festival; some of whom are no longer with us, like David "Honeyboy" Edwards, J. J. Cale, Hubert Sumlin, and Robert Lockwood Jr., who learned to play with the legendary Robert Johnson.

The show ended dramatically with a Texas-sized lightning and thunderstorm that even ZZ Top's grand finale playing couldn't withstand.

Weather is a constant companion on the road. I've been treated to tornadoes, hurricanes, blizzards, and torrential downpours and not to mention earthquakes. It's all part of the show.

Coda

Elliot Scheiner produced the mixing of the audio recordings for CD and DVD. They encountered a problem with the SMPTE time code that had been fed to the audio trucks from an outside source. It apparently was not locked to the same source as the videotape. That made for a lot of creative editing, to say the least. The good news was that the sales in the United States alone were 10 times Platinum—Gold and Platinum elsewhere in the world, too.

ERIC CLAPTON'S CROSSROADS GUITAR FESTIVAL, 2007
TOYOTA PARK IN BRIDGEVIEW, ILLINOIS, JULY 28, 2007

The success of Clapton's 2004 Crossroads Guitar Festival was repeated at Toyota Park, an outdoor 28,000-seat soccer stadium just outside of Chicago, Illinois. It sold out in minutes and was another hugely successful event and recording.

The star host for this year would be the actor Bill Murray, best known for his Saturday Night Live roles and movies like Groundhog Day. Bill really took the entertainment level for video to new heights, narrating the stage action and participating with costumes and even playing "Gloria" with Clapton. His energy and high humor helped keep the audience entertained through the 11-hour show.

Elliot Scheiner would again produce the live audio recording, partnered with Ed Cherney once again. They would also mix the show in DTS surround sound. Elliot would mix in Remote Recording's Silver Truck with me, and Ed would mix in the Le Mobile truck with Guy Charbonneau.

When Elliot recorded the famous Eagles' Hell Freezes Over reunion concert in LA, my Silver Truck was not available, so I recommended using the LA-based Le Mobile remote truck. We had excellent results; the album alone went nine times Platinum and the DVD eight times. So, we definitely had our team ready for Crossroads 2007.

The lineup had many great artists to add to the festival, including legendary guitarists like Jeff Beck and B. B. King. Country stars Willie Nelson and Vince Gill and the vocals of Sheryl Crow and Susan Tedeschi with the Derek Trucks Band.

The big finale was a super summit of guitar players, led by Clapton with Buddy Guy, Hubert Sumlin, Robert Cray, Jimmy Vaughan, and Johnny Winter.

The popularity of the Crossroads Guitar Festival continued with DVD sales reaching six times Platinum in the United States alone.

ERIC CLAPTON'S CROSSROADS GUITAR FESTIVAL, 2010
TOYOTA PARK IN BRIDGEVIEW, ILLINOIS, JUNE 23–26, 2010

This festival would be the second festival performance at this Toyota Park venue, making life a bit easier for everyone setting up as they had in the 2007 festival. Many of the same performers also returned. The ever-affable Bill Murray hosted the festival and brought his long video and film experience to the show. The long list of guitar greats included Buddy Guy, Johnny Winter, the band ZZ Top, and a rare appearance by the great Scottish folk singer/songwriter Bert Jansch. It would be one of his last performances. So many of the great veterans: Jeff Beck; Steve Winwood; Albert Lee; and the King, B. B. King, were also there. Newer players Joe Bonamassa, Sheryl Crow, Citizen Cope, and John Mayer were also there. Robert Randolph and the Family Band brought church, soul, and funk in a great performance.

As I so often advise, you have to listen to the recording because words cannot do it justice. The festival received good reviews, and the feeling was classic, maybe even old school, real guitar playing without all the showmanship. As usual, the DVDs sold well, going at least four times Platinum in the United States and sold very well worldwide.

ERIC CLAPTON'S CROSSROADS GUITAR FESTIVAL, 2013
MADISON SQUARE GARDEN IN NEW YORK CITY APRIL 11–13, 2013

The festival returned to where it started on June 30, 1999, at Madison Square Garden in New York City. This must have been a little poignant for Eric because this was where he played the last show with his mates in Cream on October 26, 2005.

I was amused to see this recording listed as Eric's 11th live album. Sales were still Platinum—only singly in the United States but did well on the worldwide charts. This would be the last Clapton Crossroads Guitar Festival for me because I retired from live recording, and it would also be the last for my friend, Ed Cherney, who passed away in 2019. His talents and soul are reflected on so many great recordings; you can find many of them in this book. All of these Eric Clapton Crossroads Guitar Festival recordings were the Els & Ed Show—always my favorite act.

Remembering Ed Cherney
June 16, 1950–October 22, 2019

THE REUNION OF CREAM WITH ERIC CLAPTON, JACK BRUCE, AND GINGER BAKER
CREAM REHEARSAL, SONY STUDIOS IN NEW YORK, OCTOBER 23, 2005
CREAM CONCERT MADISON SQUARE GARDEN, NEW YORK, OCTOBER 24–26, 2005

The band Cream was the at the pinnacle of the psychedelic rock era in 1968 when the three powerful creative talents decided to follow their own solo careers.

After hearing Cream perform live at the Electric Factory—Philadelphia's famous psychedelic concert venue in 1968—I had to go back to wearing out my vinyl copies of their records, especially *Disraeli Gears*. They were such a powerful presence playing live. When Cream was inducted into the Rock & Roll Hall of Fame in 1993, there was hope that they would tour again, but that was not to be. As the years went by, Clapton admits that he thought more about his old mates and decided to approach them again. Jack Bruce had been ill and Ginger Baker was not in much better health, but they all apparently decided, hey, we're still alive, let's do it!

When they worked out the details in 2005 and announced a Cream reunion at the Royal Albert Hall, they instantly sold out all four shows. The recordings were also a huge success, and they decided to continue the reunion tour with three more shows booked for October 2005 at Madison Square Garden, in New York, and more in the works.

I had a long track record recording Eric, and our recent successes with recording the Crossroads Guitar Festivals helped us get the booking to record these Cream reunion shows. Clapton's engineer, Alan Douglas, was already familiar with our Silver Truck, so recording the Cream rehearsal session at Sony's New York Studios went smoothly. Madison Square Garden is always a challenge, with extremely long cable runs up five floors from the street. The big modern tractor trailers can't drive up the ramps to the stage like our old Black Truck could. Millennia remote preamps on stage are now used to compensate for the long analog cable runs. Clapton and his production team still preferred analog sound, until digital recording media came along.

The shows were a huge sell-out success for their US audience, but apparently an unpleasant experience for the band, with many old issues resurfacing. The perpetual animosity between Jack Bruce and Ginger Baker kept flaring up, catching Eric Clapton in the middle. I must say, in all the shows I recorded with Eric, he was always the calm presence on stage. With the Cream shows, we could feel the strain in the remote truck, but everyone persevered to get through the shows. At least all three of our heroes played through to the end of Cream's last encore. None of us knew it would be the last one ever.

Coda

Jack and Ginger, thanks for all the years of music you played for us; we'll never forget.

Jack Bruce May 14, 1943–October 25, 2014
Ginger Baker August 19, 1939–October 6, 2019

Eric Clapton played on so many other shows that we recorded, including:

The original Live Aid concert, Bob Dylan's 30th Anniversary Concert, Atlantic Records 40th Anniversary, Chuck Berry *Hail! Hail! Rock 'n' Roll!*, and many others. There was also the *Grammy Awards* and *MTV Awards* in 1993, playing "Tears in Heaven" on a solo acoustic guitar.

When mixing those big shows with many star guitar players, I could always count on Clapton to step forward and take the final solo on those messy grand finales.

Recommended Listening

Eric Clapton, *E. C. Was Here*, 1975 Album, RSO Records
Eric Clapton, *Crossroads 2 Live in the Seventies*, RSO Records
Eric Clapton, *Give Me Strength*, 1974–1975 Polydor Records
Eric Clapton, *Crossroads Guitar Festival*, 2004, Dallas, Texas
Eric Clapton, *Sessions for Robert J.*, 2004 Reprise Records

Eric Clapton, *Me and Mr. Johnson*

Eric Clapton, *Crossroads Guitar Festival*, 2007, Bridgeview, Illinois

Eric Clapton, *Crossroads Guitar Festival*, 2010, Bridgeview, Illinois

Eric Clapton, *Crossroads Guitar Festival*, 2013, Madison Square Garden, New York, Warner Music

Babyface, *MTV Unplugged*, NYC 1997 Live (Eric Clapton solos)

5

SIX HUNDRED THOUSAND

The Allman Brothers at
Watkins Glen Racetrack to the Finish Line

My first encounter with The Allman Brothers Band was the 1973 Summer Jam at Watkins Glen, also featuring The Band and the Grateful Dead. I was there as the tech and tape op for the Record Plant New York remote truck. Our client was Capricorn Records, and we were there to record The Allman Brothers Band.

It was all a bit surreal for me, as I had attended many races at the historic Watkins Glen Racetrack, which was right behind the stage area. Memories of the snarling unlimited Can-Am racers and the unforgettable sound of Formula 1 Grand Prix V-12 engines screaming at 10,000 RPM still reverberated for me. The Grateful Dead's "Wall of Sound" would soon give them a run for their money. Sports cars were my first career, this was second.

Having experienced the crowds at racetracks, I had anticipated the crush of a Woodstock-size crowd, so I drove up early in my trusty VW Westfalia camper with my wife Dusty. She bravely assisted our outdoor adventures. I couldn't leave the remote truck unattended and depend on commuting to the crew hotel in town because traffic was already a jam. As it was, the producer and Record Plant engineers Frank Hubach and Jim Reeves had to helicopter in to make it on time.

It was astounding to see the gigantic Wall of Sound and the delay towers already set up. Owsley "Bear" Stanley, Dan Healy, and fellow audio freaks were way ahead of the curve, building "line array" speakers before there was the name. The delay towers used the early Eventide digital delay units so the sound from the stage would arrive at the same time, avoiding the "ballpark" echo that ruined live music. The Agnello brothers were at Record Plant Studios working on our monitors as well.

I don't think anybody anticipated the huge turnout because the promoters sold a little more than 150,000 tickets, but an estimated 600,000 fans showed up! It still holds the concert record for the United States. Frankly, it was a bit scary because we were parked right beside the stage with only a hurricane fence separating us from the crowd. There was not much in the way of security personnel. Much to my surprise, a large tractor-trailer pulled up and disgorged a troop of horse-mounted New York State Police. The fans seemed to love the horses, and thankfully, it turned out to be a peaceful encounter.

The sound checks started on July 27 turning into longer jams with The Band, then the Allman Brothers, and finally the Grateful Dead playing for hours. With the truck parked next to the stage, we had little isolation. The tech from Capricorn Studios was there to set up the Dolby noise reduction system for the two Ampex MM-1000 16-track tape recorders. It was an all-nighter, getting everything aligned to their satisfaction. We would find out later that an intermittent Dolby power supply caused some tape dropouts. Because tape playback isn't possible while recording Dolby, no one could hear it until later.

On July 28, the Grateful Dead went on to thunderous applause and played two long sets. There is an interesting story here about trying to record the Grateful Dead. We were hired to record the Allman Brothers, but our client had generously offered to record the Dead. There didn't seem to be much interest, but at the last minute, the Dead's recording engineer, Betty Cantor, came into the truck and was prepared to go, but the "security" guys wouldn't let our crew on stage to patch in the mic splits. Nobody was going to argue with the Hells Angels. Recordings of that show came from their PA board tapes.

There was a classic backstage acid moment that I happened to witness. Right behind the remote truck was a giant pile of plastic garbage bags that had been thrown down from the stage from the last few days. As I opened the back door of the truck to toss our bag on, I was startled to see a woman walk off the stage and fall the twenty feet onto the pile! I rushed over to give her a hand, but she was unfazed, and just wafted off with a radiant smile, communing with some spirit in the sky.

The Band had a rough time with a torrential downpour interrupting their set, but they toughed it out and played the rest of the set when it stopped.

Even though they had been off the road for some time recording in the studio, they played great.

Finally, the Allman Brothers took the stage to play two sets of all their recent hits plus new material that was recorded for the upcoming album *Brothers and Sisters*. Even without the late band members, Duane Allman and Berry Oakley, they played their hearts out to the 600,000 fans that had come to cheer them on. They continued on to an encore set with members of The Band and the Grateful Dead.

Amazingly there were no serious injuries or deaths, with the exception of an unfortunate sky diver. The New York State Mounted Police were actually well-received by most of the audience, and they certainly were appreciated by all of the concert production staff.

1976 KENTUCKY DERBY WITH THE ALLMAN BROTHERS

ABC Wide World of Sports decided they would include some of the Allman Brothers concert being played on the grounds of Churchill Downs in Louisville, Kentucky. This was sort of the opening act for the annual first leg of the Triple Crown. It has the distinction of running for 144 years before the 2020 coronavirus shutdown.

We had a great time hanging out with the horses and watching all the finely dressed folks in attendance. As we sat in the Record Plant remote truck waiting to go on the air, watching the video monitor and listening to the director's intercom, the Allman Brothers were playing on stage. The director kept finding other things of interest to shoot; in the end I think they used maybe one song out of the whole set. It probably cost them about $5,000 for us to mix that one song. We love ABC.

They also recorded a number of shows for live radio, such as at the Fox Theater in Atlanta, Georgia, on November 24, 1980, for GK Productions, engineered by Rod O'Brien and known as *A Night on the Road*.

THE ALLMAN BROTHERS REUNITE 1986

After disbanding in 1982, the Allman Brothers reunited on October 31, 1986, for Bill Graham's Crackdown Concert at Madison Square Garden, a benefit hoping to ease the crack cocaine epidemic raging in those years. Concert promoter Bill Graham had a history of helping, he produced Live

Aid in the United States and Amnesty International, among others. For this concert, he brought together a variety of stars that people would listen to because most of them had overcome their own drug addiction.

The Allman Brothers and Crosby, Stills & Nash knew all about the dangers of drugs. Run DMC, Ruben Blades, and Santana brought credit to the cause from their histories and culture. There were two shows; we recorded one to be filmed and recorded for fundraising.

The Allman Brothers and probably Crosby, Stills & Nash had not played together for some time, but they put on a great show. It was a Halloween midnight show and the finale was the high point with Santana, Steve Stills, and Mick Taylor from the Stones joining in. Drummers Butch Trucks and Jai Johanny "Jaimoe" Johanson were joined by keyboardist Chuck Leavell and really made the night.

Those were hard years in New York City for the crack addicts; I hope the efforts of these veteran musicians and concerned citizens made a difference.

Gregg Allman and Cher

Speaking of hard times, Record Plant was in New York City on West 44th Street between 8th and 9th Avenues. In those days, it was still a bit dangerous late at night with muggers, drug dealers, hookers, and the like. One night I was coming back to the studio after a remote recording in town, probably 3:00–4:00 a.m., when I saw Gregg Allman and his then-wife Cher walking out of the front door. They stopped and looked a bit shocked to realize they were alone on the dark street and this long haired, bearded guy was walking toward them. Allman didn't recognize me and Cher kind of stepped back closer to him. I had to go past them to get into the studio, so I said, "Hi, I work here at Record Plant. Can I get you a cab?" Cher was having none of that, and they bolted back into the studio. Lucky for me he didn't have one of Dickey's guns.

AN EVENING WITH THE ALLMAN BROTHERS BAND

Working with the legendary producer Tom Dowd, my Silver Truck recorded a number of shows that became *An Evening with the Allman Brothers* album. As drummer Butch Trucks once said of Dowd, "He was the greatest record producer that ever lived." You won't get an argument out of me about that. I first met him at Atlantic Records Studios in New York, visiting Daryl Hall and John Oates while they were recording their album, *Abandoned Luncheonette*, with producer Arif Mardin. What an incredible era that was at Atlantic Records, as the Allman Brothers discovered, in 1975, when Tom Dowd produced their album *The Road Goes on Forever*. It certainly seemed a possibility

Fast forward to 1991 at the City Auditorium in their former hometown of Macon, Georgia, where Tom Dowd would again be producing the band for a live album. He was joined by his longtime engineer Jay Mark and Epic Records executive Michael Caplan. Burt Holman, the band's longtime road manager, was there keeping everything organized.

The band featured original members:

Gregg Allman on B-3 organ, acoustic guitar, and vocals
Dickie Betts on lead and rhythm guitar and lead vocals
Jaimoe on drums and percussion
Butch Trucks on drums and background vocals

Newer band members:

Warren Haynes on lead and rhythm guitars, lead and background vocals
Alan Woody on bass guitars, fretless, six-string and acoustic, and background vocals
Marc Quinones on congas, percussion, and drums

The City Auditorium was going to be a special New Year's Eve for The Allman Brothers Band, returning to their former home in Macon. They spent a lot of early years there, and of course, the fans were wound up and waiting. The previous shows had sold out, and this one was SRO with a crowd outside hoping to hear a little leakage. We certainly could hear it inside the Silver Truck, the best seat available—a flawless mix of every song by Jay Mark and Tom Dowd.

The band played a great set—all the hits and then some. Everything from "Statesboro Blues" and "Midnight Rider" to "Ramblin' Man" and "Whipping Post." I thought a lot of those would end up on the albums! The parties, needless to say, went on for the rest of the night. As usual, we stayed to check the recordings, finish the paperwork, and get the Silver Truck ready to roll to New York in the morning. For a change of pace, we would be recording at the New York Metropolitan Opera with a new production of *The Ghosts of Versailles*.

The next Allman Brothers recording would be at the Orpheum Theater in Boston, Massachusetts, on March 3–4, 1992. You can see the entrance of the theater on the cover of *An Evening with the Allman Brothers* album. Built in 1852, it is one of the oldest theaters remaining in the United States. I recorded many shows there and Boston always turned out for The Allman Brothers Band. These shows would prove the rule that sellout crowds made for a great recording. Other shows fondly remembered here include: Loggins and Messina, J. Giles Band, and the original Fleetwood Mac with Peter Green on lead guitar and vocals.

BEACON THEATER IN NEW YORK, MARCH 10–11, 1992

The Beacon was a traditional stop for The Allman Brothers Band every tour, where they would play to sellout crowds for as many as 10 nights. The 2,900-seat, three-tiered balcony is a great theater for a rock show. I have recorded many shows there over the years; it was right up the street from Record Plant, which was a short drive for the Remote Recording trucks.

We recorded 2 of the 10 nights that they played, March 10 and 11, 1992. Producer Tom Dowd and engineer Jay Mark were happy with the performances, and combined with the shows from Macon, Georgia, and Boston, Massachusetts, they had more than enough for the album. In fact, it would eventually become two, maybe three albums.

They say it takes 10,000 hours to really be able to play; this band must be in the 100,000s of hours and do they play! My favorites here were Betts's *Nobody Knows*, perfect for today's world, Allman's *Dreams*, great early Gregg blues, and then the saving grace, Dickey's *Revival*. Look up these records and listen for yourself. Turn it up and join the audience!

After the show, there was a crew bus shuttling between the Beacon and the hotel, so I hitched a ride. I was sitting next to a guy that looked vaguely familiar. He was fit, with a Gold's Gym T-shirt on, which was not your average rock band look. After a few words I realized that he was the legendary Owsley Stanley, creator of the Grateful Dead's Wall of Sound and most of their LSD. He was at the Summer Jam at Watkins Glen, minding his giant sound system. Despite his reputation, he was quite pleasant and a fascinating character.

WHERE IT ALL BEGINS
THE LAST STUDIO ALBUM WITH ORIGINAL GUITARIST DICKEY BETTS
JANUARY 24, 1994–FEBRUARY 8, 1994, WITH TOM DOWD
PRODUCING AND JAY MARK ENGINEERING

The "studio" was actually the Silver Truck parked on location at Burt Reynolds's ranch in Jupiter, Florida, and it was right down the road from drummer Butch Truck's home. They had a large building with enough room for the whole band and support gear. No livestock was allowed into the studio. With a little acoustic treatment, it sounded fine. The album was successful and with popular radio play it went Gold, doing better than their last studio album. It was a great sounding album, "All Night Train" and "Everybody's Got a Mountain to Climb" are my favorites, although "Temptation Is a Gun" seemed more relevant by then.

It would be the last Allman Brothers album with their original guitar player Dickey Betts. He would continue on as Dickey Betts & Great Southern with his son, Duane Betts, on lead guitar. He did reconcile with Allman before Gregg's death in 2017.

That remote "studio" turned out to be one of those gigs where once we got everything up and running to Tom Dowd and Jay Mark's liking, there was little for me to do. Our longtime tech and recordist, Phil Gitomer, was taking care of everything in the remote truck, so I was able to go back to my "Ranch," which was a classic Pennsylvania barn that I had built for the remote truck and maintenance shop. There was always the next recording to organize, and in this case, it was a Carnegie Hall show, The Music of Pete Townshend, with singer Roger Daltrey of The Who and the Juilliard Orchestra plus guests. That turned out to be an incredible show.

THE ALBUM NETWORK SYNDICATED RADIO SHOW
RALEIGH AND CHARLOTTE, NORTH CAROLINA, JULY 1–2, 1994

These would be the last recordings we would make with The Allman Brothers Band. Live recordings for syndicated radio play were still important in the early 1990s. Video had not yet killed the radio star, but they were working on it. We once had a number of radio-related clients like the *King Biscuit Flower Hour*, but they gradually faded away in the MTV era.

Tom Dowd would be producing the recording, but Jay Mark was not available, so I was back in my engineer's chair. They had requested a 32-track digital recorder with my Studer A-820 24-track SR analog recorders as back up. Unfortunately, the rental 32-track Otari blew the remote, without which it could not go into record mode. We had to scramble to sub mix enough inputs to fit in 24 tracks. I have to grin as I remember having to fit a band onto 4-track and 8-track recorders. It didn't seem like a problem back then when it's what I had.

It all worked out in the end; the Allman Brothers played just fine, and everyone seemed happy, except the rental company. I never heard the radio show mix, but with Tom Dowd producing, you knew it would be the best possible. It was an honor to work with him, and as Butch Trucks said, "He was the greatest record producer that ever lived."

The Allman Brothers Band held their last performance on October 28, 2014, at the Beacon Theater in New York. The show marked the 43rd anniversary of Duane Allman's death—what an incredible legacy.

Recommended Listening

1973 Summer Jam at Watkins Glen

An Evening with The Allman Brothers Band
Epic Records

An Evening with The Allman Brothers Band: 2nd Set
Epic Records

Where It All Began
Sony Music

6

GOT THEIR WINGS

Aerosmith from an Opening
Act to *Rocks, Lines,* and the Oscars!

I first heard Aerosmith live when they were the opening act for a Mahavishnu Orchestra concert that we were recording in 1973. They already had a big following, and their hard rock guitar volume could match John McLaughlin's fiery jazz fusion. This recording would be for the very first *King Biscuit Flower Hour*, which became a huge success and syndicated nationwide. I would soon be seeing Aerosmith quite frequently.

Aerosmith connected with Jack Douglas as their producer at the Record Plant New York in 1974. Jay Messina joined them as recording engineer and that team would become one of the most successful in rock-and-roll history.

The album they produced together was *Get Your Wings*, and it would go three times Platinum, a trend they would continue for many years. It was this album, their second, that really locked in the Aerosmith sound and persona. By 1975 they would release *Toys in the Attic*, and it would go eight times Platinum! By now the live Aerosmith tours were selling out, and they needed to record them. My remote log entry shows us at the Boston Garden from November 13 to 16, 1976. They were hometown heroes, playing at the 1928 wooden sports arena, where Boston fans love a wild crowd. They were great shows, excessive excess everywhere, even in the remote truck, but I won't talk about that.

1976 ROCKS

Aerosmith had a large rehearsal and band storage building appropriately named The Wherehouse, and it was just outside of Boston and securely private. Rehearsals for the new album were going well and producer Jack Douglas decided to start recording tracks right there. We brought the Record Plant remote truck up to join Jack and engineer Jay Messina for a trial run. After a bit of acoustic modification, they decided to stay. We stayed at the classic Copley Plaza Hotel downtown and enjoyed the historic city of Boston. I loved that part of life on the road, seeing so many towns and cities throughout the United States. Everyone was pleased with the songs they had recorded, and the final vocals and overdubs would be done back at Record Plant New York. Indeed, they were "Back in the Saddle" again, the *Rocks* album went four times Platinum in the United States and did equally well worldwide.

1977 DRAW THE LINE

Recording the previous album tracks away from the studio environment had worked so well, producer Jack Douglas decided to up the ante and record the next album in a real mansion. I had recently recorded a Brownsville Station album with Eddie Kramer at a magnificent mansion he had discovered, not far from his home in Armonk, New York. He was planning on bringing the band Kiss there to record but was having scheduling problems. Once Jack saw the incredible mansion, he booked it straight away. We had just finished recording Frank Zappa at the Palladium in New York, and I took the Record Plant remote truck offline so we could build a temporary recording studio inside the mansion. With our resident genius designer Jim Falconer, I built a control room in what had been the Cenacle Sisters Monsignor's office. They are a French Catholic Order of Nuns who were "downsizing." You must look at the photos to appreciate this incredible acoustic environment and the endless number of rooms to play in, including a large chapel. Then the band and entourage moved into the endless rooms available. I could write another whole book on the two months we spent there, but discretion is the better part of valor. My favorite story is when the band came back from a brief trip home to Boston driving a fleet of expensive sports cars. Jack Douglas had his blazing red Lotus Esprit, Brad Whitford had a Ferrari Daytona 275 GT that we wound out on the interstate, Joey Kramer had a beautiful Ferrari 246 Dino, Tom

Hamilton also had a Ferrari (an early 308 GTB), and Steven Tyler opted for a Porsche 911 anniversary special in gold. Steven tossed me the keys and said with a grin, "I think there's something wrong with the radio, go check it out!" Great backcountry roads out there. The grand prize went to Joe's black Porsche 911 Turbo, one of the first in the United States. When he opened the trunk, it was full of machine guns, including a round magazine Thompson! I'll leave it there for now.

I loved that they all experimented with playing in the different rooms, especially the beautiful classic chapel. It was a great place for Joey's powerful drumming—what holy reverb. My favorite song is "Kings and Queens." You should listen for the ambience on all the songs. I know the album did not initially get great reviews, but they did improve with age. It was rather ironic that there were expectations that the isolated bucolic setting would relieve the drug and party habits. Unfortunately, dealers do deliver, even in the country. The basic track recording for *Draw the Line* at the Cenacle wrapped up by the end of February, and Jack Douglas took the tapes back to Record Plant for overdubs and mixing. The record did go Platinum, and the band would get a break before starting up the 1977 tour. What a unique adventure that was!

As great as the "remote studio" project was, I needed to keep our other live recording clients happy, and we only had the one remote truck back then. It took us a week to disassemble the Cenacle studio and restore all the gear back into the remote truck and Record Plant New York. Then everything had to be cleaned and tested, ready for the next live gigs. Those would be for Carlos Santana at the old Roseland Ballroom and our favorite downtown club, The Bottom Line Theater. We blew up their 1930s' overloaded electrical panel, and it took a little creative wiring to "borrow" another tenant's breaker box in the basement, but we got the recording accomplished. The *King Biscuit* radio show also became a live album.

Aerosmith also went back on the road to support the *Draw the Line* record, from July 1 to 9, 1977. We started in St. Louis, Missouri, and worked our way back up to the Civic Center in Baltimore, Maryland, having recorded six shows. Those recordings would find their way onto the *Aerosmith: Live Bootleg* album.

Jack always found things to keep the tour rolling; this time it was the opening of the original *Star Wars* film. I think it was in Indianapolis—they sometimes all run together in memory. Their ever-resourceful production manager arranged for the band to sneak into the darkened theater into front row seats without the fans spotting them and, of course, snuck them out before the lights came up again. At the time, it was a mind-boggling

sci-fi adventure, a total surprise to the senses! The fans did spot them on
the way out; it could have been the full-length sword Joe Perry was wearing. We got away in the limo without serious injury. Our last recording was
at the Civic Center in Baltimore, and we peeled off to prepare for a Bob
Seger show at our old favorite venue, Pine Knob, outside of Detroit, which
was Seger's hometown. That show was for the *King Biscuit* radio show, but
I would later record Bob right in Detroit at Cobo Hall for his hit live album
Nine Tonight. And it's funny, the things you remember; I saw Bob sneak
away from the Pine Knob show in his leathers and crash helmet to escape
on his motorcycle.

Later on, in March 1978, we would join the Aerosmith tour at the Aragon
Ballroom in Chicago, another grand 1926 theater that became a regular
stop on the rock tours. The show in Columbus, Ohio, was followed by one
of my favorite venues, the Tower Theater, just outside of Philadelphia,
where we could always count on a great rock audience. I always remember
David Live, the Bowie album we recorded there. We finished that tour at
Aerosmith's hometown theater, the Music Hall, another grand 1925 former
opera hall. The shows were sold out, signaled by the rowdy successes that
you can hear on the *Aerosmith: Live Bootleg* album.

After a short detour to record the band Gotham at Carnegie Hall, we
rejoined Aerosmith at the majestic Masonic Temple in Detroit. That is another US architectural treasure that I love to record in. The last recording
we did on that tour was at the opposite end of the architectural spectrum:
The Paradise Club in Boston. It is a 600-seat single-story rock club owned
by legendary promoter Don Law and partners. It is situated in Boston's university campus heartland. It was a great "homecoming" vibe for the band to
play in a club like where they started out their career. Several of these performances close out our recordings on the *Aerosmith: Live Bootleg* album.

LIVE TEXXAS JAM '78

The original Texxas Jam was a three-day rock festival organized by Pace
Concerts and David Krebs, manager of Aerosmith and other bands. The
concert series would go on to be a huge success; this first concert brought
in more than100,000 people to bake in the 104-degree summer sun. As it
soared even hotter on the Cotton Bowl grounds, fire hoses and first aid
became mandatory. It got worse for me and the Record Plant remote truck
crew when the overworked air conditioner failed! Down went the lights and
off came the shirts as the heat from the big Ampex MM-1000 recorders

and our brand-new 44 input API console (with massive redundant power supplies) broiled us alive. Somehow a big window air conditioner magically appeared, and we jerry-rigged it to blow some cool air through the cable door truck side. That big API console was meant for our new Black Truck, which was still back at Record Plant being constructed. There were some other hilarious stories involving some bands playing the indoor arena, which still reeked of horse manure from a rodeo; AC/DC was one of them . . . welcome to the United States.

Aerosmith was headlining the Texxas World Music Festival, better known as the Texxas Jam, so at least they got to play later in the day, after the fire hoses had cooled off the baked audience. Talk about die-hard fans, they endured Sahara Desert conditions and warm beer. Aerosmith made it through an exhausting set of 14 songs, including "Milk Cow Blues" for the Texas ranchers.

We had to record many other acts as well; my logs show Journey, Charlie Daniels, and Emmylou Harris, among others. Frankly, I don't remember much besides Aerosmith; after all, they were Record Plant family and were produced by Jack Douglas.

We then had more insanely tight remote bookings for the White Truck, all the while trying to finish building the new Black Truck. I flew back to New York and recorded Frankie Valli (of the Four Seasons) using the old RCA remote van, with Record Plant owner Roy Cicala producing. He had recorded many of the Four Seasons' 1960s' hit records. The White Truck was driven straight back to Record Plant, returned the new API console to the Black Truck, loaded the old DeMedio console in, and took off for a couple of Rolling Stones dates. My memory is a little hazy here; none of us were getting much sleep. I do recall staying up for a couple of days getting the last wiring finished on the Black Truck. It was too late to fly, and the truck had to drive overnight to make the Kansas show in Detroit, so I climbed into the brand new Peterbilt sleeper. Was I ever glad that I had ordered the expensive interior! About 3:00 a.m., a huge banging rattle startled me awake! As a former race car mechanic, I knew that disastrous sound and screamed at the driver to shut off the engine. The brand-new Cummins diesel engine had dropped a valve into the piston, blowing the engine in the middle of nowhere. This was long before cell phones, so I had to hitch a ride back to a roadside pay phone and started calling the dealers in the Peterbilt owner's manual. At dawn, I finally got a live person on the line in Nashville, who kindly found a local 24-hour road service to tow us to the venue.

Fortunately, the show venue, then called Pine Knob, allowed us to work on the engine while we were parked there for the recording. Kansas played four sold-out shows, which gave us enough time to rebuild the entire engine. I was gambling that the Cummins mechanics had flushed all the metal debris out of the oil passages and that we hadn't bent the crankshaft. They replaced the cylinders, pistons, rods, and bearings and then fired it up, while I held my breath. I had rebuilt many engines in my youthful sports car days but never a monster nine-liter diesel like this. It grumbled a bit but no loud noises.

The band hardly noticed the ruckus and concentrated on their brilliant playing that would propel the live album (*Two for the Show*) to go Platinum. They were happy with my recordings and continued their tour. Our driver gingerly aimed the Black Truck back toward New York. I had enough of the road and took the first flight back home.

Our Peterbilt dealer wanted to go through the rebuilt engine for warranty documentation. I had taken a huge chance on the quality of the emergency roadwork, but good faith paid off and that big Cummins diesel went more than 300,000 miles before I bought a new one!

With Black Truck in the shop, I had to use the White Truck for Aerosmith's show at their hometown Paradise Club in Boston. Owned by rock promoter Don Law and partners, it was a comfortable 900-seat venue, great for Aerosmith to get a break from the giant arenas and enjoy playing for friends and family. Some of those performances made it on to the *Aerosmith: Live Bootleg* album.

A few years later I was in the Paradise Club to record George Jones for the country side of the *King Biscuit* radio show. The first set went pretty well, his great band opened; and George joined them to sing a rowdy list of his hits. The second set featured an increasingly frustrated band playing away with no George in sight. They finally had to admit that George had taken a taxi out to Logan Airport during intermission; it was part of his legend.

A few weeks after the Paradise Club shows, Aerosmith was back at their infamous rehearsal studio, The Wherehouse, to record a few more performances that would end up on the *Aerosmith: Live Bootleg* album, and among them would be the John Lennon/Paul McCartney classic, "Come Together."

I wouldn't see them as I went straight out to Chicago to record a Muddy Waters and Johnny Winter album. The remainder of 1978 was extremely busy for both White and Black Trucks. Among the many back-to-back shows for the Black Truck were on the Neil Young *Rust Never Sleeps* Tour that produced the live albums and the feature film and is still one of my favorite engineering credits. The White Truck also recorded memorable shows by Santana, Frank Zappa, and others.

Jack Douglas and Jay Messina would record several more Aerosmith shows using the Record Plant Black Truck, including in Huntington, West Virginia, at the Civic Center on December 11, 1982, and in Augusta, Georgia, at the Cape Cod Coliseum on March 4, 1983.

AEROSMITH IN HOLLYWOOD

I had been taking the Silver Truck out to the *Academy Awards* show since 1993, where we were responsible for the large orchestra that plays throughout the live broadcast.

The last place I expected to see a heavy rock band like Aerosmith was there, but on April 19, 1999, they were playing "I Don't Want to Miss a Thing" from the film *Armageddon*. Aerosmith contributed four songs to the soundtrack album where it went Platinum four times in the United States and sold just as well worldwide, especially in Japan.

It was great to see Jack Douglas and those unsinkable rock stars still at the top of their game, killing the video!

Recommended Listening

Get Your Wings
Columbia Records

Rocks
Columbia Records

Draw the Line
Columbia Records

1978 Live Bootleg
Columbia Records

Live Texxas Jam '78
CBS/Fox Video

Armageddon The Album
Columbia Records and Sony Music Soundtracks

7

CSNY *RUST NEVER SLEEPS*

Neil Young and CSNY, 1974 through to the *Heart of Gold* Feature Film

Alone or together, these four musicians advanced the art of rock from the 1960s on.

Crosby, Stills, Nash & Young (CSNY) appeared as the group, in pairs, and individually. I recorded many shows with each combination of the group, including at Live Aid, Atlantic Records 40th Anniversary Concert, and the seminal environmental protest shows known as No Nukes: The Muse Concerts for a Non-Nuclear Future.

I was a believer from the moment I heard those CSNY harmonies; we already knew Crosby from his time with the Byrds (one of my personal favorites), Stills and Young from Buffalo Springfield, and Nash from the British band the Hollies. Joni Mitchell knew it the first time they sang together for her in Topanga Canyon.

I would work with them all eventually, but my first live recording experience came when Steve Stills formed his band Manassas, which was a major change from CSNY.

STEPHEN STILLS AND MANASSAS LIVE

We recorded several shows for ABC's *In Concert* TV series, first at the Academy of Music in New York City and then at the uniquely named Bananafish Gardens in Brooklyn, on February 19–20, 1973. Those shows they shared with other bands, but then as the headliner at the classic 1847 Auditorium Theater in Chicago, Illinois, they packed the 4,000-seat theater on March 8, 1974. The band featured Chris Hillman (from the Byrds), Al Perkins on pedal steel, Paul Harris on keys, Calvin Samuels on bass, and Joe Lala on percussion. The studio album was successful, as were the tours. They did issue a live album from the Bananafish Gardens show. Steve Stills also issued a live album from a second concert we recorded at the Auditorium Theater on March 9, 1994, titled *Stephen Stills Live*.

During that same period, the *Graham Nash David Crosby* album came out as did Neil Young's *Harvest* album. And Atlantic Records also issued CSNY singles.

The 1974 CSNY tour was the first real US Stadium tour in our music history. It strained the resources of every participant in sound systems, transportation, legal issues and, of course, the stars themselves. It changed rock forever.

The CSNY tour started on the West Coast and worked its way east, including two shows at the Nassau Coliseum on Long Island. Bill Halverson, who did many of their studio records, engineered these two on the Record Plant New York remote truck. I was on stage for those shows and had a rare opportunity to shoot some interesting photos (see photo section three).

The tour was legendary for its excess of everything, fueled by the enormous wealth it generated. The hard living took its toll on the musicians, and it became obvious by the time we recorded them on August 14–15, 1974. The fans loved it, the shows were packed and we got some good recordings. As often happened in those days, we went right on to the next gig and never heard about the recordings again. Forty years later, it surfaced as a CD, *CSNY 1974 Crosby, Stills, Nash & Young*.

In fall 1976, we recorded a couple of Crosby and Nash shows in New York City at the Beacon Theater, one of my favorite venues, right down the street from my West 89th Street apartment. Not often can you walk to work in the remote business. We had two super stars, each with his own engineer. That was fine, until a disagreement turned into a fist fight. Being the "adult on duty," I had to break it up; there just wasn't enough room for that in the White Truck. The next location was the Wollman Skating Rink Center in Central Park, one of my least favorite locations. It's very difficult to get a truck through the trees and soggy ground. Remind me to tell the "sunk in the quick sand, three wreckers to get us out" story. But it was a nice fall day this time and Crosby and Nash put on a great laid-back show in the autumn sun. These would end up on the next live album, and it was one of the rare easy gigs.

I started recording Neil Young and Crazy Horse in November 1976 with shows at the Palladium in New York and the Boston Music Hall. Neil impressed me from the beginning as the strongest original star in the rock galaxy. He had a laser focus, even before lasers, singing in his unique range, with confidence that defied the purists. He always found the right combination of soul and raw talent to play his music. Crazy Horse had the talent: Frank "Pancho" Sampedro on guitar and vocals, Billy Talbot on bass and vocals, and Ralph Molina on drums.

NEIL YOUNG *RUST NEVER SLEEPS*

Those earlier 1976 gigs were a good introduction, but it was the 1978 tour that produced the *Rust Never Sleeps* family of albums, feature films, DVDs, and countless remixes. The stage sets were a fantastic combination of giant guitar amps, *Star Wars* creatures, and a Woodstock acoustic setup. As one newspaper reviewer asked, "Was it an acid flashback?" if so, it was pretty good acid. Even the roadies and sound crew were in costume, including our stage manager, Phil Gitomer, who was dressed as a mad scientist in a white lab coat. Neil's longtime band of road warriors fit right in to the sets, dressed as gnomes with glowing red eyes. David Briggs, the producer, was there to keep me focused on Neil's unique sounds, engineer Tim Mulligan and crew made the venues sound great, and Elliot Roberts served as benevolent overlord.

You really must see the film or the DVD of *Rust Never Sleeps* to have any idea how incredible it was! We started recording the live shows again in October 1978, right where we left off, in Boston at the Garden. That was the first time I got to hear Neil and the band through the new API console in the Black Truck. The show has a huge dynamic range, starting with Neil playing solo acoustic guitar and singing "Sugar Mountain" for the acoustic set, followed by the electric set with the full force of Crazy Horse and Neil's electric guitars with his custom distortion effects. "When You Dance" really lit up the stage and Neil continued through his best, "Powderfinger," "Cortez the Killer," "Cinnamon Girl" . . . his set list was deep, winding down into "Hey Hey, My My (Into the Black)," and a dark coda of "Tonight's the Night," a story of losing a friend to drugs.

We didn't have much time to check the Ampex 24-track recorders, but we always ran two machines in overlap, so I was confident we had everything safely on tape. We had to be in Rochester, New York, the next day for a show at the War Memorial Auditorium. I played back the tapes for

David Briggs, and we passed the first test. Rochester was a sold-out show with a great audience, and I felt we had the basic levels and sounds pretty well dialed in.

We had to temporarily leave Neil's tour to record previously booked shows back in New York. First was a Jethro Tull live satellite broadcast from Madison Square Garden and then Frank Zappa at the Capitol Theater— always perfectly played chaos.

We picked up Neil's tour again on October 14, 1978, at the huge indoor Chicago Stadium, a 15,000-seat echo chamber that dates to 1929. Now we were back on overnight runs to the next gig. On we trucked to the St. Paul, Minnesota, Civic Center on October 15, 1978, and the show at the Coliseum in Madison, Wisconsin, on October 16, 1978. Next came a rare two-day travel to the McNichols Sports Arena in Denver, Colorado, a show on October 19, 1978.

The show on October 22, 1978, at the famed Cow Palace in Daly City, just outside San Francisco, was the last recording date we had booked. It would be one of the most important shows because most of the *Rust Never Sleeps* feature film was shot here. The album of the same name used recordings from here and from Denver and St. Paul.

I got a late call from David Briggs saying Neil wanted to record the shows at The Forum in Inglewood, California. Unfortunately, the Black Truck was already heading back to New York with barely enough time to make the Frank Zappa shows at the Palladium Theater in New York City on October 27–31, 1978.

After some frantic phone calls, I ended up with a remote truck from engineers Alex Kazanergras and John Fiore. I had worked with them recording *Loggins and Messina on Stage* at Carnegie Hall with the White Truck. Their truck had some interesting features, a red stove in the front of the truck interior, which I didn't expect to see in warm LA, and a recording console similar to the DeMedio in the White Truck. It had a strange feature for soloing the microphone inputs. The operating switch had to go through the "off" position before reaching the solo, which is not a good idea for live recording. Thanks to Alex and John, we successfully recorded the shows and I was able to get back to New York in time for the Zappa shows. Those recordings became Zappa's famous New York *Halloween* album and film.

As it always seems to go, I didn't hear the mixed records or film for some time. The film *Rust Never Sleeps* premiered in New York City on August 15, 1979, and I did get to see it, which was a different experience from watching a video monitor in a remote truck. Neil and LA Johnson really made it an adventure, being able to see all of Neil's moves while playing the entire Cow Palace show. There was also another double album released called *Live Rust* with a different set of shows. I was honored to see my engineering credit right on the record label, just below David Briggs, Tim Mulligan, and "Bernard Shakey," which was Neil's nom de plume.

By the way, that Neil Young tour was a round trip of about 6,500 miles for the remote truck crew. The new Black Peterbilt 352 with a Turbo Cummins Diesel and a sleeper cab made it easier.

We went on to record many more shows with the different bands and personas that Neil experimented with: the Shocking Pinks, the Blue Notes, and the various Stray Gators incarnations.

Concerts for a Non-Nuclear Future was a series of concerts in 1979 that Graham Nash was instrumental in organizing. It was an enormous undertaking with many of rock's influential stars (see chapter 17).

NEIL YOUNG: THE BLUE NOTES TOUR, 1987–1988

Neil put together a great band, he named the Blue Notes, with a lot of horns and attitude. It was a whole new direction that had to be heard while it's together, especially Neil's aggressive guitar playing driving the band.

The Notes featured Crazy Horse vets Billy Talbot and Rick Rosas on bass, Frank Sampedro on keys, and Ralph Molina and Chad Cromwell on drums. The horn section was Steve Lawrence on lead tenor sax, Ben Keith on alto sax, Larry Cragg on baritone sax, Claude Calliet on trombone, and John Bray on trumpet.

Neil wrote the signature song, "This Note's For You," as a parody of Budweiser's beer adds. It was a scathing put down of commercialism in an era of corporate-sponsored rock tours. The video he made featured spoofs of Michael Jackson with his hair on fire; Whitney Houston; and Spuds McKenzie, the Budweiser dog, selling product. The video pissed off MTV, but as it went public, they played it anyway!

My company, Remote Recording Services, was booked to record shows for a live album, starting with the rehearsals at the Studio Instrument Rentals (SIR) New York studios on April 15, 1988. It was quite a luxury for a remote truck to get a rehearsal before the live shows!

Neil worked hard to get those arrangements together, and that band cooked . . . a whole new chapter for him.

The first show was at the World Ballroom on the lower East Side of New York, infamous for its sleaze—squalid restrooms, just as bad as the CBGBs club, dark balcony orgies, and customary beer bottle breakage on the dance floor. A low-level stage on the ground floor was great for the crowds to be close to Neil and the band. We certainly recorded some rocking shows there, and thankfully, no one was seriously injured.

The Trocadero Theater in Philadelphia has seen it all, from vaudeville to rock and rap. I lived near here in Philly when I worked at Regent Sound and was always happy to revisit the "Troc." I've recorded shows there, and it was great for the Blue Notes band. Philly has a long history with all forms of music, from the 120-year-old Philadelphia Orchestra through jazz giant John Coltrane, who once lived blocks from there, to rock stars Daryl Hall and John Oates, who also lived close by in their early years. Philly audiences loved the big horn section and Neil's vocal energy singing with them. I think some of that Philly soul was inspirational.

The next venue was the Agora Ballroom in Cleveland, Ohio. Cleveland's reputation as a rock capitol was confirmed when the Rock & Roll Hall of Fame opened there in 1995. We recorded the all-star opening concert at the Cleveland Stadium.

The Agora Ballroom was a reminder of all the music history in Cleveland. From 1913, the building hosted everything from opera, vaudeville, burlesque, and finally rock shows. Cleveland does indeed rock, and we recorded some great shows with Neil and the Blue Notes. In fact, four of the Agora Ballroom songs made the final remix of *Neil Young—Blue Note Cafe.*

Among them were "Bad News Comes to Town," one of the darkest songs, and just right for current events. Neil's guitar solos fit as well. "Ain't It the Truth" is a little more upbeat. "One Thing" is back to dark blues, headin' for a heartache, and "Twilight" finishes with more blues, anticipating coming home to love.

You can access all of Neil's music at the http://neilyoungarchives.com. It's free to listen.

ATLANTIC RECORDS 40TH ANNIVERSARY CONCERT, MAY 11–14, 1988
CROSBY, STILLS & NASH PAY HOMAGE TO ATLANTIC

There is a more detailed story of the whole 13-hour concert in chapter 17, but Atlantic Records was so important in starting and maintaining their career, I know this concert had special meaning for them. The 1969 Atlantic album *Crosby, Stills & Nash* changed the music business and crowned their careers.

After a rousing introduction by actor Michael Douglas, they boldly played their longest and most difficult acoustic version of "Suite: Judy Blue Eyes." Just Steve Stills on acoustic guitar and the three most famous harmonies of the age. That most painful love song Stills wrote for Judy Collins filled the Madison Square Garden with the audience singing along. Stills played a brilliant solo, proving his heart was still there, despite the ache.

They had also played "Wooden Ships" and "Our House," giving all three their own composition. Atlantic founders Ahmet and Nesuhi Ertegun were proud of their artists (see chapter 17).

Other Crosby, Stills & Nash (CSN) live appearances we recorded: *Live AID* and *Crackdown*. In September 2000, we had just finished with the *Hispanic Heritage Awards* show at the Kennedy Center in Washington, DC, and had just enough time to get back to our base and change out the gear for Neil's next recording.

NEIL YOUNG, RED ROCKS IN DENVER, COLORADO, SEPTEMBER 18–22, 2000

The Red Rocks Amphitheater is one of the most incredible settings you can imagine for an outdoor concert. It's surrounded by the Red Rocks State Park mountains at an elevation 6,500 feet. It felt like home to this Montana boy; I loved being there for five days—a rare pause on the road. Getting there was not half the fun; it's a steep winding road up the mountain to the amphitheater. Our big Peterbilt Tractor Trailer had a hard time getting traction. The long wheel-base tractor was designed for carrying a heavy generator when needed, and we didn't need one, so there wasn't enough weight on the drive wheels. At the steepest turn, the tires would just spin! We had to hire an industrial duty wrecker to pull us up the last turn—very embarrassing for a trucker.

Once we got up there, everything was easy; we had worked with Neil and his longtime crew and management for many years. He had a great band, with multi-instrumentalists Ben Keith on pedal steel, guitar, dobro, lap slide, vibes and vocals; Spooner Oldham on B-3, pump organ, vibes, and vocals; Donald "Duck" Dunn on bass; the legendary Jim Keltner on drums; and Astrid and Pegi Young on vocals—what an incredible array of talent. John Hanlon, an engineer for many of Neil's recordings, would be at the console in the Silver Truck. We had recently recorded an interesting Robyn Hitchcock film with John, so he was familiar with the Neve VR console and our crew. We had the luxury of some rehearsals to dial in the sounds on Neil and the band.

There were also three shows to record, so Neil and John had plenty of material for the audio and video releases. This was called the *Music in Head Tour*, an inside classic car joke from Neil's car collection.

Larry LA Johnson directed the video of the concert, as he had so many others for Neil, including *Rust Never Sleeps*. We were able to view his live cut on our video monitor in the Silver Truck. There was a classic shot toward the end of the show when a huge storm system passed through Red Rocks, with almost hurricane force rains blasting horizontally across the stage. Neil would not stop the show; he leaned forward into the drenching rains, singing in a rage, daring the storm to stop him! That shot will always define Neil for me, thanks to the late LA Johnson's vision. Look for that DVD *Neil Young Red Rocks Live*.

CROSBY, STILLS, AND NASH *DAYLIGHT AGAIN*, 1983
UNIVERSAL AMPHITHEATER, LOS ANGELES, CALIFORNIA

This is one of those gigs that is lost in space. I do remember flying out to LA to record this show on the Record Plant LA remote truck. The Universal Amphitheater was the venue, and it was on the 1983 tour. I can't find it in my log books, but I think maybe it was a last-minute save when some other engineer became unavailable. I always loved recording that amazing group and was friends with their live mixer, Stanley Johnston, so maybe Stanley called me in?

The DVD did not come out until 2004.

NASHVILLE NOTES

Besides the love of music, there were two primary attractions for me in the remote recording business: travel and people. This next Neil gig had them all.

Nashville has long been a center of the country music business and has grown in stature over the years, attracting every genre of music. The studio population and independent producers and engineers has grown exponentially. There are now hundreds of studios, including one owned by my son, Ryan Hewitt.

I have recorded many shows in Nashville over the years, including Wynonna Judd, Kenny Rogers at the Ryman, Jimmy Buffett, and the *Country Music Awards*, but I never seemed to have time to explore Nashville and meet some of the studio and record businesspeople. Neil had recorded the studio album *Prairie Wind* with Chad Hailly at Masterlink Studio. He would also engineer the live film shoot on the Silver Truck. Hailly gave me a full tour of the historic studio, originally a church, with some unique acoustics. The album sounded great in its home studio.

NEIL YOUNG: *HEART OF GOLD*, AUGUST 14–19, 2005
RYMAN AUDITORIUM NASHVILLE, TENNESSEE
THE LATE DIRECTOR JONATHAN DEMME MADE THE CONCERT
FILM *NEIL YOUNG HEART OF GOLD* AT NASHVILLE'S RYMAN
AUDITORIUM, THE ORIGINAL GRAND OLE OPRY.

Neil had a serious medical issue that I didn't know about at the time. He was flown to New York for a delicate operation on a cerebral aneurysm. He was soon back in the Nashville studio, and as he was walking from the hotel, the artery plug from the operation failed and he started losing blood. Once again, he was saved in the nick of time. Either situation could have been fatal. Neil shrugged it off and went back to film production.

We had already set up the Silver Truck in back of the Ryman and were assembling a complicated recording system. Neil insisted on analog tape recorders and because there were quite a few inputs, we needed 48 tracks, two 24-track recorders sync locked for 48 tracks.

Because we need simultaneous backup, two more Studer 24-track recorders were rented from Blackbird Studio, who has an incredible inventory of gear. In addition, a Pro Tools system and engineer were set up in the Silver Truck's audio booth in the rear of the studio. We used all those tracks with the number of players and guests. The first set was music from the *Prairie Wind* album, which was just recently finished. The second encore set consisted of songs Neil associated with Nashville.

The first set had not only the songs from *Prairie Wind*, but also Neil telling a few stories and guest appearances by Emmylou Harris and the Jubilee Singers from Fisk University. My favorites were "It's a Dream" and "This Old Guitar," which certainly says it all. There are stories and philosophy lessons here worth repeated playing.

The second set held all the classic Neil Young songs from *I Am a Child* to *Old Man*. Most touching to me was "Comes a Time," which was played on acoustic guitars, with crew and background singers downstage. It was a tribute to the late Nicolette Larson who sang with Neil on the original recording.

On the DVD, Neil closed the set on acoustic guitar, singing "The Old Laughing Lady." He is alone on stage, playing to an empty auditorium as the credits roll on screen—a perfect Neil Young ending.

As always, I recommend listening to the recorded music, and in this case, I recommend the DVD as well for a close look at some of Nashville's finest musicians and Neil in great form after his life-threatening adventure.

WARNING: SCIENCE COMING UP

Forty-eight track analog recording requires a total of four 24-track tape recorders. Each pair of machines must record SMPTE time code and 59.94-Hz VD locked to Video. One pair will be the "A" recording, and the other pair will be the "B" recording. The 14" × 2" reels of analog tape running at 15 IPS will hold 60 minutes of music. The *Heart of Gold* performance was longer, so the machines must overlap so one pair is in record while the other changes tape. Before starting the show, I ran the "A" machine ahead a few minutes and stopped. All four machines go into record for the show: the "A" machine will run out of tape first, leaving the "B" to continue recording, while we change tape on the "A" machine. In theory, we have two complete 48-track analog recordings. Keep in mind each reel of 2" tape weighs 22 pounds maybe and must be changed and properly boxed with a collar ASAP! We use two tape operators. Don't even ask about what the studio engineers go through mixing all these tapes.

Neil loves the sound of analog tape and will pay the extra costs to make the film and audio formats live up to his standards. "Quality whether you want it or not."

This film remains my favorite Neil Young adventure. He is one of the last heroes in this live recording business.

Larry Johnson, Neil's longtime friend and film producer, passed away of a sudden heart attack on February 21, 2010. He is greatly missed by all; he was a friend indeed.

Recommended Listening

CSNY 1974 Crosby, Stills, Nash & Young

Stephen Stills & Manassas: Live

Stephen Stills Live

Neil Young Rust Never Sleeps album and film

Live Rust album

Crosby, Stills & Nash Allies

Bluenote Cafe volume eleven Neil Young Archives Performance Series

Red Rocks Live: Neil Young Friends & Relatives

Neil Young: Heart of Gold Film
Paramount Classics

PS

Life on the road can be hard on the families left at home, but there are a few opportunities where they can share in the adventure. The end of Neil's 1978 *Rust Never Sleeps* Tour gave my family a chance to enjoy some time together. The last record date of the tour for me was to be October 22, 1978, at the Cow Palace, just outside of San Francisco.

My wife and two young children flew out to San Francisco early, where I put them up in the grand old 1926 Mark Hopkins Hotel for a brief vacation. Dusty, Ryan, and Allison (Nate would come a few years later) rarely got to go on the hectic tours, so this was a nice treat for all of us. They got to see the great city up close, ride the cable cars around the steep hills, visit the zoo, splash in the Pacific ocean, or at least the bay. . . . I wanted my kids to see the world while they were young, it's so important to learn about other cultures and histories, not to mention the incredibly diverse geography in the United States. The huge difference between the West Coast and their native East Coast really thrilled them. I'm from Montana, so they would soon visit the "North Coast" and later the Southern Gulf Coast, where my Air Force family was once stationed.

Much as I loved having them visit, there was a little drama. In the grand hotel bedroom, the kids were bouncing around and I was giving my daughter an "airplane ride," holding her over my head with her "wings" flailing about. Unfortunately, her sharp little fingernail sliced my left eye! It was painful because the eye has nerves galore, and of course I couldn't keep it open to see. The concierge got me to the nearest ophthalmologist where I received my pirate eye patch and lots of pain killers. The doctor said it was not an uncommon injury and that I was lucky it wasn't too deep and would "most likely" heal. Meanwhile I had to record Neil's show the next day, a bit high on whatever pain killers the doctor gave me, and mono vision, but I had things pretty well dialed in after recording eight consecutive shows: "the show must go on," and so must the family. They would have many more adventures with me down the road.

8

THE HAVANA JAM IN CUBA 1979

The Cold War, Where American and Cuban Stars Play in Peace

The common thread of music and baseball allowed the late Bruce Lund-vall, then president of CBS Records, to negotiate a diplomatic crack in the door to Cold War Cuba. It was to be a music festival featuring US stars like Billy Joel, Stephen Stills, and Kris Kristofferson paired with Cuban stars like Irakere, Pacho Alonso, and Arturo Sandoval. It would be known in Cuba as Musica CUBA–USA and elsewhere as the Havana Jam.

I designed and built a Record Plant remote package with all the accouterments to support a dual 24-track recording of the shows. Getting it there was half the fun: the recording gear flying on a Curtis C-46 cargo plane from the World War II era. There were no legal flights from the United States, so these were charters from South America.

My crew and other production staff from Columbia Records flew in on an aging Martin 4-0-4 twin-engine charter from South America. One of the guys nervously pointed out the oil streaks behind the propeller engines. Having grown up an Air Force brat, my pilot father would have said, "you only worry when it *stops* leaking oil."

The Havana air traffic controller seemed to enjoy making us wait for permission to land, circling the airfield while there were no other aircraft in the pattern.

When we finally landed at José Martí Airport in Havana, we were made to wait in a small reception area with few chairs. In fact, I was sitting on the floor with my back against the wall, when I noticed one of the guys digging in his shoulder bag suddenly became wide-eyed and silent. He quietly got up and walked to the restroom. When he returned, he confessed that there was a small vile of leftover "recreational material" that needed to be flushed down the toilet. I can only imagine had that been discovered when we went through Cuban customs!

We were introduced to a lovely young lady who was to be our guide, actually a government minder, who let us know that she had to stay with us everywhere we went. I had traveled in communist-controlled Eastern Europe, so I knew they were dead serious.

We were staying at the Havana Hilton Hotel, a well-preserved piece of 1959 Americana. I was a little miffed to find I was sharing a room, but it turned out to be with Jack Maxson of Showco, the famed Texas company, providing sound for the concert. When his suitcase yielded a bottle of good Scotch and some magazines on vintage aircraft, we became lifelong friends! Maxson and I would work on many shows together over the years, including the Rolling Stones tours.

The shows were taking place in a 5,500-seat venue, renamed the Karl Marx Theater after the Cuban revolution. Showco brought a large touring sound system, and we built our portable recording system in a dressing room offstage.

One of the highlights of our stay was being treated to the legendary Co-pacabana dance show, in an outdoor tropical forest setting. The band was great, but of course the real stars are the scantily clad dancers! I found it amusing that the communist Castro regime allowed this leftover decadence from the US gangsters to continue. It was an important source of hard currency from the tourist trade, much of it from Eastern European communist countries. I would see these same acts years later touring with Yoko Ono in Budapest, Hungry, while it was still under Russian control.

The music performances were spread across the three-day festival, and they were quite competitive, with all the musicians upping their game for these shows.

The first show on Friday was packed, as were all three, with a mixed crowd of well-connected party members, many young fans, music business executives from both sides, and security guards. The crowd's reception was most welcoming, even though the long opening speeches by Cuban officials outnumbered Columbia Records president Bruce Lundvall's single presentation. Bruce really was the driving force behind a complicated political Cold War negotiation.

The US band Weather Report opened the show to enthusiastic hooting, a unique Cuban greeting for a band the audience knew from listening to

Florida radio stations. Cuban classic, traditional, and modern acts followed, like Orquesta Aragon, and then the Fania All-Stars—the US-based salsa supergroup, that all parties loved.

The second show on Saturday opened with the CBS Jazz All-Stars, a phenomenal group including Dexter Gordon, Stan Getz, Jimmy Heath, and many other classic jazz giants. The crowd were on their feet with applause and then welcomed the "one-time only" Trio of Doom—John McLaughlin, Jaco Pastorius, and Tony Williams. That recording was finally released only a few years ago! Another great ensemble performed with Jimmy Heath, Hubert Laws, Arthur Blythe and was propelled by Richard Tee, Eric Gale, and John Lee. Those were some tough acts to follow!

The Cubans answered with a 25-piece percussion group of all-stars backed by the Frank Emilio quartet. It was an amazing performance that kept our tape recorder VU meters on red alert!

Steve Stills brought US rock to the stage with his band that included Bonnie Bramlett and Mike Finnegan to sing background vocals for the Crosby, Stills & Nash songs! Steve Stills finished with a song he wrote in Spanish for the occasion . . . "Cuba El Fin!" He waded into the crown to finish it, much to the alarm of the Cuban security guards!

The Cuban band Erakere, with Chucho Valdez on piano, was the rightful headliner and were later joined by the American All-Stars for a grand finale that lasted till 3:00 a.m., when the powers that be shut us down.

The final show on Sunday started with Cuba's legendary singer, Elena Burke and the Orquesta Santiago de Cuba. She was warmly welcomed by the audience. Florida's radio stations made fans in Cuba for Kris Kristofferson and Rita Coolidge. The audience was chanting a chorus of "Kris and Rita!!" Billy Swan and the band played a great set of their many hits. The Cuban singing star Sara Gonzalez and the Pablo Milanes Grupo Manguare performed a powerful set to an appreciative audience.

The Grand Finale for Musica Cuba—USA was to be Billy Joel's long-awaited performance. The packed house was chanting "Bil-lee Yo-ell" and clapping furiously! The Cuban security guards were overwhelmed by the crowd rushing the stage because that was not permitted in Castro's Cuba!!

As Billy was about to appear, we had to take the tapes off of the Ampex 24-track recorders. I had been ordered by the production staff in advance to make sure there were no recordings made of Billy's performances. The blame game for that "No Record" decision was never quite resolved, but it was deeply regretted ex post facto!

We did get to listen to Billy's set in the control room, and having recorded his live shows on numerous occasions, I thought it was one of his best performances ever. He definitely won the hearts of Havana! Unfortunately, I have only my memory to go on; I could find no recordings anywhere.

The grand finale went on until 3:00 a.m., but then they just moved everyone over to the hotel for an all-night jam party that lasted until dawn! Of course, the Record Plant crew and I had to pack up all the remote studio gear for the flight back to the United States; there were no more mojitos for us.

It was a wonderful adventure that became known as the "Bay of Gigs." For those of you too young to get the pun, look up Bay of Pigs.

Leaving Havana was even more difficult than arriving. On the day of departure, my crew had all packed up and met in the lobby of the hotel. Unfortunately, the official bus had left for the airport without us. So not wanting to miss our flight, I hailed a Cuban taxi. We found the rest of the cast in the airport restaurant celebrating with our last chance at Cuban rum and beer.

A short time later, our poor government minder came frantically running up to us. She was in tears with panic, crying, "Thank God I found you! If I lost you I would have been arrested!" We promised no one would report her to Castro.

After endless delays, the airport police finally guided us toward the loading gate. Our chartered Boeing 707 jet was waiting out on the ramp, but so was a Russian IL-62 jet. We soon found ourselves merging with the Russian passengers, who were mixed military and "plain clothes," heading for their flight. This was a deliberate set up to clash the Russians with us in a narrow passageway! The Cold War was still on and with a red grin.

I drew a Russian officer with all kinds of rank but was in no mood for this treatment. He did not get past me. Fortunately, there were no serious physical altercations and we got on a bus to go to our Boeing 707. Then we sat there, waiting again. With a brilliant stroke of humor, Steve Stills played his guitar and narrated the Rod Serling intro to the television show *The Twilight Zone*! That cracked everybody up and released the tension.

Phil Gitomer had stayed to supervise our Record Plant studio gear being loaded on the cargo plane back Stateside, as there had been innuendos that we really should "donate" the recording gear to the cause. Bruce Lundvall had already donated a lot of Columbia Records swag.

It was quite an adventure and I had hoped that some progress had been made toward peace. I know that many of the musicians felt that way, and it did result in some Cuban musicians being able to leave Cuba to tour internationally. Cuba needed the hard currency, and the musicians needed the opportunity to escape Castro!

Irakere and a few other artists did manage to defect later on.

There are compelling stories about Billy Joel's family involvement in Cuba after fleeing Nazi-occupied Europe and why Billy was so keen to play here.

Recommended Recordings

Havana Jam 1 and *Havana Jam 2*
Columbia Records

Trio of Doom John McLaughlin, Jaco Pastorius, Tony Williams
Legacy Recordings

Havana Jam '79 Documentary
Ernesto Juan Castellanos

(https://www.facebook.com/havanajam79)

PS

I want to add a recent story that surfaced about a Jaco Pastorius recording we did in 1982.

This is from a blog I wrote for Audio-Technica, a favorite audio equipment manufacturer. I own the material and have their permission to use it here. This seemed like an appropriate home for it.

Jaco Pastorius on *Jazz Alive*

The recent discovery of Jaco Pistorius's ultra-rare Big Band recording from a 1982 NPR program called *Jazz Alive*, really brought back memories of this self-proclaimed "Greatest Bass Player in the World." It was special to me for a number of reasons; first, because I was there in charge of the Record Plant New York Black Truck with NPR engineer Paul Blakemore as it was recorded live at Avery Fisher Hall in New York City. Second, because it was still in a "Golden Era" of live music when great jazz ensembles like this would suddenly appear. Third, because all this great jazz was once available free for the listening on NPR via the *Jazz Alive* program.

I recently called on Paul who is now in charge of mastering at the Concord Music Group. We had a great time talking about that highly charged session. You can find an in-depth interview on NPR (http://www.npr.org/2017/05/27/530194946/in-a-lost-concert-jaco-pastorius-sounded-the-rhythm-of-the-city).

Paul had wonderful stories of meeting Jaco in clubs in the 1970s, when Paul was a drummer, so you can imagine his pleasure in being able to meet him again as a recording engineer. There were so many great shows recorded for *Jazz Alive*, like the complete 1981 Monterrey Jazz Festival and quite a few in New York that I remember. Paul went on to an illustrious career as a recording, mixing, and mastering engineer.

What began to intrigue me was the story of how a public and privately funded nonprofit sanctioned by congress could produce these great jazz recordings.

I also called on longtime friend and co-conspirator on many a remote, Jim Anderson. Jim was one of the original NPR live engineers, starting with the New Orleans Jazz & Blues Festival in 1977. They spent two glorious weeks recording the likes of Ella Fitzgerald and Stevie Wonder for *Jazz Alive*'s first radio broadcast.

Jim also explained how the National Endowment for the Arts provided grants to produce radio programs like *All Things Considered*, still on the air today and a program so many people depend on for a wider worldview. I know I do, as do my adult children.

The National Endowment for the Humanities provided grants from 1976 to 1980 for recording live classical and jazz concerts in Europe to air on NPR. Jim traveled to Paris and Berlin in those days engineering those shows. So, you can see how these institutions contributed to our greater music industry. Some may know Jim as a past president of AES, Chairman of the Clive Davis Institute of Recorded Music at NYU, and for his many Grammy-winning recordings. I was privileged to be the engineer when Jim produced several episodes for *In Performance at the White House*, back when musicians were welcome there.

Those wonderful music programs were made available to all of NPR radio station affiliates in the United States. This was before so many public schools started to cut funding for their own music education programs. All three of my kids played in public school bands and arts programs, as well as listening to NPR (they had no choice, it was always on at home!). Although none of them became professional musicians, it was a major part of their education. Just ask my oldest son, Ryan, who has gone on to a successful career as an engineer and producer.

In this era of drastic cuts in funding to the arts and proposals to *eliminate* these agencies, all of us in the music business, regardless of politics, *must* do whatever we can to support these programs. Please let your local, state, and national officials know how valuable these agencies are. You can find them on the web; please tell them you will watch how they vote!

Music matters!
David W. Hewitt

BILLY JOEL:
NEW YORK STATE OF MIND

Carnegie Hall, Yankee Stadium, Boat
House Studio, *River of Dreams*

Billy and New York have been synonymous for so long, it's hard to remember when that started. But for me, Billy's stardom actually started in Puerto Rico at the 1972 Mar y Sol Pop Festival. This was still in the era of Woodstock-style rock festivals, and there were several dozen major acts booked, including the Allman Brothers; Emerson, Lake, and Palmer; B. B. King; Dave Brubeck; and a rising star named Billy Joel.

My girlfriend at the time was a stewardess for Eastern Airlines based in San Juan, so I flew down to attend the festival with her. The whole event was quite a debacle, out in the jungle with a hostile government and irate locals, not to mention stranded musicians and disappearing promoters! We were fortunate to get through it unscathed, but the music was great! Bill Hanley engineered the PA on the same system that he provided for Woodstock, and I was able to park on the mix position as a fake press photographer. John Lennon's band Elephant's Memory was there, and although John couldn't travel because of his visa problems, he sent a tape-recorded greeting. I particularly enjoyed jazz great, and Billy's idol, Dave Brubeck with Gerry Mulligan. Emerson, Lake, and Palmer played their classically tinged progressive rock to majestic effect, and Alice Cooper stunned the crowd with his showmanship.

Billy put on a spirited performance and received good reviews in the *New York Times* for lighting up a rain-*soaked* audience with a rendition of Joe Cocker's "The Letter" and kept them rocking through his set.

Rumor has it there were Columbia Records reps in the audience and that would pay off later. Apparently, word did get back to label president Clive Davis.

There was a remote recording truck there all the way from Heider Studios in LA. Years later engineer Tom Scott would tell me the story of the truck and crew being locked backstage by enraged locals who hadn't been paid. They had to drive the truck through the hurricane fence to escape! There was a Mar y Sol album released on ATCO in 1972, but unfortunately without Billy's performance. If he was recorded, the tapes have not surfaced as yet.

Back home in Philadelphia, where I was still working at Regent Sound, Billy Joel would play a now legendary live radio show over WMMR from Sigma Sound Studios. Listeners kept requesting replays of "Captain Jack," and other radio stations soon picked up on the popularity, even Clive Davis heard about it. Billy's fortunes were about to change.

The Recordings

Mar y Sol Festival
Originally issued as a two-record set on ATCO Records in 1972

WMMR Billy Joel Live
Released as a bonus CD in 2010 with the *Piano Man* reissue.

NEW YORK CITY AND CARNEGIE HALL

Fast forward to June 1977, where Billy Joel and his band, now signed to Columbia Records, were hot off the road promoting his *Turnstiles* album and booked into Carnegie Hall for four nights. That was a major accomplishment in those days; rock acts were not always welcome in the classic venues because of too much gear, too loud, rowdy fans, and nonunion roadies! However, they were always glad to see us because Carnegie Hall and the union charged hefty fees for the privilege of recording and using the hallowed name.

Billy had been working on new songs for his next album while on tour and would be showcasing them in these concerts with orchestral accompaniment. Now he needed a star producer.

There is the famous story of Beatles producer George Martin auditioning one of Billy's earlier shows and being interested in producing him, albeit with his studio musicians. Billy had been disappointed in polished session players before and insisted on using his touring band, so George Martin demurred, for which he would later admit regret. Actually, so would Billy; was it the right decision in the long run? It seems to have worked out.

The next candidate for producer was one Phil Ramone, who Billy Joel admired for his work with Paul Simon and Barbra Streisand. She had recorded his "New York State of Mind" for her own album and made it a hit. Ramone was invited to attend a Carnegie Hall performance and was knocked out by the high-energy performance and the raucous audience reaction. That was enough to have Don DeVito, who was Billy's Columbia Records A&R producer, book the Record Plant New York remote truck to record the show on June 3. We had worked with Phil Ramone before, recording John Lennon and Judy Collins, but this was my first time meeting Don DeVito. DeVito would become a good friend and client over the years. He was the consummate rock-and-roll A&R guy: a street-smart, former guitar player (in Al Kooper's band) who really understood the artists. He had already produced live albums for Bob Dylan and knew all about the road. DeVito would tell me years later that he remembered this show as one of his all-time favorites, and I have to concur. By 1977 I had recorded many shows at Carnegie Hall, including Ray Charles, Ella Fitzgerald, and even Frank Sinatra, but this was the first rock star I would hear playing the hallowed hall. But hey, he did bring an orchestra and is a classically trained pianist. Listening to this recording today makes me realize what an amazing performance it was. These shows really confirmed his place in New York stardom.

Billy was already playing in concert some of the songs that would appear on *The Stranger* album. Within a month Phil Ramone would be producing Billy's new album at his A&R Studios with Jim Boyer engineering. This was the start of a long personal and professional relationship that would yield seven albums.

Because of the concentration on the new studio album, the live recording from Carnegie Hall languished in the vault until 2008. I highly recommend it, if you can find it!

The Recordings

The 30th Anniversary Edition of The Stranger with the Live at Carnegie Hall Show 1977.
Issued on Columbia Records in 2008

BILLY JOEL PLAYS A HISTORIC SHOW IN CUBA
THE HAVANA JAM FEBRUARY 26–MARCH 7, 1979

The previous chapter was dedicated to the extraordinary adventure that was the Havana Jam, so here I will dwell on Billy's performance as the headliner for the US artists playing the show. They would share the concerts with an equal number of Cuban musicians. Remember this was still during the "Cold War" era after the Cuban Missile Crisis with Russia. A cultural exchange like this was a rare opportunity for peaceful dialogue.

The entire Cuban project was orchestrated by Bruce Lundvall, then president of Billy's label, Columbia Records. They had invested a large amount of capital, both financially and politically, to make these concerts a reality. We were part of that investment. As director of remote recording at Record Plant New York, I had designed and built a portable recording studio that would provide studio-grade audio for live albums to help recover those expenses. It was a bit of a shock when the Columbia engineers and I were definitely told, "Do not record Billy Joel's performance."

There are conflicting stories about why this happened; one version was that Billy and his manager/wife Elizabeth refused to participate in the financial exploitation of what was supposed to be a nonprofit cultural exchange. This may also have been about the Joel family history in Cuba. Billy Joel's father, Helmuth Joel, fled Nazi Germany with his Jewish parents, Karl and Meta Joel in 1939. They were among the fortunate few who made their way to England and sailed to Cuba, hoping to emigrate to the United States from there. Other less fortunate family members are known to have perished in concentration camps.

The Joel family lived in Cuba for several years while waiting for visas, during which time Helmuth was allowed to attend a Cuban university. Finally, in the early 1940s, the family was allowed entry into the United States and moved to New York City. Suffice it to say, Billy had reason to feel a special connection to Cuba. He still had family members living there, and he was able to visit with them. I don't know if they attended the show, but you can be sure that many Cubans did know about his family's Cuban history.

There were other US stars performing, including Stephen Stills of Crosby, Stills & Nash; jazz fusion pioneers Weather Report; and country star Kris Kristofferson with his wife, singer Rita Coolidge, but the audience was thirsty for some US rock and roll and Billy Joel's band delivered. Castro's government kept a tight lid on music, so the kids at the Karl Marx Theater almost rioted when they finally got to hear a real rock band through a huge sound system mixed by Showco founder Jack Maxson. It was a bit tense with the soldiers with machine guns keeping the fans from storming the stage, but the show was a huge success. *People* magazine reported a young Billy Joel fan saying "We listen to him on radio and when the weather is clear we can see *Soul Train* on television. But now here's Billy Joel, this is the most important thing to happen in twenty years." Fidel Castro did not attend.

All of the Columbia Records staff and my crew monitored Billy's triumphant performance back in our control room with the JBL speakers cranked up. I had to stand there and watch the two big Ampex 24-track recorders looking forlorn without any tape loaded. I was told that Billy later regretted that Elizabeth had made the management decision not to record the concert. You can always decide not to release it later, but now it's gone forever. . . . Never stop tape.

The Recordings

Havana Jam and Havana Jam 2
Original two record set issued on vinyl in 1979 by Columbia Records

Trio of Doom John McLaughlin, Jaco Pastorius, Tony Williams
Issued on CD in 2007 by SONY BMG

BILLY JOEL IN BLACK AND WHITE

In July 1981, we got a call from Phil Ramone to bring the Record Plant Black Truck out to Sparks Tavern on Long Island, where Billy used to play in his early career. The band had grown since the small club days. It was tight squeezing them in among all the cameras and recording gear. Getting everything placed and the lighting focused to the director's satisfaction was difficult. They were still working at it while Billy Joel was impatiently waiting to play. After several false starts and stops, the associate director called "Roll sound, roll cameras, slate . . . Action!" We were watching the video feed in the recording truck and saw a close up of Billy grinning and saying "Hold it! Let's just waste a little more time." He then crossed his arms and made the whole production wait for him! We thought it was hilarious; the film crew, not so much.

They did successfully shoot four performances in black-and-white film that were then made into worldwide promotional videos for Billy Joel's singles. Some of the audio recordings were also released in later CD collections. Record companies love to have extra tracks for something to release in between studio albums.

BILLY JOEL AND NELSON MANDELA PLAY YANKEE STADIUM

By June 1990, my company, Remote Recording Services, was operating its brand-new Silver Truck, a large tractor-trailer with the latest custom API console and a matched pair of Swiss Studer A-820 24-track recorders. This was the pinnacle of analog audio technology before the long decent into low sampling rate digital.

Columbia Records producer Don DeVito booked us to record Billy at Yankee Stadium, the first rock star allowed to play there. This was considered to be his homecoming to the Bronx where it all began. It was a perfect setting for a major video special. Director Jon Small was Billy's original drummer and who better to capture the show on camera. Billy was known to be a big baseball fan, but there was a bit of controversy over his preferences between the Yankees and the Mets. His fans didn't seem to care and the shows were a huge success. The two shows sold 103,000 tickets and the concert video and CD were certified Platinum by RIAA and were nominated for a Grammy for Best Music Video.

Nelson Mandela, the South African revolutionary politician, recently released from 27 years in prison, was in New York to be honored and to stage anti-apartheid rallies. They had trouble with Yankees owner George Steinbrenner over trying to book Yankee Stadium, until Billy Joel offered one of his tour dates and donated his staging and sound system. After Mandela's powerful rally speech, New York mayor David Dinkins draped Mandela in a Yankees jacket, to which Mandela responded, "You now know who I am. I am a Yankee!" The next day Steinbrenner offered to reimburse the event's expenses.

The Recordings

Billy Joel—Live at Yankee Stadium
DVD issued in 1990 on CMV
CD issued in 1990 on CBS Records

David W. Hewitt late night mixing at Regent Sound Studios, Philadelphia, PA.
Photo courtesy of Lynn W. Hewitt

David W. Hewitt, first live recording in the Record Plant Remote Truck at the Academy of Music, Philadelphia, PA.

Record Plant Studios NY owner Roy Cicala in a rare peaceful moment. More than just great records, he helped make the careers of so many people, including mine. Rest in Peace, Roy.

Recording *The Who Tour 1982* on the Black Truck: David W. Hewitt, David DB Brown, Kooster McAllister, Phil Gitomer.
Photo courtesy of David DB Brown

David W. Hewitt mixing on the API console in the Black Remote Truck.
Photo courtesy of David DB Brown

At the 1982 Tony Awards, Kooster McAllister and Phil Gitomer dressed up for the stage.

Record Plant Family beach picnic celebrating Lila and Ruby's anniversaries.

The Culture Crew: David with Producer Jay David Saks and Broadcast Director Bill King. Usually seen at the NY Metropolitan Opera, but now at the Washington National Opera.

The legendary Engineer/Producer Eddie Kramer and David W. Hewitt recording one of his many Kiss albums.

The man who invented so much of modern recording, Producer Tom Dowd (R), Sony Music Exec Michael Caplan (C) and Engineer Jay Mark, recording the Allman Brothers.

Neil Young's long-time Producers, Larry Johnson and David Briggs flanking Engineer David W. Hewitt in center.

Yoko Ono's birthday party for her son, Sean Lennon, while on her 1985 Starpeace tour in Budapest, Hungary.

Woodstock '94, or Mud-stock as it became known . . . with a band of great Engineer/Producers: Ed Cherney, Dave Thoener, and Elliot Scheiner, with me and Phil Gitomer keeping it all in record.

Woodstock '94 in the modernized Record Plant Remote Truck: Recording Boss Chris Stone, Producer Mitch Maketanski, Engineer Dave Thoener, Engineer Kooster McAllister and the multi talented Paul Prestopino.

Rolling Stones 1998 *Bridges to Babylon Tour* Buenos Aires, Argentina. Remote Recording crew Ryan Hewitt, Sean McClintock, Phil Gitomer, David W. Hewitt and Producer/Engineer Ed Cherney.
Photo courtesy of David W Hewitt

Hewitt Remote

The Academy Awards Broadcast lobby, Kodak Theater in LA: Tech Phil Gitomer, Engineer David W. Hewitt, and Orchestra Mixer Tom Vicari.

The Hewitt Dynasty in our Silver Remote Truck: Ryan Johnathan Hewitt and David W. Hewitt.

This was taken at an *In Performance at The White House* PBS Show by my friend and the Audio Producer, Jim Anderson.
Photo courtesy of Jim Anderson

Esteemed Producer/Engineer Bruce Botnick and wife Marie recording the mega-show *King David* on Broadway in New York.

Rolling Stones live broadcast from the Super Dome on the West Wood One Truck with Biff Dawes and David W. Hewitt engineering.

The *Eagles Hell Freezes* Over Tour with Master Producer/Engineer Elliot Scheiner and David W. Hewitt on the Silver Truck.

Ed Cherney and Rose Mann Cherney at the Technical Excellence & Creativity (TEC) Awards, both richly deserving their induction into the TEC Hall of Fame. They are royalty in our music recording world!

Kooster McAllister, much loved and missed, mixing in the Black Truck, which he helped me build at Record Plant NY. R.I.P.
Photo courtesy of David DB Brown

David DB Brown in the Black Truck, multi tasking between Tech, engineering, mixing, photography and 10 other things!
Photo courtesy of David DB Brown

RIVER OF DREAMS: BILLY JOEL'S 12TH AND LAST ROCK ALBUM

My next encounter with Billy was in 1992 when he decided to start recording for his new album, then titled *The Shelter Island Sessions*. Rather than
commute to a New York recording studio, Billy decided to use a former
boathouse as a rehearsal and recording space. It was at Island Boatyard,
not far from Billy's waterfront home, so he could commute by boat. A portable recording system was brought in by Dave Wilkerson of Right Coast
Recording to start the project and as always seems to happen, the demands
of the band quickly mushroomed. I was called by Columbia A&R chief Don
DeVito to supply a larger recording console to meet Billy's needs and co-
producer Danny Kortchmar. By now it was decided that a full-blown studio
console with automation was required. Fortunately, I was able to procure
an SSL 4000 console that the famous Power Station Studios had available.
It had been upgraded sonically and was up to date on automation. An SSL
4K is a big, heavy board, and it did require disassembly, a moving crew, and
bit of work getting it commissioned out at the Boathouse. I must say it was
a pleasant change of pace from the hectic live shows to be able to hang out
with Billy and the band. He is such a high energy, caustically funny cat and
kept everyone on their toes. Once everything was up and running, I was
able to leave it in the capable hands of Billy's crew and engineers.

I'm told that most of the album that became known as *River of Dreams*
was recorded at the Boathouse at the Island Boatyard with additional sessions at Cove City Sound Studios and the Hit Factory. This would be Billy's
twelfth and last rock studio album. It also turned out to be one of his most
successful, going Platinum five times, according to RIAA, and earned a
Grammy Award for Album of the Year 1993.

The Recordings

River of Dreams
CD issued in 1993 on Columbia Records

A Voyage on the River of Dreams
3 CD box set issued in 1993 on Columbia Records

BACK ON THE ROAD

Now of course to support the album, the River of Dreams Tour for 1993 and
1994 started up. The first recording we did on the 1993 tour was actually

booked by the New York PBS station WNET/13 *Great Performances*. Our friend Mitch Owgang would be producing. Billy would allow portions to be used for public television fundraising; he has a long history of support for the arts and education. Another thing he has a history of is keeping the band razor sharp at sound check by calling out anything but the usual songs. Obscure 1950s pop songs, jazz standards, and you guys better get those background vocals too! He pulled a funny one on me at this sound check as I was engineering in the Silver Truck. After a few songs at the piano, it looked like he was heading offstage, so I called for my stage manager to ask for a level check on the downstage mic. Billy dutifully runs over and grabs the mic, and sings at full show level "I'M SINGING ON THE MIC, I'M SUCH A FUCKING KIKE!!" . . . How's that, he says with a big grin. Being Jewish, he can get away with it and cracks up the MOTs and us goyem.

This show was held in the old Boston Garden, a classic wooden sports arena built in 1928. Boston is a great rock-and-roll town, and we recorded many a show there over the years, including Boston favorites The J Geils Band, Aerosmith, Bob Seger, and even Frank Sinatra. All of those recordings would make it onto live albums selling millions of records. This was the last time we would record there because it was torn down a few years later. The modern Fleet Center replaced it, and we would record Fleetwood Mac there, but the old Garden still lives on in my memory with all the other lost legends of live theater.

Starting in 1994, Billy teamed up with Elton John on the Face-to-Face Tour. That tour sold just under two million tickets and grossed more than $48 million. When they arrived at Giants Stadium in New Jersey for five shows, we joined them with the Silver Truck to record more songs for the *Live from the River of Dreams* CD. Our old friend Don DeVito, who has been Billy's A&R director at Columbia since the 1977 Carnegie Hall recording, would produce this project. If I said Boston was a great rock-and-roll town, then the unlikely burg of East Rutherford, New Jersey, is a monster rock town. Situated right outside of New York City, the Giants Stadium can attract crowds like the 300,000 fans that attended these shows. The logistics of recording this kind of giant show can be daunting but rewarding when you capture performances like Billy and his band turned in. We shared recordings on this live album with my old friend Kooster McAllister and his Record Plant remote truck. Although extensively expanded and updated, it is based on the original 1970 White Truck that I started on at Record Plant Studios New York. McAllister worked with me there for many years until I formed my own company, Remote Recording Services. Kooster stayed on to continue the fabled Record Plant remote legacy, now in modern purple livery.

The Recordings

Billy Joel Live from the River of Dreams Tour '93–'94
My Lives/Live from the River of Dreams (Special Limited Edition 5-Disc
    Advance CDs issued in 1994 on Columbia)

BILLY JOEL HOSTS PIANO GRAND!
A SMITHSONIAN CELEBRATION OF THE 300TH ANNIVERSARY OF THE PIANO
A PBS *GREAT PERFORMANCES* SPECIAL, MARCH 8–9, 2000

The Smithsonian complex of museums is the world's largest and among their collections are more than 5,000 musical instruments, and included in this anniversary celebration is a 1722 Bartolommeo Cristofori grand piano (Cristofori is believed to have invented the Piano), Irving Berlin's upright piano, and even one of Liberace's Baldwin grands.

True fans of Billy will know that his father was a classically trained pianist and his mother started him on classic piano lessons at the age of four. Of course, by his teens he was playing in rock bands, but he was also tuned into the great jazz artists of his era.

We now know that Billy had paused his song writing career to concentrate on composing more classically oriented music, like his album *Fantasies & Delusions*. So Billy was the perfect choice to host this celebration with star pianists from every musical genre.

Billy opened the show with his tune "Baby Grand" and proceeded with grace and humor to introduce a wonderfully diverse cast of performers. Jerry Lee Lewis rocked the mostly formal Washington crowd with "Whole Lotta Shakin' Goin' On," but most of the performances were more classic, like the beautiful sisters Katia and Marielle Labeque's duo piano performance of "America" and a wonderful arrangement of Billy Joel's "Fantasy Film Noir" by pianist Hyung-Ki Joo. But the real star of the evening was Billy's hero, 79-year-old jazz master Dave Brubeck. He mesmerized the audience with a thoughtful introduction and a solo rendition of his thank you to Chopin, "Dziekuje."

There were many other wonderful performances, and of course, Billy Joel closed with "Piano Man."

The Recordings

Piano Grand! A Smithsonian Celebration
DVD issued in 2000 on Sony Home Entertainment

WORLD TRADE CENTER ATTACK, 9/11
THE CONCERT FOR NEW YORK CITY, OCTOBER 20, 2001

In the aftermath of the World Trade Center attack, the United States was still in shock. The entire music community, especially those of us whose lives centered around New York City, came together to put on a benefit concert for the victims and survivors. It was the most difficult, heartbreaking, exhausting, and monumental show of my life.

There is a whole chapter dedicated to the concert, so here I focus on Billy Joel's performance. If ever there was a time for Billy to show his New York chutzpa, this was it.

Coming on stage after his hero Martin Scorsese, Billy placed a first responder's helmet on the piano and storms into an ironic rendition of "Miami 2017: Seen the Lights Go out on Broadway" to the tears and rage of recognition in the audience. When he finished, Billy famously said, "I wrote that song 25 years ago. I thought it was going to be a science fiction song; I never thought it would really happen. But unlike the end of that song, we ain't going anywhere!" The audience of first responders and survivors cheered wildly in agreement. With typical Billy Joel attitude he then played his signature "New York State of Mind" as testimony to the resilience of all New Yorkers, indeed, all of the United States.

Just before Paul McCartney's headlining appearance, Elton John played several songs and then reintroduced Joel. Billy gathered up police and fire captains' hats tossed up on stage for them to wear. Together they played "Your Song," a powerful love song to remember the fallen.

In an intense night of brilliant, heartfelt performances by great artists, Billy's was uniquely New York. As I write this in 2017, Miami 2017 still plays in my memory with thoughts of those who perished on 9/11.

The Recordings

The Concert for New York City
CDs issued in 2001 by Sony Music
DVDs issued in 2001 by Columbia SMV

BROADWAY BILLY JOEL
MOVIN' OUT: THE MUSICAL AUGUST 13–14, 2002

This would be my last Billy Joel adventure, albeit without Billy singing. The esteemed choreographer and theatrical director Twyla Tharp had a vision of creating dances to illustrate Joel's characters and songs. The concept of a "rock ballet" was original and dramatically different from other contemporary musicals like Elton John's *The Lion King* and The Who's rock opera *Tommy*. Other producers had approached Billy about writing a Broadway musical to no avail, but he took an interest in Tharp's concept.

The turning point came when Billy discovered a young Michael Cavanaugh performing his songs in Las Vegas. After joining Cavanaugh on stage for a few numbers, Billy was convinced he found his Broadway surrogate.

We were booked by Columbia Records to record the original *Movin' Out* show at the Shubert Theater in Chicago. Management wisely planned to have an *Original Cast* album available for sale by the time the show opened on Broadway in New York. I was pleased to find that Ed Rak would be engineering and mixing the live cast album. Ed founded Clinton Studios in New York and had recorded many great jazz and R&B records.

After all the years of recording Billy and his various bands we were a bit suspicious of a "Broadway" cover band, but they were really good and Michael Cavanaugh sang convincingly with his own style. The band was elevated upstage where you could see them and the sound design by Brian Ruggles, Billy's live mixer, was real rock and roll. Twyla Tharp's production designs and choreography were brilliant and really brought Billy's stories to life as a rock ballet.

Movin' Out did move on to New York's Richard Rogers Theater and played more than 1,000 performances. They also played London and Tokyo along with three national tours in the United States. Tharp won a Tony Award for Best Choreography and Billy Joel won for Best Orchestration.

The Recordings

Movin' Out Original Broadway Cast
CD issued in 2002 on Sony Music

Live Recordings with Billy Joel

Billy Joel Live at Carnegie Hall June 3, 1977 (*The Stranger* 30th Anniversary)
Havana Jam February 26–March 7, 1979, Billy Joel Headlined, Bootleg only
Billy Joel Live at Sparks (film) July 21–24, 1981
Billy Joel Live from Long Island (video) December 29, 1982
Billy Joel Live at Yankee Stadium (all formats) June 22–23, 1990

Billy Joel, Boat House tracks for *River of Dreams* July 12, 1992–May 27, 1993

Billy Joel, *A Voyage on the River of Dreams* (studio and live)

Billy Joel, *No Man's Land* 1993 Tour

Billy Joel Live at The Boston Gardens, PBS TV September 16–17, 1993

Billy Joel, *Live from the River of Dreams* Tour '93–'94

Billy Joel and Elton John, Live at Giants Stadium July 21–25, 1994

Piano Grand! A Smithsonian Celebration of the 300th Anniversary of the Piano Hosted by Billy Joel, March 8–9, 2000

The Concert for New York City, October 18–20, 2001, Billy Joel, Paul McCartney, The Who, Eric Clapton, David Bowie, Elton John, Keith Richards, and Mick Jagger

Movin' Out Original Broadway Cast Album August 13–14, 2002

Many thanks to Billy Joel and Columbia Records for the great music!

IN MEMORIAM

RIP Producer Don DeVito September 6, 1939—November 25, 2011
    Billy Joel, Rosanne Cash, and many others played for a joyful celebration of Don DeVito's life at his hometown Brooklyn Theater.

RIP Producer Phil Ramone January 5, 1934—March 30, 2013
    Legendary engineer, producer and studio owner, Phil Ramone produced many of Billy Joel's albums and was loved by all, a giant in music recording history.

🔟

RECORDING AT THE MANSIONS

Eddie Kramer, the Art
of Rocking in the Grand Acoustics

There is a long history of recording classical music in the grand mansions of Europe, and in recent times, rock bands have discovered the advantages of spacious acoustics and privacy.

The British engineer and producer Eddie Kramer recorded classic rock albums with Led Zeppelin and The Rolling Stones in their English mansions. Now Eddie was living out in the country north of New York City, and he had found a number of classic mansions that were available to use as recording studios. The first recording I did for him was actually a closed theater-in-the-round that he used to record the band Kiss. We moved all the gear out of the Record Plant remote truck and built him a control room. That was the gig where Ace Frehley shot out a bunch of the ceiling lights with his gun. The record, *Rock and Roll Over*, was a direct Platinum hit as well and the first of many.

The Woolworth Family Mansion out on Long Island, was another one of Eddie's discoveries. It was a phenomenal place to record, especially the formal living room with its high ceilings. Behind the ornate carved wooden wall panels lay the ghost of the largest indoor pipe organ in the United States. It was a magnificent collection of un-playable instrumental art. Kramer and I share a love of ancient instruments and electrical designs—a love of copper for this Montana kid from Anaconda.

Eddie produced and engineered the English band Foghat's album *Stone Blue* here. He engineered the recording in the Record Plant remote truck, parked regally between the formal columns of the grand entrance. I remember that session going right up to Christmas Eve of 1977. Santa brought some "white cheer" for the band; Eddie was not amused. He always looked out for the band's well-being and kept their focus on the music, which was rare in those days.

He would also record the band Air Raid in this same mansion a few years later. I was off recording a Frankie Valli and the Four Seasons show on the RCA remote van so Eddie could use the Record Plant remote truck. They had a great custom Neve console, but some wiring problems that had me going for a bit—crossed numbers.

Eddie's next discovery was a colossal mansion that had been the home to the French Order of Cenacle Nuns. The band was Brownsville Station, and they had a great time living in the mansion and recording in the many large acoustic spaces. Eddie stayed in the remote truck for this recording. Eddie was going to bring the band Kiss there to record, but scheduling conflicts prohibited that. Producer Jack Douglas gladly booked the time to bring Aerosmith in to live in the mansion and record the album *Draw the Line*. There are some great photos (see photo section two).

Eddie Kramer loved recording live shows as well, and he was always off to another gig; this time it was a tour with the Atlanta Rhythm Section, one of the greatest groups of session players around. I hated to miss hearing them play, but I was in the middle of designing and building the new Record Plant Black Truck. My two favorite mechanical arts: high performance road machines and large-scale analog recording studios.

BUDDY GUY AND THE *SATURDAY NIGHT LIVE* BAND

I would get to record a few more great live shows with Eddie. One of my favorites was the greatest blues guitarists ever, Buddy Guy! And to top it off, he was backed up by G. E. Smith and the *Saturday Night Live* band. What a combination; they were playing the Erving Plaza in New York City to a sellout crowd of blues aficionados.

LES PAUL'S 88TH BIRTHDAY PARTY
THE IRIDIUM JAZZ CLUB, JUNE 8–9, 2003

Every electric guitar ever made at some point in its life probably wished it was a Les Paul guitar. Look at all the great company it would keep and maybe even have an expensive guitar case to boot!

I first met Les Paul when I recorded the Modern Jazz Quartet for their live *Last Concert* album in 1974. Les had been working on a direct pickup for acoustic instruments and offered them for use at Atlantic Studios, where Les's son, Gene, worked as an engineer. Gene was with me as I recorded the show and mixed the tapes back at Atlantic Records Studio. Les is such a generous, gregarious gentleman and a clever inventor, those pickups sounded great. We became friends and I saw him at Atlantic Records Studios, AES Conventions, and at his home, which is also his studio. What an incredible mansion of music it was. I think he kept every single thing he ever built; it was a treasure vault of studio gear, musical instruments, and mountains of inventions. At the time he had an API console, similar to one of mine, which needed some attention. I remember listening to the *Les Paul and Mary Ford Show* on radio and television back in the late 1940s and 1950s—how did he get those incredible sounds?

I would gradually learn about all of Les's inventions and techniques, but the most important element was just Les himself. So, you can imagine how glad I was to have famed engineer/producer Eddie Kramer call to book the Silver Truck for Les Paul's 88th birthday party at the Iridium Jazz Club. Les had been playing there for many years, and I had visited a few of his shows, so knew what to expect. Eddie had also worked with Les, so we were quickly set up. Les's other son, Rusty, also helped with the PA. Les had a great band with Lou Pallo and Frank Vignola on guitars and the lovely Vicki Parrott on uptight bass and saucy humor to tease Les. They also had guest guitarist Russel Malone and Monty Alexander on piano. Guitar legend Pat Martino appeared as well. With Les graciously leading, everyone enjoyed their turn playing all the great songs of his era. I think "Somewhere over the Rainbow" described it all.

The second set went well into the morning, and then there was the after show party and guests waiting to pay respects to Les Paul on his birthday.

Meanwhile, the crew and I were wrapping the Silver Truck, securing all the gear, finishing up files and documentation. When we're ready to go, I always made one more round of the club to see if we missed anything. The club was almost empty, but I hear Les and some guests laughing and realize it's after 2:00 a.m. and 88-year-old Les Paul is still charming three young female fans—a Les Paul coda. What an incredible life he led; it was an honor to know you, Les.

Lester William Polisfuss, aka Les Paul, June 9, 1915–August 12, 2009

A NOTE FROM EDDIE KRAMER

I met Dave Hewitt in 1972 when I lived in London Terrace Towers in Chelsea, New York City.

I had recently bought a vintage Ferrari, which was a bit ropey, but I loved it.

I took Dave for a ride up the West Side highway at probably close to 100 mph; he really dug it and we bonded over the love of great sports cars and racing!

My first taste of recording with Dave was with the Record Plant mobile unit that he was running. We recorded the band Foghat in the magnificent old Woolworth Mansion on Long Island.

Dave always had the most amazingly even-keeled demeanor even when all about us things were coming apart or mics and cables were malfunctioning, Dave always had an answer and was calm as could be under fire.

I loved to record bands in unusual spaces like old mansions, and there were quite a laundry list of the most odd buildings I found that on the surface one would say "You gotta be kidding—it will never work out!" way too reverberant, etc. But Dave was always there for the adventure and with a gung-ho attitude of "Let's try it!"

A great example was Ace Frehley's solo album for Kiss. I found the Colgate mansion in Connecticut with fabulous different sounding acoustics for each room. Ace's amps in the main living room, bass in the parlor, and the drums on the first landing of a massive staircase! Oh, and plenty of ghosts to keep everyone unhappy at night!!

What great sounds we got with you, Dave; you are the king of remote sound recording!

—EHK
(Eddie Kramer, Engineer, Producer, Designer)

GLENEAGLES HOTEL AND THE KING AND QUEEN'S GOLF COURSES

The palatial Gleneagles Hotel in Auchterarder, Scotland, was built in 1924 by the Caledonian Railway and had many lives, including a hospital in

World War II and was once owned by Guinness Breweries. The famous golf courses were unofficially named after the royal couple and have been successful with the PGA. Formula 1 champion Jackie Stewart has a shooting school nearby. He was a champion at that before his racing crown.

As a celebrated big band venue, the Gleneagles Hotel had the perfect stage and audience accommodation for Sony Music to hold its worldwide convention in 1994. Sony Music boss Tommy Mottola's motto was "whatever it takes!" I flew over the year before to advance the theater for his use. Vice presidents Al Smith and Bill Beatty agreed the historic hotel was perfect for our use. Being located outside of Glasgow, Scotland, was a bit of a challenge for me to get enough recording gear there for the multiple Sony music stars and personalities.

Harry Braun of Sony Classical in Germany was able to find a Swedish remote truck that could cross the borders and meet the tech specs. They had a large British Raindirk console and all the gear necessary for a great live recording, including a great crew and a built-in Bier stube in the back of the trailer!

We came back in March 1994, and Sony had their crews turn the stage and formal pastel dining room into a dark, drape-hung video shooting stage. The hotel and golf course accommodated several hundred Sony Music members, plus dozens of musicians. Among them my favorites were, October Project, a haunting, harmonic band with the incredible singer Mary Fahl, who has thankfully continued as a solo artist, and a young Jeff Buckley singing solo with an acoustic guitar. He was quite strange to me, having been a fan of his father, Tim Buckley, but the raw talent was there. The big British rock stars of the day, Oasis, really brought the house down and became a huge success for Sony Music.

We had a great collection of rock-and-roll road crews, including W'evens, the Rolling Stones longtime monitor mixer. So, it really turned out to be a great series of shows to fire up the worldwide Sony Music sales force. Thank you, Tommy; you had what it takes!

There is a 1994 video of Oasis at Gleneagles showing the hotel online.

COMIC RELIEF!

Gilda Radner and Father Guido to
George Carlin and Eddie Murphy

New York City was home to so many great comedians, and I had the opportunity to work with some of the best. Before there were many dedicated comedy clubs, there was the Bottom Line Theater down on West 4th Street in the Village. Owners Alan Pepper and Stanley Snadowsky made room for some of the wilder comics between all the musical acts we recorded there.

The comedic genius of Firesign Theater, a successful recording act on records, made for a great stage show. Proctor & Bergman, two of the founders, regularly brought the house down. I recorded their album *What This Country Needs* there—and we still need it!

Another wickedly funny comedian regular was Richard Belzer, now known for his role as Munch on TV's *Homicide*, but then as a stand-up and radio comedian. The line I remember from the album: "My hair has a mind of its own; why yesterday it went bowling all by itself." But I can't print most of his jokes here.

FATHER GUIDO SARDUCCI. LIVE AT ST. DOUGLAS CONVENT
JANUARY 18–20, 1980

Saturday Night Live made the careers of Gilda Radner and Don Novello, better known as Father Guido Sarducci. I worked with Don on a number of different shows, including *Saturday Night Live* and Gilda Radner's movie (which had several names before they settled on *Gilda Live*), but this was his star's turn, performing to an all-female (almost) audience, who were acting as "Sisters" at "St. Douglas 'Convent,'" which was actually the University in New Brunswick, New Jersey. The young ladies were into it, but the guys got upset about it and protested. Ha!

The staff worked that out somehow, and we recorded the show to make the live record for Don called, of course, *Live at St. Douglas Convent*. When Don Novello came out to the Record Plant Black Truck after rehearsal, he showed me a realistic handheld sprinkler used for exorcisms, so we figured it would be appropriate to chase all the leftover demons out of the studio. After all, we had recorded Ozzie Osbourne with Black Sabbath and Blue Oyster Cult! There is a great photo in the book of Father Sarducci blessing the API recording console, and we had no further demon visits until a certain evangelist booked us for his concert.

Don gave a terrific performance in his guise, still wearing the tinted glasses and chain smoking away as he performed his classic skits, like my favorite, Father Sarducci's "Five Minute University." He introduced a series of classes like: Business? "You buy a some-thin' and you sell it for more." I wish I had learned that earlier in life. Other life lessons included mass confessions by the "Sisters" in the audience. My favorites were "The People's Space Program" and "How to Deal with Alien Invaders."

I highly recommend looking for this solo record and his many video performances available online from *Saturday Night Live* and *Gilda Live*. Don was great fun to work with, especially his off-camera banter on the wireless microphone.

GILDA RADNER LIVE FROM NEW YORK OR LATER TITLED GILDA RADNER LIVE ON BROADWAY

There were several recordings of Gilda Radner's stage show and several name changes. Of course, it all originated at *Saturday Night Live* with founder Lorne Michaels producing. The live stage shows and film was directed by the esteemed Mike Nichols. Music Promotor Ron Delsener was also producing for the theater.

I brought in the Record Plant Black Truck to record the Broadway play at the Winter Garden in New York August 9–11, 1979. We also recorded the additional shows in Boston September 25–29, 1979. I also show a log entry for December 13, 1979, at the Palladium in New York.

They had essentially brought in the *Saturday Night Live* band, with Paul Shaffer, Howard Shore, and a great cast of players, including G. E. Smith on guitars—guaranteed performances there, and it was later mixed at Phil Ramone's A&R Studios by Jim Boyer. That's a combination that can't be beat.

As I write this, I'm listening to my mint copy of Gilda's vinyl record. It's really bittersweet to hear her delirious comedy routines like "Let's Talk Dirty to the Animals" and hear her tap dancing through "I Love to be Un-happy." Anyone addicted to *Saturday Night Live* can visualize her classic routines like Emily Litella or Roseanne Roseannadanna and gladly listen to the record without visual cues. But of course, I grew up listening to radio.

The live play with Gilda was successful, but the record bombed. It was the last days of the 1970s and video was in the process of "Killing the Radio Star," along with voice-only comedy records. The public could no longer sit still and listen; we had to watch. As Roseanne Roseannadanna would say, "Oh . . . never mind it's always something."

Thank you, Gilda, great to hear you again . . .

RODNEY DANGERFIELD *NO RESPECT*

This album was recorded at Rodney Dangerfield's comedy club, named Dangerfield's, over on the East Side of New York. There were more than a few funny happenings on that gig.

I was still working at Record Plant Studios New York while recording Rodney's live album. Gene Simmons, the lead singer for the band Kiss, happened to be in the studio and found out about the gig. Being a big Rodney fan, he immediately asked if he could meet him. Producer Estelle Endler was kind enough to arrange it and I brought Gene over to the unmarked door leading to Rodney's private room, in the basement of the club. Just like one of his comedy routines, the door opened to find Rodney Dangerfield dressed in a sleeveless T-shirt, boxer shorts, garter-suspended stockings and smoking a little hash pipe! When introduced to Gene, he smiled, offered him the pipe and said, "I don't know who the fuck you are, but glad to meet you!" Estelle made a few pleasantries and excused Rod-ney to get dressed. Gene and I cracked up, grateful for a perfect Rodney scene. I had worked on many live Kiss recordings, most of them with Eddie Kramer.

The album won the Grammy Award for Best Comedy Recording, which is well worth looking for, even if you do respect him.

GEORGE CARLIN'S *WHAT AM I DOING IN NEW JERSEY?*
AN HBO SPECIAL RECORDED IN UNION CITY, NEW JERSEY, MARCH 26, 1988

The Park Performing Arts Center was a former Catholic Church complex built in 1931. The 1,400-seat theater has been preserved, as had the classic Moller Pipe Organ. All George Carlin needed was his stool and a microphone. This was one of 14 HBO specials that Carlin made, and as always, his brilliant, dark comedy captivated the audience like no other comedian. He was an orator, who should have been president.

Just as I say that you must hear musical performances yourself, trying to describe George Carlin live just makes me grin and throw up my hands in surrender! Go find him online.

I also provided a digital recording system at this theater for the performance artist Laurie Jim's film earlier in 1985. Was it part of *United States Live*? I know we worked on that as well.

JERRY SEINFELD *I'M TELLING YOU FOR THE LAST TIME*
THE BROADHURST THEATER IN NEW YORK, AUGUST 6–9, 1998

When the booking came in for Jerry Seinfeld's retirement HBO special, *I'm Telling You for the Last Time*, I was already scheduled for a long overdue break. This was an important client and a huge television star, so it had to be covered properly. I was relieved when Ed Greene was selected as the audio engineer. I use to jokingly call Ed Greene, "Mister Television Audio," because he was. Ed had done more to bring quality audio techniques to live television than anyone I know. He was a successful recording engineer and studio owner in the 1950s; he made the move to LA and MGM Records, where his work with Frank Sinatra brought him into the Grammy Awards; and he soon became the master of that genre. I could go on for pages with his accomplishments, but suffice it to say, I knew he would be the perfect man for the job.

Here is where I abdicate my responsibilities as writer, just like I did on that 1998 show. I jumped into my new BMW M3 (I finally stopped driving the company utility Land Rover) and headed for Denver, Colorado. There

I attended a reunion of my German High School class of 1963; we were all either military or diplomat brats who scattered after graduation and never expected to see each other again. Military families move every two or three years. It's a long story, but I did make it back home in time to record Wynton Marsalis and the Jazz at Lincoln Center Orchestra, always a great program with some of the best musicians on the planet. Back to work . . .

So, I'm confessing that I never got to see the Seinfeld show, I will have to ask you to look at it on YouTube. I have seen some of Jerry's incredible car collection, and I highly recommend looking into that.

(12)

VIDEO KILLED THE RADIO STAR

MTV and the Award Shows:
Emmys, Tonys, Oscars, Grammys . . .

When MTV started in 1981, it really was Music Television. I recorded their first live show with the Charlie Daniels band in Saratoga, New York; there were some teething problems. When the 24-track analog tapes were mixed back in the band's studio, edits and overdubs were done that made syncing the audio with the edited video, shall we say, challenging. It's one of the many reasons why I liked to stay in my remote truck! After that show, we just rolled down the road to record Simon and Garfunkel's big reunion show in Central Park.

The next MTV booking featured Karla DeVito, David Johansen—always a great act (post–New York Dolls, pre–Buster Poindexter)—and another unusual British act, Bow Wow Wow. All this was played out in the dilapidated remains of the New York Diplomat Hotel Ballroom. It had a vintage look on camera, but it was a bit shaky. I believe it collapsed not long after that.

THE MTV NEW YEAR'S EVE SHOWS

MTV soon created an annual New Years' Eve concert with multiple bands that went live to each of the three US time zones. It made for a long day for me as the music mixer. The first one was the 1982–1983 show with the British bands Duran Duran and Flock of Seagulls at the Savoy Theater in

New York, formerly the Hudson Theater. Duran Duran was a huge success for MTV, as video stars came into vogue. Both of these bands were at their peak here.

The following year, MTV expanded the show and moved it to the Manhattan Center, which originally was built by Oscar Hammerstein in 1903 for his Manhattan Opera Company. The upstairs ballroom was all that remained of the original hall and was now owned by Sun Myung Moon's Unification Church—more on the Moonies later. The ballroom was up on the highest floor, which made for difficult cable runs from the audio and video trucks parked down on the street.

One of my favorite stories here was about Grace Slick of the Jefferson Starship née Airplane, getting bombarded with ping pong balls! Some production genius thought it would be great to fly huge nets filled with ping pong balls over the audience and then dump them as the new year hit at midnight! Those balls are hard plastic, and the audience was pissed when they were bombarded with hundreds of them! They retaliated by throwing them at the band on stage, the cameramen, and anybody else in sight. Singer Grace Slick blasted the offending audience members over the PA and stormed offstage—and all that went out to the world on live television. There were many great moments with "Weird Al" Yankovic as he perfected his act over the years. There was also the Beastie Boys spraying there shaken-up beer bottles into the television cameras—best solo of the evening. Dave Edmunds and Lone Justis were quite good as well. We did many more shows there until they developed their own studio. Remind me to tell you about the Moonie's big show at Yankee Stadium; on second thought, don't remind me.

We did prerecord two more New Year's Eve shows for later playback on the actual calendar date of the New Year, December 11–12, 1990, and December 7–9, 1991.

MTV MUSIC AWARDS

The *MTV Music Awards* were very much the youth culture's version of the *Academy Awards*, but with loud music and outrageous costumes. The shows became hugely successful, selling out the classic New York theater, Radio City Music Hall. I have great memories of the hard-rocking Texas band, ZZ Top, driving their Hot Rod Deuce Coupe right across the stage. Who was the female star who rolled across the stage, losing half of her costume in the process? Lots of great moments of MTV history.

Radio City Music Hall, September 12–14, 1984
Radio City Music Hall, September 10–13, 1985
Palladium Theater, September 4–5, 1986

THE *MTV UNPLUGGED* SERIES

Back to focusing on the music. My favorites of the many *MTV Unplugged* shows we recorded were:

Mariah Carey
Kaufman Astoria Studios, March 15–16, 1992

It has been said that Mariah's *MTV Unplugged* performance not only boosted her career to a new level, but also put the *Unplugged* show on the map. The album went four times Platinum in the United States and multiple Gold around the world (see chapter 22).

Pearl Jam's *Unplugged* session was recorded the following day and went on to great success in worldwide distribution.

Neil Young
Ed Sullivan Theater, December 14–15, 1992

I was pleasantly surprised when Neil Young agreed to play an *MTV Unplugged*, especially after some of the skirmishes he has had with them. This show would be staged at the historic Ed Sullivan Theater, where so many great stars had performed, including where the Beatles made their US television debut. The *David Letterman Show* and now Stephen Colbert's *Late Show* have also performed their shows there.

Neil was playing with his band known as The Stray Gators, lineup 6, just for clarity. It was a classic bunch, with Nils Lofgren on guitar, Ben Keith on steel, Spooner Oldham on keys, Tim Drummond on bass, Kenny Buttrey on drums, and vocals by Nicolette Larson and Astrid Gilberto. Neil played his acoustic guitars, piano, harp, and that great old pump organ.

To me, Neil can play no wrong; it's just Neil. The rehearsals were a bit difficult, and he was not happy. I thought the show was classic, with everything from Hank to Hendrix, "Harvest Moon," to "Old Man," and "After the Gold Rush." Apparently Neil did not agree.

After the show ended, David Briggs, Neil's longtime producer, came running out to the remote truck yelling "Neil says don't release those tapes!

He will take care of it. DO NOT GIVE THEM UP!" I knew what was next. MTV's production manager came in to collect the tapes and I had to tell him I couldn't release them—the proverbial rock and a hard place. I've been working with Neil going back to CSNY and *Rust Never Sleeps*; I couldn't let him down, even to a great client like MTV. Neil had been unhappy with the band's performances all through rehearsals and the show.

After much heat, MTV finally gave up and Neil paid for it all. I can't think of many other artists who have that kind of integrity, fiercely living up to their own standards, no matter what the cost. He is one of the few heroes I have left in this business!

Later on, Neil restaged the show out in LA on February 7, 1993, and that became his *Unplugged* album and video. I was sorry to miss that show, but I would get to record him a few more times.

K.D. Lang
Ed Sullivan Theater, December 16, 1992

The day after Neil's show, we set up for K.D. Lang's *Unplugged* on the same stage at the Ed Sullivan Theater. I had just recorded her show at the Tower Theater in Philadelphia, so we were well-prepared, even though her band this time would be "unplugged." She is such a unique artist, singer, writer, and actress. Look up this performance if you are a fan.

We also recorded her *Live by Request*, for the A&E Television Network, which was released as a live album. That was on December 13–14, 2000, at John Jay College in New York.

Nirvana *Unplugged*
Sony Music Studios, New York 12/18/93

This was one of Kurt Cobain's last performances with Nirvana. It was a difficult session that took several days. Cobain was known to be going through drug withdrawal and was argumentative with the producer. Song decisions and rehearsal times were contested. The band Meat Puppets were Cobain's guests—yet another issue. Cobain insisted on playing his acoustic guitar through an amp, which was disguised as a stage monitor.

After many changes, the band did play the entire show in one take but refused to play an encore. It was a dark looking set that matched the mood. The performance included a number of their hits and several Meat Puppet songs, finishing with a Lead Belly song, "Where Did You Sleep Last Night."

The *Unplugged* episode was aired shortly after, in December 1993. Kurt was found dead of a self-inflicted gunshot wound in April 1994.

"Everyone loves a dead artist," is a sad truth in the record business. The album debuted at number one and went on to sell Platinum eight times and won a Grammy Award. It has been reissued several times, including a remastered vinyl edition. Kurt's Martin acoustic guitar sold at auction for $6 million.

Frank Zappa was right.

The Eagles, *Hell Freezes Over*
April 16–21, 1994

This was an MTV concert, technically not an *Unplugged* show, because they played mostly amplified instruments. That said, they all play acoustic guitars brilliantly.

There is a complete story of this extraordinary show in chapter 19.

The Wallflowers and Jewel, Majestic Theater in Brooklyn
May 4–7, *MTV Unplugged*, New York City, 1997

Babyface *MTV Unplugged*, New York City
Manhattan Center, September 24–26, 1997

This was a live album by the R&B Star Babyface, with many guests, like Eric Clapton, Sheila E., and Stevie Wonder. Eric did some astounding solos that Babyface loved. As a matter of fact, so did I. Another big attraction were the string arrangements by Michael Kamen that really fit musically and visually. It is well worth watching and listening.

THE ROCK & ROLL HALL OF FAME FOUNDATION

The foundation was started by Atlantic Records head Ahmet Ertegun in 1983.

When we started recording the Rock & Roll Hall of Fame Awards, they were still just a record industry celebration at the classic Waldorf Hotel Ballroom in New York City—a formal dinner and lots of champagne before and after the awards. There were some theatrical moments, including some drunk speeches by industry titans. All that changed when Lorne Michaels of *Saturday Night Live* began producing it for television. It gradually grew into the giant Rock & Roll Hall of Fame complex in Cleveland, Ohio.

Early Rock & Roll Hall of Fame Awards Inductions we recorded
Various Theaters, 1989–1995

Pardon my rough notes from the shows.

1989 Inductees: Dion, the Rolling Stones, The Temptations, and Stevie Wonder
Speakers: Daryl Hall and John Oates on The Temptations, Pete Townshend on the Rolling Stones with Mick Jagger and Keith Richards response

1990 Inductees: The Four Seasons, the Four Tops, the Kinks, Simon and Garfunkel, and The Who
Speakers: Phil Spector

1991 Inductees: the Byrds, John Lee Hooker, Wilson Pickett, Ike and Tina Turner
Notes: Bush bombs Baghdad but that doesn't stop the show
Speakers: Quincy Jones, Don Henley on the Byrds, Bonnie Raitt on Hooker
Performances: Byrds jam

1992 Inductees: Bobby "Blue" Bland, Booker T. and the M.G.'s, Jimi Hendrix Experience, Sam & Dave, Leo Fender, Bill Graham
Speakers: Neil Young on Hendrix, Keith Richards on Fender
Performances: Guitar jam on "Purple Haze"; Neil jams "All Along the Watchtower"

Rock & Roll Hall of Fame Opening Concert HBO Live to World
Cleveland, Ohio, August 9, 1995

Chuck Berry, Bruce Springsteen, Aretha Franklin, Booker T., with Bob Dylan as surprise guest

THE *GRAMMY AWARDS*

Radio City Music Hall in New York, February 25–March 1, 1994
Shrine Auditorium, LA, February 23–March 1, 1995

THE *ACADEMY OF COUNTRY MUSIC AWARDS*

Nashville Arena, November 1–6, 2006

THE *TONY AWARDS*
VARIOUS NEW YORK THEATERS, 1981–1986

Mark Heller Theater
The Imperial Theater
Uris Theater
Gershwin Theater
Shubert Theater
Miskoff Theater

I had started working on live television award shows with Bob Liftin of Regent Sound in New York. He had a long history in television audio, and as the shows grew more complicated, he was happy to hire me and the remote truck to do the live shows. Of course, it helped that I had worked as an engineer at the Philadelphia branch of Regent Sound. The shows on network television were a different world from the purely music shows. We were well-acquainted with the technical interface with video, but the politics were quite different. The New York theater world and the Los Angeles film world were different universes.

Bob Liftin knew all the players and could keep up with the constantly changing script and stage moves. My 44-input API console was augmented with outboard sub mixers, and we still had to do some fast-patch cord dances to keep up with the rehearsals. When we finished the final run through, Bob would call the crew together and run down his script. There were hundreds of cues! Each one was a major move for Bob as the mixer and me as the patch master and sub mixer. I was stunned! Live music shows may be mix intensive, but these award shows are endlessly changing cues with announcers, guests, an orchestra playing, cues on tape, actors and singers on radio mics, and audience mics augmented with an applause machine!

It may look simple watching it on TV, but it's a real rodeo in the audio truck!

THE *TONY AWARDS*

Mark Heller Theater, June 4–6, 1981
Imperial Theater, June 4–6, 1982
Uris Theater, June 2–6, 1983
Gershwin Theater, May 31–June 4, 1984
Shubert Theater, May 30–June 2, 1985
Minskoff Theater, May 27–June 2, 1986

THE *DAYTIME EMMYS*

Sheraton Center, June 28–30, 1987, ABC TV
Waldorf Astoria Ballroom, June 27–29, 1988

THE *ACADEMY AWARDS*

The *Academy Awards* have been going on in Hollywood since 1929 and were first televised in 1953. It is the granddaddy of award shows, followed by the Emmy Awards for television, the Tony Awards for theater, and the Grammy Awards for music. I have to admit being rather proud of having worked on all four of them.

My turn at the *Academy Awards* came by chance. Record Plant LA had been providing audio remote trucks for the show with their chief engineer Lee DeCarlo. The Record Plant was changing hands, and Lee couldn't be sure that the trucks would be available for the 1991 show. I knew Lee from his time at Record Plant New York, and we worked out a deal to bring my new Silver Truck out to LA for him to mix the show. Lee was happy with the new API console, not to mention the brand-new state-of-the-art appointments of the custom tractor-trailer.

Ed Greene was the long-time engineer in charge of audio for the broadcast, and of course we knew each other from the Frank Sinatra tour, the United Nations, and the Summer Olympics. We were off to a good start.

The Oscars, like everything else in television, had grown in complexity over the years. There were now too many musical acts for Ed Greene to mix, in addition to the big live orchestra that played all the complex themes from the movies and not to mention the "play-ons and play-offs," cued by the director. So, our job was to interface with the show production, house sound reinforcement, Ed Greene's audio control room and engineer Lee DeCarlo to make it all work for live broadcast to the world. No problem.

The orchestra was composed of all the A-list players in LA, veterans of the film and television industry, and the record labels. They had to play everything from muscular rock themes to romantic full orchestral compositions. That required complicated miking techniques and lots of inputs. Our large collection of microphones and direct pickups connected to the API and Studer recording consoles could handle it. We would record the rehearsals for fine-tuning our mixes, but it's the live to air television broadcast to the world that counts and there's no remixing!

Just like the recording studios, my remote trucks were there for the client. I was the "house engineer," and I was there on most every live recording to see that everything worked to a high standard. If the client had their own engineer, I supported them, otherwise I did it.

Lee DeCarlo was the man for the first few Oscars we did, and then several changes of producers and orchestra conductors brought other engineers. When Tommy Vicari came in, he became the preferred mixer and is to this day. When the politics and technology changed, my services became too expensive to bring in to LA from the East Coast, but twenty-one years was a good run. Tommy Vicari continues to mix the Oscars on the newer digital consoles, which are better suited to the changing productions.

The Oscars are, of course, all about movies, and music is an important but often unnoticed aspect. There were far too many stories, but I will tell a few after this list.

Here are the live *Academy Award* shows mixed on the Silver Truck:

63rd Annual Academy Awards, 1991, Shrine Auditorium
65th Annual Academy Awards, 1993, Dorothy Chandler Pavilion
68th Annual Academy Awards, 1996, Dorothy Chandler Pavilion
69th Annual Academy Awards, 1997, Shrine Auditorium
70th Annual Academy Awards, 1998, Shrine Auditorium
71st Annual Academy Awards, 1999, Dorothy Chandler Pavilion
72nd Annual Academy Awards, 2000, Shrine Auditorium
73rd Annual Academy Awards, 2001, Shrine Auditorium
74th Annual Academy Awards, 2002, Kodak Theater

75th Annual Academy Awards, 2003, Kodak Theater
76th Annual Academy Awards, 2004, Kodak Theater
77th Annual Academy Awards, 2005, Kodak Theater
78th Annual Academy Awards, 2006, Kodak Theater
79th Annual Academy Awards, 2007, Kodak Theater
80th Annual Academy Awards, 2008, Kodak Theater
81st Annual Academy Awards, 2009, Kodak Theater
82nd Annual Academy Awards—I don't have it in my log book
83rd Annual Academy Awards, 2011, Kodak Theater
84th Annual Academy Awards, 2012, Kodak Theater

One year that really stood out to me was 1998, when the incredible blockbuster film *Titanic* stunned the world and dominated the Oscars. Everything about that show was gigantic, including the huge stage set for the orchestra, which was designed to look like the *RMS Titanic* deck. It was so high that the horn players in the back were getting vertigo. Normally the orchestra is in the classic orchestra pit in front of the stage. You never get to see all the backstage work that goes into these complex sets; it is astounding what these Hollywood set magicians can build. It takes hundreds of specialty trades to produce what you see on TV. It was always fascinating, but of course, our focus was on the music, which was constantly changing. The musicians had to be prepared with scores for all the music of the nominated films and then play the winning film's score. The music director and conductor, Bill Conti, is certainly the calmest, most unflappable maestro I have ever seen. Of course, some of the musical cues and other acts requiring prerecorded music are played by Ed Greene in the complex audio booth, located in the video truck. This is where all of the production elements are mixed. There are endless playback audio tracks from the nominated films, the live announcer in a separate trailer, guest musicians playing on stage, and then most important, all of the stars appearing at various podiums to introduce the nominees and open the winner's card! And then there is the obligatory audience applause, mixed from many strategically placed microphones and sometimes, a little prerecorded enthusiasm.

It's an amazing circus, nothing quite like it anywhere else in the galaxy.

All the while, I had been preparing to leave on a flight to Buenos Aires, Argentina, to join the Rolling Stones tour in 1998. I had previously assembled our large "fly pack" recording system and arranged to have it fly down with the band's touring gear. There I would meet up with world-renowned engineer/producer Ed Cherney, with whom we had been recording the tours. After recovering from the travel, we headed out of the hotel into the magnificent sunny weather of historic Buenos Aires and walk right into billboards and walls plastered with ads for the film *Titanic*, already boasting about its big Oscar awards! Another huge reminder of the worldwide reach of US culture. The Brits aren't doing too bad either; of course, they had a head start colonizing the world.

You can pick up the Rolling Stones stories from their live recordings in chapter 14.

The Rolling Stones? Maybe video couldn't kill all the radio stars after all.

(13)

JAZZ: AMERICAN ROOTS

The Newport Jazz Festival Comes to New York and Miles Comes Back, Too

I had the good fortune to have come of age in 1960s' Europe, where my Air Force father was stationed. Among the many cultural lessons I learned was how respected US jazz and blues musicians became after World War II. Ironically, my first US jazz albums came from a German record store.

Back Stateside, but now in the Air National Guard doing active duty at Otis Air Force Base on Cape Cod, I was able to attend the nearby 1969 Newport Jazz Festival. That year, impresario George Wein had booked not only jazz greats Miles Davis and Dave Brubeck, but rock acts Frank Zappa and Led Zeppelin. I was shocked by Miles Davis's new electrified band and the fence-crashing hippie Zeppelin fans. "Music should be free, man!"

By 1973 the Newport Jazz Festival had moved to New York City and I was now working for the Record Plant's remote recording truck. Producer George Wein spread the shows across New York's many venues. I scrambled around the city with the remote truck, recording the likes of Ella Fitzgerald at Carnegie Hall, Count Basie at the Roseland Ballroom, B. B. King at Philharmonic Hall, Ray Charles, and many more. It was a breathtaking, mind-expanding experience when Chick Corea's Return to Forever and Weather Report played their electrified version of jazz!

The music lives on in those recordings and much better than my words can describe. The stories of getting those shows recorded are easier to write.

One show with Ray Charles makes me smile now, but it was a disaster for the recording at the time.

Back then, the PA and monitor systems were minimal, especially for jazz shows. It was all mono and bare bones sub mixes. That really clashed with Ray Charles's needs on stage. Ray did not want his piano in the stage monitor, only his vocal. Trouble was that the PA system could only send the mono house mix to his monitor. In the sound check, Charles demanded no piano and the house engineer pulled it down, but for the show he had to bring it up so the audience could hear Ray's piano!

Recording the opening acts went fine, but then Ray came on as the head-liner and started to play. He immediately heard his piano in the monitor! The poor PA mixer had the audience yelling if he turned it down and Ray yelling if he turned it up! He had to keep it up enough for the audience to hear something and Ray is livid! He calls his bodyguard over and demanded that he pull our Neumann microphones out of the piano—I'm yelling at our stage manager to stop him, until he points our stage camera at the 300-pound bodyguard! Boom, bang . . . No more piano sound. Then Ray goes to play the Fender Rhodes electric piano, and it, too, is in the moni-tors! Ray is trying to play and gesture to his guy to pull the plug. It takes him a while to find the direct boxes but finally yanks them out with a big boom in the PA! So now nobody could hear Ray play except himself. . . . We had no recording and everybody was pissed! I just kept the tape rolling because you never stop tape!

After the festival, it was back to recording rock-and-roll shows until Frank Sinatra at Carnegie Hall! I remember that April 1974 gig for the fact that no recording contract had been signed with the hall, and they refused to power up the remote truck! After much hand-wringing and panicked phone calls, they got their ink and we barely got mikes plugged in for the last of a rehearsal with the big band. I just kept my head down and scrambled to get the show recorded. Sometimes it was a hostile environment out there. We would catch up with Frank a bit later.

After that trauma, I was glad to get back to the rock world with a crazy schedule: ZZ Top in New Orleans, Mott the Hoople with some new band called Queen opening, a King Crimson tour, David Bowie's live album, the last US show of CSNY tour, and Sly Stone's concert/wedding at Madison Square Garden, where I had to get Record Plant's chief engineer Pen Ste-phens to cover me while I attended the birth of my first son Ryan!

In fall 1974, veteran engineer Ed Greene booked us to record Frank Sinatra's return to touring with Don Costa leading a blazing big band. I must confess that until then, I thought of Sinatra as 1940s' history, mom and dad music . . . but by the time we got to Madison Square Garden for *The Main Event*, I was a convert.

We had recorded only two shows when there was a major interruption in the Sinatra recording schedule because of a previous booking. Imagine the jump from Frank Sinatra to the rock band Blue Oyster Cult! Blue Oyster Cult was a good client at Record Plant and we had to honor the booking. It meant driving straight from snowbound Buffalo back to the Academy of Music in New York. It was a great rock show, except for one thing; their band crew managed to load one of our road cases in their truck and disappeared with all the Neumann microphone shock mounts for Sinatra's orchestra! In the days before cell phones, there was no way to reach the band truck, and I had to scramble to find enough mic mounts to record Sinatra's next show! I was already unpopular at Record Plant for borrowing all the Neumann mics for Frank's orchestra, now I was really in deep shit! Plus, some local punks stole the rental tuxedos our stage guys had to wear for the Sinatra show. Fortunately for me, Sinatra was well-loved by Record Plant owner Roy Cicala and other admirers, like senior engineer Jay Messina, so I wasn't fired.

We recorded shows in Philadelphia and Pittsburgh with tremendous sellout crowds and finally made it to Madison Square Garden in New York. This would be my baptism by NYC union rules: it took three guys from separate departments to move a mic stand from the remote truck to the stage, and I could not even touch it. But again, Frank Sinatra was so loved that we were allowed a few transgressions. Over the years, we recorded many shows at Madison Square Garden, so I eventually learned the rules and even made a few union friends.

Ed Greene had worked with Sinatra in the studio and also had long experience in live television, much of it with the ABC network. Before the live broadcast, Ed took me up to the huge New York ABC studio complex to check out the audio chain where our live audio feed would land. It was my initiation into the world of big-time international television, a far cry from the single TV channel of my youth in Butte, Montana! Ed was always calm and respectful of other professional's turf but carried the confidence and authority to get to the reality. Case in point: Ed knew there would be limiter/compressors in the audio chain, and he found them hidden away behind a door. If I remember correctly, they were URIE LA-3As and had some pretty severe settings. He may have made some adjustments in our favor. Working with Ed was a master class in diplomacy and mission accomplishment—very much like my Air Force pilot father.

There would be some adjustments in the Record Plant remote truck as well. The DeMedio recording console was a bit of a hybrid; it had started life at Wally Heider Studios, working on the Johnny Cash television show in 1965. It was a bit obsolete by the time it landed in this remote truck, which had been built and owned by Wally Heider Studios in 1970. It was a 24-input, 8-mix bus console for 8-track tape recording. It had been modified for 16-track recording by wiring the last 8 faders for direct out, adding outboard sub mixers and a 16-bus monitor mixer. A large patch bay allowed flexible interfacing of outboard gear and the two Ampex MM-1000 16-track tape recorders.

Ed would mix the main console faders and outboard mixers down to the 16 monitor buses, as he had during all our shows. Doug Nelson was the designated union engineer for ABC TV and would do the live-to-air 16-fader monitor mix for the broadcast. Now those mono and stereo mixes would have to find their way from 33rd Street at Madison Square Garden to the 66th Street ABC television studios. Remember, this is 1974, and audio had to be patched through telephone lines, which meant another whole world of companies, unions, and who knows how many patch bays! The Record Plant tech gurus, chief Pen Stephens and Paul Prestopino, had built interface boxes to match our audio outputs to the telephone system, "Ma Bell," as they were called then. We handed our lines to the Bell Telephone guys, who patched into the Garden's phone lines. It took several days to get it reliably sent 33 blocks uptown in New York City!

The show would go out live via ABC satellite, in one of the first stereo simulcasts from ABC television and local FM radio. In those days, television sound was only mono, and you had to have a local stereo radio station that carried the live feed. There were not many stations that could; it was complicated and expensive to do.

Frank Sinatra delivered an amazing performance that I find it impossible to describe in words. I have to ask that you look for the recording, vinyl, CD, or watch it on YouTube to appreciate the moment. It's worth it for the Howard Cosell (the famous sports announcer) *Main Event* introduction into "The Lady Is a Tramp," that starts the show. A special highlight for me was "The House I Live In," a song which resonates today more than ever, about his Italian father coming to the United States as an immigrant. The lyric "Especially the people, that's America to me," says it all.

He followed that with his classic standard "My Kind of Town," and even though it was written about Chicago, everyone here knows it's about New York! In 1974, I was a New Yorker, living up on West 89th and Broadway

and working at the original Record Plant down on West 44th and 8th—
thanks for the song Frank!

Some 45 years later, I was working on a personal project restoring a 1958
Magnavox Magnificent Console, with a new turntable to test the original
tube electronics. This took place at the appropriately named company, the
Art of Sound, owned by my friends John and Patti Nirmaier.

John was discussing one of his ultra hi-fi systems with another client,
when they heard the record I was playing. It was from a stack of albums I
had brought to play on John's systems . . . It was my original 1974 copy of
Sinatra, The Main Event Live. The client hurried over to exclaim that he
had seen and heard the original stereo TV broadcast on his home system
from Boston stations. He was so happy to tell us how watching and listening to that Frank Sinatra event live changed his musical life and opened up
his ears to orchestras and jazz. That made me pretty happy, too, to think
that the music I recorded did have meaning, even sometimes to a wide
audience.

As if to answer Frank Sinatra's *Main Event* concert, Aretha Franklin
staged an incredible show at Radio City Music Hall several weeks later on
November 1, 1974. This was in her slimmed down "Foxy Lady" period,
and she had some outrageous costumes. She took some heat for that, but
nobody could criticize Aretha's soulful singing and her piano power!

We recorded the show for Atlantic Records, and I have this great memory of producer Jerry Wexler going out to buy me a pack of cigarettes when
I ran out! We all smoked back then and gummed up the patch bays with
nicotine.

It was a great month for recording jazz. Stan Getz, Chet Baker, and
Gerry Mulligan performed at Carnegie Hall, where we recorded several
individual albums for Creed Taylor's CTI Records. As often happened in
those days, I never heard the finished records. I finally tracked down original vinyl copies last year in an antique store!

My personal favorite of all the live jazz recordings we did back then is the
Modern Jazz Quartet's *The Last Concert*. It was my first major jazz recording as chief engineer. Because they were such seminal artists for Atlantic
Records, all the brass were there . . . Ahmet and Nesuhi Ertegun and Ilhan
Mimaroglu as producer. Guitar genius Les Paul was there with his new
pickups for the bass and piano, and his son, Gene Paul, would mix the tapes
we recorded back at Atlantic Studios. To top it all off, the dean of jazz critics, Nat Hentoff, made a special note about Gene and me for how well they

were recorded; although it might have had something to do with how well they played after 22 years together!

The album was so successful that they released a second album from that show and then the complete package. Of course, they toured after the success of the album and continued to perform in one form or another until 1997. They are all gone now, but their music will live on in the grooves. I am playing my original vinyl record as I write this.

The concept of the endless *Last Concert* became a standing joke in popular music, I remember the Eagles announcing to the audience, "Welcome to the sixth annual last concert tour."

We finished 1974 by recording the great Blues guitarist Roy Buchanan and the jazz poet/singer Gil Scott-Heron.

As the 1970s progressed, rock and pop music dominated the bookings, but there were bright individual live recordings for modern jazz players like guitarists George Benson and Al Di Meola.

We recorded the legendary vocalist and civil rights activist Nina Simone at what was then Avery Fisher Hall at Lincoln Center, right across the street from the Juilliard School of Music, where she had studied. Her Bach-flavored rendition of "You'd Be So Nice to Come Home To" is astounding!

DEXTER GORDON AND WOODY SHAW VILLAGE VANGUARD
COLUMBIA RECORDS, DECEMBER 31, 1978

STUFF
MIKELLS, DECEMBER 14–17, 1979

You may not recognize the band named Stuff, but you will have heard these musicians on thousands of records. They were among the most successful studio musicians in New York. I used to see them individually at Record Plant often, playing with everyone from Aretha Franklin to Paul McCartney. You may know these names: bass player and founder Gordon Edwards, Richard Tee on piano, Eric Gale and Cornell Dupree on guitars, and Chris Parker and Steve Gadd on drums. As a band, they sold out every show they played at their favorite New York club, Mikells. That is where I recorded their album *Live in New York* over four dates, two shows per night. The sets were all instrumental and that soulful funk that defined New York to so many of us.

My favorites were "Sometimes Bubba Gets Down" and "Duck Soup," but make up your own mind; find it and listen! I still do after some 40-odd years.

BOB JAMES, ALL AROUND TOWN
DECEMBER 18–22, 1979

This title is worth an explanation, Bob James always has multiple projects to juggle, in between running record labels, producing artists, and playing piano, he managed to come up with this project, appropriately named: *All Around Town*—New York, of course.

We started recording downtown at the Bottom Line Theater, a relaxed, informal bar and with plenty of round tables right up against the stage. Owners Alan Pepper and Stanley Snadowsky knew their music and brought in a great variety of talent. You will see that club name many times in this book.

Bob James's core funk band featured Gary King on bass, Idris Muhammad on drums with soloists Wilbert Longmire, Mark Colby, and Hiram Bullock on guitar. The theme from the hit TV show *Taxi*, had to start the show, followed by the lovely "Westchester Lady." It was a great way to start the record.

Moving uptown to the more upscale Town Hall, a formal surprise of three grand pianos lined up across the stage. A black nine-foot grand for Joanne Brackeen, another black one for Bob James and a white one for Richard Tee. The rhythm section was full of Steve Gadd and Billy Hart on drums, plus Eddie Gomez on upright bass. It was an extraordinary concert, with the diverse styles of three extraordinary pianists! "Stompin' at the Savoy" and "The Golden Apple" made the live album, but there are plenty more in the vault.

The grand finale was appropriately held at Carnegie Hall and had a full big band powered by repeat rhythm players Gary King, Idris Muhammad, and Hiram Bullock plus Earl Klugh on guitar. LA Tom Scott and Mark Colby on saxes, Tom Browne and Mike Lawrence on trumpet, George Marge on woodwinds, and my next-door neighbor, the incredible Jimmy Maelen on percussion rounded out the sound. What a band; they really brought the house down with Bob's hits "Touchdown," great horn sections and solos. Bob's patented keyboard solos brought it home with the beautiful composition "Kari."

We had a great time working with all the different groups, plus Bob brought some brand-new machines back from Japan that Sony just introduced, called the Walkman. Gee, I thought, "who's going to buy a dinky handheld cassette machine like that?" That was 1979, and a friend just told me they are now worth thousands as collector items.

Thanks Bob, everyone had a great time with all your musicians and your music.

ALL THAT JAZZ, BOSTON
NEW ENGLAND AQUARIUM, MAY 28–30, 1980

This was an incredible gathering of legendary jazz stars, spread over three days in Boston. There were so many of my favorite musicians from the 1940s to the present. They included: Carmen McRae, Dizzy Gillespie, Stan Getz, Art Blakey, George Benson, Gary Burton, Ramsey Lewis, and the Marsalis brothers—Wynton and Branford.

I really enjoyed the relaxed atmosphere of the Boston Aquarium in May and the golden opportunity to record these legends of jazz.

As a note, no fish were injured in the production of this recording.

MILES DAVIS

In July of 1981 we were booked by Columbia Records executive producer George Butler to record Miles Davis's official return to the concert stage after a five-year absence. Miles's Columbia engineer Don Puluse and producer Teo Macero were there to supervise the recording. Teo wanted to use a tape delay effect on Miles using an older Ampex recorder brought from their studios. It was breaking down in rehearsals and Teo's temper was boiling over. As they tried to fix it, I attempted to assuage him by admiring his big gold chronograph watch. He turned on me, and smoldered, "I killed a fucking Nazi officer for this watch!" Gulp, end of conversation.

There was a classic Miles moment just before the show. Jim Rose, Miles's road manager, had brought his yellow 308 GT Ferrari around the corner from Avery Fisher Hall so Miles could step out of his limo and drive the Ferrari up to the stage door for his grand entrance. The awaiting crowd and the press cameras loved it.

The band was a new lineup featuring Mike Stern on electric guitar and Bill Evans (not the pianist) on soprano sax. Drummer Al Foster and Marcus Miller on bass completed the drive to amplify Miles. There was a new wireless mic on Miles's horn, which was later perfected by multitalented engineer, Ron Lorman, who would also mix his live sound. Now he could famously turn his back on the audience and still be heard.

The shows were packed with celebrities and musicians eager to hear the return of Miles Davis. They were two dynamic, sometimes loud shows. Reviews were mixed, but hey, the album won a 1982 Grammy Award for Best Jazz Instrumental Performance by a Soloist. The album's name? *We Want Miles*.

Miles recorded several albums at Record Plant New York, where I was director of remote recording. My office was on the tenth floor, right down the hall from Studio C where Miles was recording. The 1983 Columbia album that became *Decoy* came from those sessions. My friend Ron Lorman was now engineering and mixing with Miles himself, producing a band with Robert Irving III driving the keyboards and John Scofield on electric guitar. Funk was gaining on jazz with Darryl Jones on electric bass.

Even though I was often gone on remote recordings, I did stop by the sessions occasionally to see Ron Lorman, who I knew from his years at the Bottom Line Theater and touring with Frank Zappa.

Miles returned to the Record Plant in 1984 to record *You're Under Arrest* featuring John McLaughlin alternating with John Scofield on guitars and additions like Sting speaking in French and playing some surprising pop songs like Cyndi Lauper's "Time After Time." Leave it to Miles to find the beauty in that tune. Reminiscent of his interpretation of "Someday My Prince Will Come," from the Walt Disney film *Snow White*.

Miles was a different person around the studio where he was comfortable, especially around the ladies. The accounting office was right outside of Studio C and he would often stop by to charm Fran and Terry. He had a wicked sense of humor.

The New Orleans Jazz Festival in 1986 featured Miles Davis playing at the classic Saenger Theater, and I was there to record him with the Record Plant Black Truck, which I now owned. Those shows would be part of a PBS *Great Performances* documentary, *Miles Ahead: The Music of Miles Davis*. As often happened in those days, I never saw the completed documentary with all the interviews and history, but I sure do remember the thrill of Miles's electric band playing full volume through my API console to the Bryston amped Westlake custom monitors!

Even though my perennial Miles favorite is the *Kind of Blue* period, I always had to listen to everything the man played, and that show was yet another creative era for him. That would be the last time I saw him. Miles passed away on September 28, 1991.

There was a memorial service for Miles at the "Jazz Church," St. Peter's Lutheran Church at 54th and Lexington in New York City. Many musicians and friends spoke, but it was Quincy Jones's quote that stayed with me, "The death of Miles will leave a bigger hole than we know in twentieth century music."

WE DID GET A FEW JAZZ GIGS IN 1981

Johnny Griffin, Richie Cole, Chico Hamilton, Nat Aderly at the Village Vanguard
Grover Washington Jr. at the Shubert Theater in Philadelphia
Paquito D'Riviera and Arthur Blythe at the Town Hall in New York
Art Blakey and Mike Manieri at the Seventh Avenue South Jazz Club in New York

THE BUDDY RICH SHOW

Certainly, one of the most colorful drummers in big band history was Buddy Rich. I was pleased when we were booked to record his new television show pilot in December of 1982. With Buddy as the host and his band backing up the many stars he attracted, this had to be great!

Attending an early production meeting, I realized we had a tight schedule with a lot of changes. There was not a lot of rehearsal time available. One thing I asked for was that the grand piano be delivered the day before so it would have some time to stabilize from the January cold before being tuned. To save money, they brought it in the day of the show. The piano tuner was not amused. He tuned it, but, of course, it would go out as it warmed up.

Ray Charles complained about the tuning in rehearsal, so the tuner came back again. By the time Ray came on as the headliner, the piano was out of tune and he delighted in finding every bad note and playing it extra loud!

There were many great moments with Buddy engaging his guest stars in conversation with the live audience and, of course, playing with them on his drums. There were some wonderful performances by Lionel Hampton, Stan Getz, Gerry Mulligan, and Woody Herman, not to mention the velvet voice of Mel Torme.

After the final show, I presented my bill and was paid in cash, by two stern-looking gentlemen. The production company had professionally videotaped three episodes and certainly had some good material, but as far as I know, it was never released. Buddy was a colorful character.

AL DI MEOLA AT THE SAVOY

Al Di Meola at the Savoy in New York on January 30, 1982, and at the Tower Theater in Philadelphia on February 2, 1982, made the album *Tour de Force* on Columbia Records with an all-star band: Jan Hammer on keys, Anthony Jackson on bass, and Steve Gadd on drums, among others.

It was indeed an all-star Tour de Force, incredible performances!

BOBBY SHORT AT THE CAFE CARLYLE
FEBRUARY 15, 1982

Short was one of the last great Caberet pianists and singer of the great American Songbook. I had just finished recording the *Night of 100 Stars*, a four-day marathon television production over at Radio City Music Hall. The final show ran for more than three hours and then there was the wrap. I stayed as long as I could, but about 4:00 a.m., I hailed a cab for the next adventure.

We already had a show booked for the following day across town at the legendary jazz and cabaret club, the Café Carlyle. I had the Record Plant White Truck already parked there and rooms booked at the classy Carlyle Hotel. I was exhausted and just wanted to shower and get a few winks before the morning call time. Crossing the elegant lobby to the elevators, I saw the doors open to a boisterous group of well-dressed patrons, just leaving. To my surprise, the great actress and singer Pearl Bailey strode out with them, took one look at my disheveled figure and declared, "Honey, you look like shit! Best you get upstairs and use that expensive shower!"— hardy laughter ensued and created a much-loved memory of mine. Pearl had just returned from the *Night of 100 Stars* as one of the stars.

The Carlyle performance "stage" is a small riser, maybe a foot tall, in a rather low ceiling dining room. It was beautifully furnished and decorated with artfully painted murals but was a bit tight with all the fancy dining tables . . . it is a restaurant after all.

Bobby Short had been playing regularly at the club since 1968, so we had only to set up my choice of microphones for the trio and audience/ambience mics. The video producer and director had a much harder task: trying to find room for the cameras and lighting gear. The lighting trusses that were necessary for the shoot were difficult to place and had to go right up against the ceiling and across the room, side to side. Because the supporting vertical poles were blocking some of the camera shots, the director had several of them removed. It would become a near fatal disaster.

We had just finished the rehearsal, and Bobby Short, along with drummer Richard Sheridan, had walked out. Bass player Beverly Peer had just carefully laid down his magnificent double bass and was heading for the door when I heard a tremendous crash in the remote truck speakers! I whipped around to look at my video monitor, and to my horror saw the collapsed lighting trusses had narrowly missed hitting Beverly! We all ran in to see if anyone was hurt, and miraculously Beverly was only shaken but not injured!

Of course, everyone on the production crew were in shock, but quickly got down to the task at hand, "the show must go on!" The Carlyle management were not amused, but rose to the occasion, and we got everything back up and running. It's hard to believe they didn't throw us out! All I could think was, what if it had crashed down on the audience.

I did manage to get a good show recorded, thanks to the veteran Bobby Short and band, who were the consummate professionals, just relaxed and playing for their upper-crust audience, who never knew that could have come down on their heads! We were all glad to finish that adventure.

I was invited to meet with Bobby Short at his magnificent apartment in The Osborne, an edifice across from Carnegie Hall that dates to 1875. He was gracious and briefly discussed the show and his concerns.

Postproduction was booked at Regent Sound, owned by Bob Liftin, my original employer at his Philadelphia studio. We quickly mixed the audio for the edited video on Regent's console with his automation system. It was quite advanced for the day and was run by Ken Hahn and Bill Marino, who would later open a new major postproduction studio, Sync Sound. Bob Liftin had worked in television and film audio for many years and often had my remote trucks booked on his shows, like the *Night of 100 Stars* that we had just finished before recording Bobby Short. He also brought us in for shows like the *Daytime Emmys*, the *Tony Awards*, the *Parade of Stars*, and many others. Bob was a real innovator in audio for television, he pioneered

SMPTE code and many other important innovations. He had the unfortunate habit of about three packs of cigarettes per day. I was sorry to lose him.

BETTY CARTER: *WHATEVER HAPPENED TO LOVE?*
THE BOTTOM LINE CLUB, NEW YORK, MARCH 27, 1982

This was a special show by one of the most unique singers ever to grace the stage, and this was the perfect stage for her. The Bottom Line Club owners, Alan Pepper and Stanley Snadowsky, worked with conductor David Amram to arrange Betty's songs with an orchestra, including strings. That was a close fit on their club stage, but it all worked fine and sounded great, with a very intimate sound. Add to that, her favorite engineer, Joe Ferla, would be at the console in my Black Truck. Betty was so charming and gracious, it was a wonderful gig. Joe did a great job of mixing the 24-track analog tapes and the record came out beautifully. It was nominated for a Grammy— Best Jazz Vocal Performance, Female. I highly recommend looking for this performance as it is well worth listening to. No one scats like Betty Carter.

JACO PASTORIUS
"WORLD'S GREATEST BASS PLAYER"

The recent discovery of Jaco Pastorius's ultra-rare Big Band recording, from a NPR program called *Jazz Alive* from June 26, 1982, really brought back memories of this self-proclaimed "greatest bass player in the world." I was there in charge of the Record Plant Black Truck with NPR engineer Paul Blakemore as it was recorded live at Avery Fisher Hall in New York City.

Jaco was already renown for completely changing the paradigm of bass playing in jazz, most famously in the group Weather Report with original members Joe Zawinul and Wayne Shorter. My Record Plant remote crew had recorded them in Havana, Cuba, for the 1979 *Havana Jam* for Columbia Records. In addition, Jaco played with John McLaughlin and Tony Williams as the Trio of Doom. Chapter 8 gives a complete account of that adventure. We also recorded the Jaco Pastorius Big Band and Sonny Stitt at Carnegie Hall on July 1, 1982.

Other great shows followed:

Jazz Fusion greats Spyro Gyra, at the Stanley Theater in Pittsburgh,
    Pennsylvania, August 27, 1983
Ben Sidren, one of the most innovative producers, writers, composer and
    players in jazz, recorded, at the Seventh Avenue South Jazz Club, New
    York, on September 20–22, 1983.

ORNETTE COLEMEN, PRIME TIME AND THE FORT WORTH SYMPHONY
SEPTEMBER 28–OCTOBER 2, 1983

Ornette Coleman was certainly one of the most original and innovative jazz
musicians in the United States; after all, he invented the term "free jazz."
From his Texas roots playing tenor sax in 1940s' bop and R&B bands, he
switched to alto sax with jazz bands in LA and New York. His album, *The
Shape of Jazz to Come*, was prophetic indeed. Followed by his invention of
free jazz and "harmolodics," he was astoundingly prolific. I first took interest in his music with the orchestral *Skies of America*. He would continue
innovating and playing with and gaining the respect of everyone from Louis
Armstrong, the Grateful Dead, and Sonny Rollins, to Lou Reed and Yoko
Ono.

In 1985, Ornette returned to his hometown of Fort Worth, Texas, for
two important performances. The Texas billionaire Bass family opened an
incredible club called Caravan of Dreams, with a performance stage and
the Fullerian Desert Dome on the roof, where Ornette could also perform.
We recorded his *Prime Design/Time Design* album there.

The main event would be held at the Tarrant County Civic Center,
where Ornette would perform with his band Prime Time playing with the
Fort Worth Symphony Orchestra. The audience would be the unlikely
combination of wealthy socialite supporters of the symphony and avant-
garde jazz supporters of Ornette's brand of harmolodics.

We were fortunate to have been recruited by Ron Saint Germain, Ornette's engineer, to record the performances. Ron and I have Air Force
backgrounds and he still flies his own airplane; plus he has wide ranging
experience on the road recording orchestral, jazz, and rock music. And he's
got a wicked sense of humor, so we got along great. Remind me to tell you
about the stuffed chair.

I have tried repeatedly to describe Ornette's performances in these dramatically different musical environments, but like all unique artists, Ornette must be seen and heard to understand him. Please look up the film *Ornette: Made in America.*

OTHER GREAT LIVE JAZZ BROADCASTS FOR WBGO RADIO 88.3 FM

Carmen McRae, Zoot Simms, Blue Note WBGO , December 31, 1983
Jazzathon WBGO, April 29, 1984
Jazzathon WBGO, February 28, 1985

ONE NIGHT WITH BLUE NOTE
TOWN HALL, NEW YORK, FEBRUARY 21–22, 1985

There was a relaunch of Blue Note Records by executive Bruce Lundvall and music director Michael Cuscuna, who were two of my heroes in jazz history. These LPs, CDs, and DVDs are a treasure chest of Blue Note artists and music. Over three hours of historic Blue Note music played by the musicians who knew it best. It included an all-star cast that included pianists Herbie Hancock, McCoy Tyner, and Cecil Taylor; Jimmy Smith on organ; bassists Ron Carter, Cecil McBee, and Reggie Workman; drummers Tony Williams, Jack DeJohnette, Grady Tate, and Art Blakey; Freddie Hubbard and Woody Shaw on trumpets; Joe Henderson, Johnny Griffin, Charles Lloyd, and Grover Washington Jr. on tenor sax; Stanley Turrentine, Lou Donaldson, and Jackie McLean on alto sax; Curtis Fuller on trombone; James Newton on flute; vibes by Bobby Hutcherson; and Kenny Burrell and Stanley Jordan on guitar.

LES PAUL, TAL FARLOW, AND BUCKY PIZZARELLI
AT THE MASON GROSS SCHOOL. NEWARK, NEW JERSEY, JULY 24, 1985
THREE GURUS OF THE GUITAR

I did not often engineer in the audio section of video remote trucks. Today's trucks can have incredible gear, but back then, not so much. When my friends at WNET/13 asked me to mix this show they were taping, I jumped at the chance. I had met Les Paul when I recorded the Modern Jazz Quartet, and certainly knew Bucky's many great records, but Tal Farlow was a rather mysterious guitar player, often not credited for his unique playing. This combination of players I had to hear.

Jersey Jazz Güitars was the name of the 1985 concert held at the Rutgers University Nicholas Music Center in New Brunswick, New Jersey. As advertised, they had Les Paul, Tal Farlow, Bucky Pizzarelli, and Pizzarelli's son, John. The concert was aired on New Jersey's PBS station as part of their three-part *New Jersey Summerfare* series. Bucky and Les Paul had played together before and they were local "Jersey Boys." John contributed guitar and vocals and would go on to forge his own career, not only as a guitarist, to make his dad proud, but as a star entertainer and singer. I would enjoy recording his shows at the legendary Algonquin Hotel later.

You can still see that show in the PBS archives; it is well worth a visit, especially the jam at the end—Jersey Boys having fun!

BENNY GOODMAN
THE KING OF SWING RETURNS

PBS flagship station WNET/13 has produced so many phenomenal live concerts and musical events, many of which help preserve the legacy of US artists. When they decided to produce a special concert with the legendary Big Band leader and clarinetist Benny Goodman, I knew the perfectionist Goodman would bring in great musicians. Even in his late 70s, he was still the King of Swing.

I was summoned to meet Benny at his East Side of New York residence to discuss the recording. Directed to his floor, the door was answered by a charming lady, wearing, er . . . a bathrobe. She smiled and called for Benny to come and meet me. I couldn't help but notice his collection of French impressionist paintings on the walls. Benny immediately wanted to show me something and led me to the master bedroom, where there were a number of clarinets spread out on the bed! With a big smile, he asked which one I thought he should play for the television show—quite a sense of humor. He also showed me his collection of classic tube microphones, which we agreed were too valuable to use on the show. In the same closet was a box of his famous 1938 Carnegie Hall records, and he asked if I would like one, but somehow never gave to me. After discussing his strong views on modern recording techniques, we happily looked forward to working together.

The concert would be staged at the brand-new Marriott Marquis Hotel, just off of Times Square. My 10th floor office at Record Plant looked out on 46th Street as I watched them bulldoze a number of classic New York Broadway theaters to build this hotel. New York has a bad habit of eating its own children.

The Marquis Hotel ballroom was barely finished and acoustically, ah . . . modern industrial, so it was difficult adhering to Benny's minimal distant miking demands. The ambiance was awful. I got around some of it by discreetly hanging closer mics from the lighting trusses, but the music was fantastic! Benny's manager and a band leader himself, Loren Schoenberg, had assembled a great big band with A-list players and guest Dick Hyman on piano and drummer Louie Bellson. They played all the great Fletcher Henderson charts and of course Benny Goodman solos! Benny was still in classic form and really enjoyed himself, as did all the folks who paid $1,000 a seat for the benefit concert, that later would be aired on PBS as *Benny Goodman: Let's Dance! A Musical Tribute*. He went out in style and would pass away less than a year later on June 13, 1986. A truly great US musical treasure who started in the 1930s to integrate his Big Bands based on talent, period.

MORE GREAT DATES FROM THE LOG

Guitar Great, Roy Buchanan, at Carnegie Hall, December 6, 1985, primarily known as a blues player, he influenced many a jazz musician.

Jazz legends Art Farmer and Benny Golson at Sweet Basil, in New York with Producer Helen Keane, February 21–22, 1986

JVC Jazz Festival at Newport, Rhode Island, August 23, 1986, with an all-star cast of Gerry Mulligen, John Scofield, Miles Davis, Stanley Jordan, Al Di Meola, David Sanborn, George Howard, Natalie Cole, and the Wayne Shorter Quartet.

Dave Valentin, the great Jazz flautist, at the Blue Note, New York, May 31–June 1, 1988, for GRP records

The legendary Chick Corea at the Blue Note, New York, December 29–30, 1988, for GRP records

LFLC Ray Charles, State Theater, April 9–12, 1989

CHARLES MINGUS *EPITAPH* REDISCOVERED
JULLIARD ALICE TULLY THEATER, MAY 31–JUNE 1–3, 1989

The 1962 recording of *Epitaph* was a star-crossed adventure that Mingus abandoned. After his death, a score was rediscovered, and Sue Mingus managed to get the composer/conductor Gunther Schuller to brave a mission impossible to record the full score. The WNET/13 *Great Performances* producers brought in John McClure and me to try recording it again with a serious orchestra. This was a once-in-a-lifetime chance to play this legendary composition.

Now I was a wary admirer of Mingus; he was a bit over my head musically but glad to have a chance to hear this now legendary composition. The problem was that my Black Truck had crashed badly (with me in it) only a few months previously. Fortunately, Chris Stone at Record Plant LA, had leased me one of his remote trucks, so I could stay in business. It was a bit older, but we made it work. John McClure was one of the most competent, confident engineers in live orchestra recording I've ever seen. Nothing fazed him; he had the scores and made it all work!

If you are also brave musically, listen to the Columbia Records album *Mingus Epitaph.*

MANY OTHER GREAT JAZZ PERFORMANCES WE RECORDED IN NEW YORK

Stanley Turrentine, Village Gate, August 8, 1989
Wynton Marsalis, Avery Fisher Hall LFLC, December 20–22, 1989
Marsalis Family, Alice Tully Hall WNET/13, October 31,1990
Jimmy Smith, Kenny Burrell, Fat Tuesday's Fantasy Records, November 16–17, 1990
Buddy Rich Tribute, *NFL Films*, April 7–8, 1991
Stepane Grappelli, Carnie Hall, June 9, 1993

HUGH MASEKELA BLUES ALLEY
WASHINGTON, DC, TRILOCA RECORDS, JULY 30–AUGUST 1, 1993

This was a special recording for me because my old friend and mentor Paul Sloman was producing this important show. The South African jazz trum-

Touring the Maserati factory in Italy 1963, when this Tipo 151 race car returned from LeMans. They wouldn't let me test drive it.

This very same Maserati Tipo 151 race car shows up 53 years later right next door, at Leydon Restorations. They still won't let me drive it.

Record Plant NY White Truck as it looked in 1971 when recording George Harrison's Concert for Bangladesh.

Eddie Kramer recording the British Band Foghat at the magnificent old Colegate Mansion. Eddie loves the great acoustics of these rooms.
Photo courtesy of David DB Brown

The Colegate Mansion living room was set up for Foghat's recording, also using other isolated rooms as well. The world's largest indoor pipe organ was sadly not playable.

This recording studio we built using the Record Plant Remote equipment for Jack Douglas and Jay Messina to record Aerosmith. The Cenacle was a huge mansion where the band stayed while recording their album *Draw The Line*.

The magnificent Cenacle living room was used for Aerosmith's drummer, Joey Kramer. What an incredible sound!

This flyer announced my purchase of the Record Plant Black Truck to join my company, Remote Recording Services. I loved Taxi Briell's photo from the Rolling Stones show in Chicago.
Photo courtesy of Thomas Taxi Briell

Stevie Wonder's 1984 *Homecoming in Detroit* was a huge show, one of the first all digital audio broadcasts. These are early 3M Digital 32 track recorders, requiring lots of care. A lot of fun stories from that gig!

The Havana Jam in 1979 Cuba was a huge adventure. It was an attempt at easing the cold war with music. We assembled a large portable recording system to be flown down. Long interesting story in the book.

Recording the Prince *Purple Rain Tour* on the Black Truck: Susan Rogers, David Tickle, Sal Greco and Fritz Lang having a laugh. PRN was such an incredible talent.

Highest Remote ever, on the helicopter pad of the South Tower, the World Trade Center in New York.

We moved all the recording gear from the Record Plant Remote Truck up 110 floors to build a studio. The band was called Year One and they were filming performances In places like the Grand Canyon. Great story in the book.

Producer/Engineer Jim Anderson mixing live to air for Jazz Radio WBGO, a brilliant combination!
Photo Courtesy of Jim Anderson

The 1982 Who Tour was a grand farewell, leading up to a live international TV broadcast. The results, and the live album and video, were so successful they didn't retire!

Over 500,000 people gathered by the Washington Monument for the Beach Boys 4th of July 1980 concert. It was an incredible experience mixing them live to air.
Photo courtesy of David W Hewitt

Ornette Coleman was certainly the most innovative jazz musician of his time. Recording him with Ron St. Germain was a career high point. Look up Ornette: *Made in America*.
Photo courtesy of David W Hewitt

The Rock and Roll Hall of Fame in 1982 on stage at the Waldorf Astoria Hotel in New York, before it became a TV show. A great gathering of artists and record biz moguls.

The Black Truck on the 1980 Winter Olympics field. We were there to record bands playing for the athletes. I got to see the famous hockey game where the Americans beat the favored Russian team.
Photo courtesy of David DB Brown

The Silver Remote Truck at the opening of the Hard Rock Casino in Las Vegas, 1995.

When the SARS epidemic struck Toronto, Canada in 2003, a benefit concert was organized. The Rolling Stones, Rush and others drew 450-500,000 to a grateful audience.

Audio Producer Jim Anderson brought us in for the PBS series *In Performance at the White House*, back when there was real music in the house, like this one with B.B. King. Hopefully, there will be again.
Photo Courtesy of Jim Anderson

The Silver Remote Truck snowed in at Carnegie Hall early 1990s; note the old movie marque, before the original 1891 basement rehearsal hall was rebuilt as Zankel Hall.

The Cathedral of Saint John the Divine in NYC (1892) is one of the largest in the world. I have recorded mostly classical music there, but this was for Mariah Carey's 1994 Christmas video peter, Hugh Masekela, was returning to the United States with an incredible ensemble of musicians from his home country.

Masekela had arranged a show covering his long musical history to be played by musicians who grew up listening and playing it. I knew some of Hugh's more popular compositions, but these were deep songs from his life, more like a theatrical event; there was so much color and nuance to the playing. It was mesmerizing—a reaction I have heard from many listeners of the recording in the years since. It has become a collector's item among audiophiles around my area. No wonder Paul Simon took him out on the *Graceland* Tour.

I highly recommend giving this a listen: *Hugh Masekela Hope.*

PS

Paul Sloman was our studio manager at Record Plant New York in the 1970s. He was instrumental in helping me build up the remote recording business. He would go on to manage Atlantic Records Studios, Sony Studios in New York, and record labels like Triloca.

MORE GREAT JAZZ PERFORMANCES THAT WE HAVE RECORDED

Lionel Hampton, Tribute at the Kennedy Center, Washington, DC, September 10, 1995

Theolonius Monk, Competition at the Kennedy Center, Washington, DC, November 20, 1995

John Pizzarelli at the Algonquin Hotel, New York, February 28–March 1, 1996

Count Basie Band with Joe Williams at the Blue Note, New York, August 20, 1997

Theolonius Monk, Institute at the Kennedy Center, Washington, DC, October 23–26, 1997

Tito Puente at Bird Land, New York, RMM Live Album with John Fausty, May 8, 1998

Miles Davis Tribute at Bird Land, New York, N2K Live Album, May 26, 1998

Wynton Marsalis, LCJO at the Supper Club, New York, August 24–27,
1998

Harry Connick Jr. at the Warner Theater, Washington, DC, January
26–29, 2000

PIANO GRAND! A SMITHSONIAN CELEBRATION
BET STUDIOS, WASHINGTON, DC, MARCH 8–9, 2000

I have visited the Smithsonian museums many times during my gigs in
Washington, DC, so I was happy to participate in their celebration of the
piano's 300th anniversary. Smithsonian Productions and Maryland Public
Television, in conjunction with WNET/13 in New York produced a grand
show indeed.

Billy Joel was the perfect host for this celebration because he plays classical, jazz, rock, and his own compositions on piano. His musical knowledge
and stage presence made for a great production. Of course, he opened the
show with "Baby Grand" and later "Piano Man." There were classical performances of "Grieg's Piano Concerto in A Minor," by Jean-Yves Thibaudet
and the Smithsonian Chamber Orchestra and fantastic "Baroque Impres-
sions" by jazz pianist Cyrus Chestnut. There were wonderful vocal and
piano performances by Diana Krall and Elaine Elias and would you believe,
by1950s' rocker Jerry Lee Lewis, pounding out "Great Balls of Fire!" There
were many other great performances to hear, but the most heartfelt performance to me was by jazz legend Dave Brubeck. His composition "Thank
You (Dziekuje)"—well, you just have to hear it.

Pianist Hyung-Ki Joo performed Billy Joel's composition "Fantasy" and
the Smithsonian students and artists closed with "Heart and Soul."

WYNTON MARSALIS
POLYMATH MUSICIAN AND DIRECTOR OF JAZZ AT LINCOLN
CENTER IN NEW YORK.

Wynton Marsalis has done so much to preserve and advance jazz in the
United States and throughout the world. His efforts with Jazz at Lincoln
Center (JALC) and the subsequent construction of JALC's theater complex
at Columbus Circle in New York have elevated the culture to new heights.
I've had the honor to record performances with his many groups. Among
them were these recordings:

Jazz at Lincoln Center Gala
Apollo Theater, June 1–2, 2003

Jazz Foundation Gala
Apollo Theater, October 28, 2004

Jazz at Lincoln Center Gala
Apollo Theater, June 5, 2006

Recommended Recordings

The Buddy Rich Show
https://drummagazine.com/the-buddy-rich-show-1982-finally-comes-to-
    life-with-new-dvd-release/

Ella Fitzgerald
Newport Jazz Festival Live at Carnegie Hall

Stevie Wonder, Aretha Franklin, Donny Hathaway, and Ray Charles
Recorded Live at Newport in New York

B. B. King and Friends
The Blues . . . a Real Summit Meeting
Recorded Live at Newport in New York

Frank Sinatra
The Main Event Live

Stuff
Live in New York

Miles Davis
We Want Miles and *Miles Ahead: The Music of Miles Davis*

Weather Report
Havana Jam

Jaco Pastorius
Truth, Liberty & Soul Live in New York

Wynton Marsalis Quartet
Live at Blues Alley

A note from the author:

Of all the musical genres, jazz has long been my personal favorite. I was privileged to have recorded with many great jazz artists and tried wherever possible to accommodate the budgets and dates they required. As my remote recording trucks grew in complexity, cost, and almost solid bookings, it became impossible to compete with the smaller portable digital recording operations.

It was thanks to publicly funded television programs like PBS's *Great Performances* and special productions from institutions like the Smithsonian, that there were still a few opportunities for us to be involved with the great jazz being played.

Here are a few examples:

Benny Goodman "Let's Dance"
WNET/13 *Great Performances*

Charles Mingus *Epitaph*
Gunther Schuller conducting a 30-piece orchestra, plying Mingus's long missing masterpiece.

Piano Grand! A Smithsonian Celebration
The 300th Anniversary of the piano hosted by Billy Joel with guests Dave Brubeck, Vladimir Meller, Diana Krall, and many others—p.s. don't wait for the 400th anniversary.

(14)

THE ROLLING STONES: WE FINALLY GOT THE GIG

And Kept It through Many Adventures, Tours, Films, South America, Tokyo . . .

When the Rolling Stones 1972 US tour descended on Philadelphia, I was still working at Regent Sound, but I got a call from Frank Hubach aboard the Record Plant New York remote truck. He needed to borrow some gear for the live recording, so I gladly came down to the Spectrum Arena to deliver it and hang out for the show. Frank had some great stories, most of which I can't repeat here!

When I finally did go to work for Record Plant remote division in January1973, I hoped to be onboard for the next Rolling Stones US tour, but the legendary British engineer Eddie Kramer was working with them again, and he had a deal with the Fedco Remote Truck. My chance wouldn't come until the 1981 tour.

There was one surprise Rolling Stones recording in May 1978. They had recorded at Record Plant New York in the past, but this was a quick film shoot to promote the current record. It was taking place over on the East Side of Manhattan at a film studio. They needed to playback a prerecorded track and record Mick Jagger's live vocal with it while filming his performance. Senior Record Plant engineer, Jay Messina, who had worked with Mick before, would be engineering. I just had to assemble the gear, get it over there, and set it up for Jay. Simple, right? A four-track Ampex 440, a small console, speakers, and some mics and then hit record. Of course, Mick kept adding things, and I had to call Record Plant to have the White

Truck bring over more gear; we were still building the new Black Truck at that time.

I should have cabbed it back to the studio and driven it myself, but they were in a hurry, so a studio assistant who knew how to drive a truck brought it over. I met him at the curb and dug out the gear for the union hands to bring in, but the poor assistant stopped me and pointed up at the top of the truck. He had crashed the roof of the truck into a stone bridge arch in Central Park, where trucks are prohibited. He was a nice Midwestern farm kid, who was new to New York City. I told him to leave the truck, I'd take care of it and sent him back to the studio.

I carried some extra gear up to our makeshift control room, but when I opened the door Mick was fast asleep in the lap of a lovely young lady, who gave me the "shush" sign. Mick knows how to pace himself; lesson learned. Jay, the ever-serene adult on duty, made it all work to Mick's satisfaction. I went back to the studio to work on the Black Truck design.

The crashed roof story gets worse; the White Truck had to go record the jazz guitarist Al Di Meola at the New York Palladium and then drive to Saginaw, Michigan, for an Alice Cooper show! We had gaffer-taped a tarp over the smashed roof, but that didn't stop a torrential rainstorm on the way back to New York. We had to park the truck late that night at the Bottom Line Theater for a Lou Reed Show the next day. As the truck approached the venue, they saw a tow truck pulling away with our competitor, the Fedco remote truck on the hook!

My schadenfreude wouldn't last for long, when we opened up the truck door, all the water that had leaked into the roof cavity was running down the slanted interior walnut roof! It was like a shower, but fortunately the slant directed the water just past the faders of the DeMedio recording console. The 1970 San Francisco Hippie shag rug was soaked, so we sent somebody out to buy hair dryers.

Miraculously, no water got on the console or the Ampex MM-1000 tape recorders, so we just did the show in a damp, chilly studio. I don't think we told Lou. The client was Arista Records, so it was for the live album *Live: Take no Prisoners*.

My logs show the Record Plant White Truck recording the Rolling Stones in New Orleans on July 13, 1978; and Boulder, Colorado, on July 16, 1978; but I was frantically trying to finish building the new Black Truck, which had to leave to meet the band Kansas, whose live album we had already started on the White Truck. That is another nightmare story! The new Peterbilt truck blew up. Complicated? You bet; see chapter 6 to see how it interfered with their recordings as well.

THE ROLLING STONES 1981 *TATTOO YOU* TOUR

Mick Jagger had heard engineer Bob Clearmountain's work with Nile Rogers and Chic at the Power Station studios in New York and wanted him to mix the disco version of "Miss You." After that success, Bob was asked to record the 1981 Rolling Stones *Tattoo You* Tour.

Being as we were just nine blocks down the street at Record Plant, it made sense to call me and book the Black Truck for the tour. I finally had my chance to record the Rolling Stones live shows! I would manage the remotes and engineer the dates Bob couldn't make; he was always busy working on multiple studio albums.

Impresario Bill Graham was promoting the tour, so I started by meeting the Stones' production manager, my old friend Michael Ahern, at the Eagles Stadium in Philadelphia. They were building and modifying the giant stage sets for the tour. There had to be two identical stages, leapfrogging along, to keep up with the tight concert schedule. As you will see from any of the show videos, it was a monstrously complex stage production.

Michael was busy directing the insanity, with hundreds of production crew members and contractors. When he finally got a free moment, I asked how it was going, and with the calm understatement he was known for, said, "This thing has too many moving parts" and went back to making both stages work.

Brendan Bryne Arena, New Jersey, November 4–7, 1981

My Record Plant crew and the Black Truck caught up with the Stones tour at the Brendan Bryne Arena, just outside of New York City. It was our first interface with the touring sound system by Showco, one of the most advanced companies of the period. Fortunately, the Stones' live mixer was another good friend (and a co-owner of Showco), Jack Maxson. There were the usual interface issues with a new show, sorting out remote truck parking and power, union jurisdictions, and getting all the band inputs shared for the first time. Then, of course, there was the interface with film and video crews. In the predigital era, synchronizing sound and pictures was a risky business!

The Record Plant New York crew was experienced. Phil Gitomer had the Black Truck parked, powered, and secure; Phil Gitomer and Kooster McAllister made sure all the band and crew interface went smoothly. David DB Brown kept all the analog tape machines recording and in sync with the video.

Recording engineer Bob Clearmountain knew the members of the band and all the important management figures from his studio work, so everything went smoothly. Bob had the music mix together on the API console in short order, so we had a great first show recording. The New Jersey and New York crowds roared their approval!

One of my favorite road sayings is, "The show is that little inconvenience between the load in and the load out."

Muddy Waters's Checkerboard Lounge, November 22, 1981

Our next stop would be in Chicago, a city famous for the many blues artists living there. Chief among them was Muddy Waters, who had long been an inspiration for Mick Jagger and Keith Richards. While in Chicago, they decided to join Muddy at his Checkerboard Lounge and film the show. This was all rather last moment and Bob Clearmountain was not available to engineer. I told the worried producer that I could take care of it; he looked me in the eye and said, "I'll be the judge of that" and walked away. A short time later he came back with a grin and said, "Somebody likes you; do it!"

If you watch the film, the lounge is small, and adding the Stones made it real tight! There was not enough power for the extra gear, so I went looking for any mains electrical panels next door in an open parking garage. This was a rough neighborhood and when I interrupted two men exchanging a small package, they were not happy to see me. One of them made the gesture of reaching into his jacket—'nuff said.

I ended up ordering an extra generator! The setup and rehearsal were a bit tense, as you can imagine—rich rock stars showing up in a tough neighborhood blues club, but it was all about payback for all that Muddy Waters had given to the music world, especially for Mick and Keith.

Once everybody was playing together, it was an incredible night. For whatever reason, the CD and DVD recording was not released until 2012, but you can see it now on YouTube. Bob Clearmountain mixed it, and it is a gas!

Horizon, Rosemont, Illinois

The Rolling Stones show that we came to record was at the Horizon Arena just outside of Chicago. The late night at the Checkerboard Lounge made the following setup day a bit strenuous, especially when it was decided that the PA had to be rehung with an expensive overtime union call! We finally got a sound check and the show went fine; Chicago always turned out a great audience.

Silverdome, Pontiac, Michigan, November 30–December 1, 1981

Super Dome, New Orleans, Louisiana, December 5, 1981
Stones Rollin' on the River

We were still outside the Super Dome loading the rental station wagon full of Rolling Stones Ampex 24-track tapes to go back to Record Plant New York. The "A" rolls go, the "B" rolls stay with the Remote Truck for back up in case of accident.

Just as we finished loading, I was informed that a huge party would take place on the River Boat, which was conveniently moored close by. And the Rolling Stones would play after the hometown Neville Brothers set. Oh, and I needed to record it on multitrack for the film being shot! And I had x hours to get ready before the River Boat sails.

The Black Truck couldn't fit on the boat and the API recording console was bolted down, but fortunately Jack Maxson agreed to let me borrow his Showco Superboard! The crew unloaded it from the case, which won't fit up the three flights of stairs to the only room available to us. My crew and the deck hands managed to get the two 450-pound Ampex 24-track recorders up the stairs and we frantically drug multicable and outboard gear to set up the control room. We just finished plugging in the last mic as the Neville Brothers start playing. We had no sound check and just winged it on an audio console I've never seen before!

Miraculously, everything worked, and we recorded some great Neville Brothers sets. Unfortunately for the film, the Stones were having such a good time at the party that they never got around to playing, but I did make it downstairs to see the show for a few minutes.

I'm playing a few bars of the Stones singing "Honky Tonk women, Gimme, gimme, gimme, the honky tonk blues!"

MICK THE BARTENDER

There was a large party at the next theater. The large bar in the lobby was quite crowded by the time I got there. I managed to belly up to the bar and was looking to catch the bartender's attention. When he turned around, I realized with a shock, it was Mick Jagger in a white uniform! He didn't say anything, and I just played along and ordered a beer. I'm sure some other patrons must have caught it, but none had the balls to say anything. After a few minutes, Mick disappeared behind the bar. I think he was a bit disappointed.

Capitol Center, Landover, Maryland, December 7–9, 1981
Sun Devil, Tempe, Arizona, December 13, 1981

The Rolling Stones 1981 *Tattoo You* Tour Finale Show, December 19, 1981

The Rolling Stones were getting into the habit of ending each US tour with a big live pay-per-view TV show. This time it would be on December 19, 1981, at the Hampton Coliseum in Hampton Roads, Virginia.

Adding to the excitement for the live television broadcast and video and audio albums, they added the hard rocking George Thorogood and the Destroyers. I added a second remote truck, the White Truck, with engineer Rod O'Brien to mix, so we didn't have to interfere with Bob Clearmountain's Stones' setup in the Black Truck.

The rehearsals had gone well, and despite months of touring, the Stones were in top form. We did not get to rehearse the opening sequence because they wanted it to be a surprise. . . . it sure was! None of this made the film, but after the handheld cameraman followed the stage manager around to raucous dressing rooms, desperately looking for the band, he ended up in the sports team's bathroom, just as a large sheep, dressed as a honky tonk woman in fishnet nylons walks out! Another honky tonk woman stood facing a men's urinal while a giant python wrapped itself around the next urinal! No, I don't have any pictures.

Clearmountain and I were in the remote truck trying to stop laughing long enough to keep the opening act mix going until the band hit the stage!

I don't think the concert audience got to see that part of the show, but the rest of it was great.

It did turn out to be a spectacular show to end the 1981 *Tattoo You* US Tour. In addition to the estimated $52 million in concert revenues, it's reported that the Hal Ashby film *Lets Spend the Night Together* also grossed $50 million. The live *Still Life* CD went Platinum and has been reissued several times.

LETS SPEND THE NIGHT TOGETHER FILM MIX

The postproduction audio mixes were complicated due to editing and sync issues, not to mention too many cooks and crazy schedules for all involved. I've heard conflicting stories about who did what.

There was a big premier showing of the film in New York City, to which I was invited. The film was quite good, but there were so many problems with the sound, that I had to leave. Record Plant got some critical calls about it, but we had nothing to do with the postproduction. It did get corrected for the full theatrical release.

A few bars of Mick singing, "I can't get no satisfaction!"

Recommended Recordings

Still Life
Rolling Stones/Atlantic Live
Vinyl and CD Remastered by Virgin Records and Universal Music

Let's Spend the Night Together
Rolling Stones Feature Film
Also released on VHS and CED Videodisc and DVD in Japan

Live at the Checkerboard Lounge, Chicago 1981
CD and DVD Eagle Vision

Live: Take No Prisoners
Lou Reed
Arista Records

THE KEITH AND CHUCK MOVIE: *HAIL! HAIL! ROCK 'N' ROLL*

Keith Richards had long admired Chuck Berry and his guitar playing, so the celebration of Chuck Berry's 60th birthday was a perfect opportunity to honor his career with an all-star concert at the magnificent Fox Theater in his hometown of St. Louis, Missouri. Keith organized the event and recruited an incredible group of like-minded musicians, including Eric Clapton and Robert Cray on guitars, Steve Jordan on drums, and Joey Spampinato on bass. Plus, featured singers Etta James, Julian Lennon, and Linda Ronstadt were also there and a feature film was planned with Taylor Hackford directing.

Filming started at the Cosmo Club in East St. Louis, then Chuck's private club at Berry Park and finally the big show at the Fox Theater in St. Louis.

I brought the Black Truck, which now belonged to my company, Remote Recording Services, to all three locations. We were joined by recording engineer Michael Frondelli, who would also mix the music for the feature film, home video, and a live record.

The rehearsals were recorded at the Berry Club, a 1950s' style venue located on Chuck's estate. It no longer functioned commercially, but still served as Chuck's recording studio. The building had a lot of water leaks and mildew. There were piles of old recording gear on the floor, including Ampex 300 tape machine parts. When we ran out of limiters in the truck for Michael Frondelli, I asked if we could use some of Chuck's from his studio, and we could—for $100 per day.

The big celebration show and film shoot was at the Fabulous Fox, St. Louis, a magnificently restored 1929 movie palace, modeled after the Palace of Versailles. For many years, the Fox movie theaters were a monopoly that ruled US screens. The Fox empire didn't last, but thankfully, this theater survived. And it turned out to be a pretty good venue for rock and roll.

There were two shows and plenty of great takes for the film, even with some of the stops and starts for the filming. Keith Richards was the real producer of this birthday salute to Chuck Berry, but he and the band, along with the guest stars, played following Chuck. That is no easy task because Chuck Berry plays what he feels at the moment. There were many great performances, and Chuck could still "Duck Walk" play that guitar! I loved watching the musicians trying to keep up with the 60-year-old rocker. My own favorites were Linda Ronstadt singing "Back in the USA" with Chuck; "Too Much Monkey Business," just Chuck; and, of course, "Rock and Roll

Music" with Etta James singing and Keith, Robert Cray, and Eric Clapton on guitars.

The film is what you need to watch to really get the message of long overdue homage to one of rock's founding fathers.

PS

For you die-hard Keith fans, I recommend watching the movie *Hail, Hail Rock 'n' Roll*—especially the ending where an exhausted Keith gives his final salute to the master. I heard the unedited version backstage; Keith is a rock-and-roll mensch!

THE CRASH OF '89

The year 1989 was difficult for me and my small band of road rangers. In the early morning hours of February 6, the Black Truck struck black ice on a high crowned country road and rolled over. Thanks to the skill of driver Phil Gitomer, we avoided crashing into a spinning car in front of us or the surrounding trees.

My seatbelt failed, and I was thrown into the bunk instead of the windshield, saving me from more serious injury but knocking me unconscious. Phil survived with lots of bruises and valiantly directed salvage operations to get the Black Truck home.

As the medics hoisted me up out of the sideways cab, I tried desperately to remember what happened and where we were supposed to be going!

By the time I arrived at the emergency department strapped on the board, I started to remember: We were heading for New York to record Harry Connick Jr. at the famed Algonquin Hotel!

I grabbed a passing intern and got him to call my wife Dusty and told him do not tell Dusty what happened! Just call my friend Kooster McAllister and get him and the Record Plant White Truck over to record the gig! She did, and he did, and saved the day for Columbia Records and Harry Connick Jr. That show would help launch Harry's career, and we would record him many times as he became a star. My son Ryan just finished engineering Harry's album *A Celebration of Cole Porter*. It's a glorious return to his Big Band roots.

RIP Black Truck, my faithful road companion.

THE ROLLING STONES *STEEL WHEELS* TOUR, 1989

Canadian concert promoter Michael Cohl was now in and Bill Graham was suddenly out after all those years. Bill Graham had a few choice words about that I can't print here. Jake Berry was now the production manager, replacing my friend Michael Ahern, who was actually happy to spend time with his wife Mady and their two young daughters. His company, Michael Ahern Production Services had a number of clients to keep him busy.

Despite having lost our prized Black Truck, I was saved by Chris Stone, the original cofounder of Record Plant and still the owner of the Los Angeles and Sausalito Record Plants. Chris had three remote trucks and magnanimously offered to lease one to my company, even though we had long been East Coast–West Coast competitors. Chris had always been a graciously tough and farsighted businessman. He knew that I was an ally he could count on. I would later join his World Studio Group, formed after he sold Record Plant Studios.

With his help, I was then able to retain the Rolling Stones as a client and start recording the *Steel Wheels* Tour. We recorded the following Rolling Stones shows with the various remote trucks listed. I engineered unless otherwise noted.

> CNE Stadium, Toronto, Canada, Record Plant LA Remote Truck, September 2–3, 1989
> Jacksonville, Florida, Record Plant LA Remote Truck, November 25, 1989
> Clemson, South Carolina, Record Plant LA Remote Truck, November 26, 1989
> Stade Olympique, Montreal, Effanel Remote Truck, December 12–14, 1989
> Bob Clearmountain Engineer

The Rolling Stones 1989 *Steel Wheels* Tour Finale Show
Convention Center, Atlantic City, New Jersey, December 16–20, 1989
Bob Clearmountain Engineer

As they had in the past, the Rolling Stones staged the final show of the US tour as a live television broadcast. This time tour producer Michael Cohl had negotiated a deal with Donald Trump to stage the show at his Atlantic City, New Jersey, casino. The Stones did not want Trump involved, so the contract specifically stated Trump was not to be involved in promoting or even to be present at the live television broadcast.

The story I heard there on location was verified by Cohl during TV interviews later on with *Vanity Fair*, among others. Before the Rolling Stones show started, Trump staged his own press conference at a building next door to take credit for their concert broadcast. When Michael confronted him, Trump refused to leave and said the sponsors had begged him to stay. Cohl quotes this from the band: "They call me back [into the dressing room], at which point Keith pulls out his knife and slams it on the table and says, 'What the hell do I have you for? Do I have to go over there and fire him myself? One of us is leaving the building—either him, or us.'" I said, "No. I'll go do it. Don't you worry."

Trump did finally leave, and you can read the whole Julie Miller interview from March 18, 2016, at vanityfair.com. There were some other colorful quotes that I heard about on location but won't repeat here.

Bob Clearmountain and I were in the Effanel remote truck with owner Randy Ezratty and didn't hear about this until later. Being the end of the tour, now being called the *Urban Jungle Tour*, spirits were high and so were the sold-out crowds. It would be the last live show with original Rolling Stones bass player, Bill Wyman, so that was a historic show for the fans.

It was great listening to Bob Clearmountain mixing the Rolling Stones on the SSL console. That is his longtime preference and what he owns in his mixing studios. He really has a unique sound of his own. There were guest appearances by Eric Clapton on "Little Red Rooster" and John Lee Hooker on "Boogie Chillun." Some of these performances made it on to the live record released later called *Flashpoint*.

This tour grossed an astounding $175 million in 1989–1990. I guess Michael Cohl earned his keep.

THE ROLLING STONES JAPANESE TOUR
TOKYO DOME, JAPAN, FEBRUARY 24–27, 1990
RS RECORDS

I got the call for recording the Tokyo shows to add to the Rolling Stones live albums. Fortunately, the Japanese remote truck had a Neve VR console and Studer sub mixers similar to my own Silver Truck. Their engineers were helpful, and the recordings were just fine. I was able to stay when they recorded for Japanese television, and they demonstrated their considerable skills—very impressive.

It was one of those rare on-the-road coincidences, my old friend Jack Maxson happened to be in Tokyo on business. He had retired from live mixing for Showco (as he use to do for the Rolling Stones) but was dealing with Vari-Lite in Japan, in which he had an interest, along with Showco. We had a wonderful dinner at a restaurant high above Tokyo that replicated an old English Pub. Kobe beef and excellent Japanese beer made for a great evening of remembering our music history. Jack was a unique Texas gentleman.

The other perk was a tour of Tokyo's incredible electronics market, where I bought my first portable DAT recorder. That was big news back in the day.

The recording was later issued on vinyl as Rolling Stones *Steel Wheels Live at the Tokyo Dome*

THE ROLLING STONES 1994 *VOODOO LOUNGE* TOUR
SUPER DOME, NEW ORLEANS, LOUISIANA, OCTOBER 9–10, 1994

I got the call to mix the live radio broadcast over the Westwood One Network, although I had to use their remote truck. That was fine because I knew their engineer Biff Dawes from his Wally Heider Remote days, and he would save me from any embarrassing mistakes on the Euphonix Console. Well, almost; I did have a sax solo erupt before I could find the pad. It was an early digitally controlled analog console.

Mick Jagger called me in for a conference before the show. He certainly knew that I had been the remote truck engineer for the last few tours and the mixer when his studio engineers were not available. I would be mixing the live-to-air show, and he wanted to discuss a few concerns and expectations.

It certainly was a lesson in show production as various department heads came in for Mick to make decisions. The one that really interested me was how he notified the beer concessionaires to expect a rush crowd when Keith would sing his songs!

Things went well enough for a live Rolling Stones show, except I remember the video director kept calling for more audience applause in the mix, which was already too loud and washed out in a big stadium. Of course, the band didn't like the mix because of that—the usual dilemma of music versus picture.

ADDITIONAL STONES LIVE RECORDINGS

Tampa Stadium, Tampa, Florida, Silver Remote Truck DH, November 21, 1994

Sun Life Stadium, Miami, Florida, Silver Remote Truck DH PPV, November 24, 1994

Remote Recording Services Studio, Lahaska, Pennsylvania, January 24–February 5, 1995

Rolling Stones Mix, David Hewitt Engineer

Julliard School Bridge, New York, Tour Announcement Show, May 10, 2005

THE ROLLING STONES *BRIDGES TO BABYLON* TOUR
ED CHERNEY JOINS THE RECORDING

Engineer Ed Cherney had recently been working in the studio with the Rolling Stones, so I was pleased to hear he would be the mixer on the next live pay-per-view show. I knew of Ed's great studio recordings with artists I admired, like Bonnie Raitt, but mixing live-to-air full concerts is a challenging test for studio engineers who have some control over their time. I needn't have worried, Ed was as calm, collected, and in control of his mix as any veteran I have worked with. We would become great friends and record many live shows together.

This pay-per-view show was at the Trans World Airlines Dome in St. Louis, Missouri, on December 12, 1997, using my Silver Truck. Ed was comfortable with the Neve VR console and the broadcast went fine with great reviews.

The next recordings were at the Qualcomm Stadium in San Diego, California, on February 2–3, 1998, with the same successful results.

THE ROLLING STONES SOUTH AMERICAN *BRIDGES TO BABYLON* TOUR
RIVER PLATE STADIUM, BUENOS AIRES, ARGENTINA, MARCH 26–APRIL 7, 1998

My crew and I had just finished the *70th Academy Awards* broadcast in LA and flew down to join Ed Cherney and my son Ryan Hewitt in Buenos

Aires, Argentina. We had earlier assembled a rather complex portable recording studio and had it flown down to the venue with the Rolling Stones stage gear in the chartered Russian cargo plane. As you can see in the photographs, it was a complete analog recording studio, albeit with digital tape recorders. It took several days to put up acoustic treatment on the cement walls of the stadium room and assemble all the gear. The main console was a Studer 963 with additional 961 and 962 mixers. (I would later sell that 963 to Neil Young for his studio.) It was a formidable studio, with a lot of vintage outboard gear that Ed Cherney had requested. Once we had everything functioning and interfaced with the Clair sound system and the outgoing feeds for radio and television, we could concentrate on the more important task of finding a runner to go out and buy plenty of the local gelatos! At one point, we were suspected of drug trafficking because of the number of bags being brought into the studio.

The River Plate Stadium is the biggest in Argentina, seating more than 76,000 soccer fans. The Stones sold out five shows, just as they had in 1995.

It's hard to describe the incredible power of the Rolling Stones energizing a stadium full of 76,000 fanatic fans! Ed Cherney just smiled and mixed a great show.

There were some wonderful days off, in between shows, where we explored the city and its culture, enjoyed the restaurants with their legendary steaks, and listened to local musicians. I found rare books on the legendary early jets in Juan Peron's Argentine Air Force. I'm an Air Force brat and a vet, so I love the aircraft of that era.

So, after a successful series of shows, the tour packed up and prepared to move to Rio de Janeiro for the next series of shows. All our studio gear was on a plane flying back to the United States. We were about to fly home too, when I was informed that Mick wanted to record those shows because Bob Dylan was to be playing with them. With help from tour production and lots of phone calls (no Internet) I found a remote truck and made all the arrangements. The remote truck and crew were able to make it on time and get interfaced with the show. I wish I could remember their names, but the paperwork is long gone. There were some dodgy moments, especially when Bob Dylan's vocal mic kept dropping out! The Stones engineers had it, so the problem was with the remote truck and they couldn't find it. I got through it, and I think the Stones recordings were OK, but I don't know if they ever used the recordings.

I went straight to the hotel bar and joined the crew.

THE ROLLING STONES
SAN JOSE ARENA, SAN JOSE, CALIFORNIA, APRIL 19–20, 1999

THE ROLLING STONES HBO CONCERT SPECIAL
MADISON SQUARE GARDEN, NEW YORK, JANUARY 15–18, 2003

The Silver Truck was not available in time to make this show, so we once again brought our "portapack" recording system that we had used for the Rolling Stones recording in Buenos Aires. This time we had to set up in a sports locker room with even worse acoustics and no time to deal with it. Thankfully Ed Cherney's sense of humor pulled us through.

I was also fortunate to have the multitalented Daryl Bornstein volunteering to help with the digital multitrack recorders; he was up for a change from the classical music world.

ROLLING STONES *STEEL WHEELS* LIVE RECORDING
MADISON SQUARE GARDEN, JANUARY 15–18, 2003
THE HOCKEY DRESSING ROOM

HERE DARYL BORNSTEIN REMEMBERS WORKING THESE SHOWS

For most remote recording dates at Madison Square Garden, we parked the remote truck in the parking area adjacent to the entrance to the very long ramp that winds around the circular arena, rising from street level to arena level—approximately four stories up. Video and audio production trucks parked in the permanent production area between the building and the street, which is most often filled with a sea of sports television and production trucks.

For this recording, a fly pack consisting of several Studer analog consoles, two Sony 3348 digital multitrack recorders, a stack of Tascam or Sony DA88s, DAT machines, CD recorders, video cameras and monitors, intercom equipment, boxes of recording tape, and a pair of powered speakers had to be brought up from the street and assembled in the Rangers locker room. It smelled like the team had left moments before we arrived!

The load in and set up went smoothly, the interface with the Rolling Stones' monitor engineer went off without incident, and then we waited for Cherney to show up for the sound check.

Eddie, easily one of the most talented and nicest people you would ever meet, strolled in at the last minute (literally) and, coincidently, stoned. After brief introductions, Eddie started at one end of the first console and worked his way through all of the inputs on both desks in a matter of minutes. And what was coming through the monitors sounded like a finished record.

I asked Eddie how he was able to get such great sounds so quickly. He replied, modestly, that it had nothing to do with him and everything to do with the drum and guitar techs, and, of course, the members of the band. He said the drums sounded the way they did because Mike, the drum tech tuned the drums brilliantly, the Stones' sound crew placed the mics in exactly the right position, and Charlie was the most consistent drummer on the planet. The same could be said for the guitar techs, and of course, Keith and Ronnie.

Needless to say, Eddie had something to do with the sound, but this was typical of him. He was recognized by artists and colleagues alike as one of the best in the business. If he had an ego, we never witnessed it. Eddie showed up, did his work—brilliantly—and then left.

Eddie was also supportive of young engineers and producers, generous with sharing his knowledge, and making sure that everyone received credit for their contributions to a project. I was there as the tape op and appropriately nervous. I was thrilled when David asked me if I would like to join the party. He thought I might enjoy a day with Eddie and the Stones. David was equally generous with his time and knowledge. Frankly, I had no idea what I was doing. When I alerted Eddie to some "overages" on various drum channels, he wasn't the least concerned. He said that the peak LEDs on the 3348s needed some exercise!

The concert recording went flawlessly, but the load out, not so much. A Rolling Stones Tour is comprised of a large organization, with the best production and road management crew in the world. They have to be because their tours include two complete stages and crews and a fleet of more than 80 tractor trailers. A typical Stones stadium tour has more than 80 equipment trucks: 40 for each crew. The advance crew builds the stage in one city, while the show crew loads in and runs the live performances.

The Madison Square Garden arena is significantly smaller than the stadiums in which the Stones perform, with only a portion of the set used for the show. After the Madison Square Garden date, the equipment was being split between two different cities and had to be loaded into specific trucks for a specific location as designated by the Stones' production management. Coordinating more than 40 trucks to coincide with the order of equipment coming "out of the air" and down the long, winding loading ramps is a tour d'force—a real art. We were given specific instructions on what to do with our gear and told to wait to push it down the ramp until the designated truck was in position in the loading dock. As you may have guessed, our stagehand decided on his own to start pushing our gear down the ramp prematurely. In fact, he pushed a portion of our gear, had it loaded on the wrong truck and headed to the wrong city before we could stop him. It was a huge inconvenience to production to have to interrupt the load out to get the truck back in the bay and pull the gear off of it.

It's a long story, which I don't want to go into; suffice it to say, we finally got our gear back and the remainder of the load out went without incident. All the "flypack" portable gear would go back to the Silver Truck garage. The next Rolling Stones recording wouldn't be until July 28–30, 2003 at the SARS Benefit in Toronto, Canada.

Thanks for your view of the Stones recording Daryl!

THE ROLLING STONES HEADLINE A CANADIAN SARS BENEFIT
DOWNSVIEW PARK, TORONTO, CANADA, JULY 28–30, 2003

In summer 2003, Toronto, Canada, suffered an epidemic of severe acute respiratory syndrome (SARS), which is similar to the current coronavirus epidemic. In Canada, it was primarily contained in hospitals but did damage the economy. The Stones headed up a large number of bands for a benefit to aid the damaged economy. The Guess Who, Rush, and AC/DC, among others, performed with the Stones, playing a full 90-minute set as the headliner. We brought the Silver Truck, and I recorded a few bands while Ed Cherney mixed the Stones.

THE ROLLING STONES PLAY AMERICAN FOOTBALL WITH THE NFL
COMERICA PARK, DETROIT, MICHIGAN, AUGUST 30–31, 2005, BELIEVE OR NOT, A HALF-TIME SHOW!
GILLETTE STADIUM, FOXBORO, MASSACHUSETTS, SEPTEMBER 19–20, 2006

THE ROLLING STONES HBO LIVE RECORDING
ZILKER PARK, AUSTIN, TEXAS, OCTOBER 23–24, 2006

DARYL BORNSTEIN REMEMBERS WORKING THESE SHOWS

We arrived in the stadium in Austin after the massive stage had been erected and just as the sound speakers and upstage video wall were being flown. As impressive as the enormous Rolling Stones stage is, the crew and fleet of trucks is equally impressive. But what I noticed immediately was Dave Natale, the Stones' sound mixer, getting his hands dirty, hanging speakers. This is typical of everyone who works for the Stones. The crew, many of whom have been with the band for more than a quarter decade, are not only talented but are also totally committed to making the shows a success, and no one sits by and watches someone else work.

The crew is organized and disciplined, with many things happening simultaneously in a predetermined order designed for efficiency and safety. Adding an outside television production to their already complicated technical show could be an enormous inconvenience to the well-oiled machine. But the crew understood the importance of lucrative television and recording projects to the tour and were singularly accommodating to us interlopers.

Prior to our arrival, the production team and sound crew allocated for us space, power, and "tails" with a split from all the onstage mics. Dave Natale took a minute away from his load in and set up to meet with us, introduced us to the rest of his sound crew, and made us feel at home. We set up and patch our equipment, and then did a line check with the Stones' audio stage tech. Sadly, I can't remember his name, but I will never forget him. He was a former Special Services member and moved faster and more efficiently than anyone I have worked with before or since. He was friendly, accommodating, and when he was doing his normal preshow line check with Dave and was moving faster than the remote truck could follow, he let me know that he would go back and pick up any channels the truck missed after he was done with Dave's check out.

Part of the line check included moving the satellite stage from its home position by the main stage to its performance position mid arena. I was invited to tag along as the satellite stage motored over the tracks from the stage to the performance position and back, with the Stones' roadies playing the part of the band—literally!

Ed Cherney was on hand as audio engineer for this show, and as always, he set the festive and stress-free tone.

One cannot understate the magnitude of what undertaking a Rolling Stones production is like. It is huge, it is complicated, and it is emotionally charged. And yet, it runs as smooth as clockwork and is managed by people who know what they are doing and know how to keep the insanity to a minimum.

Our position was backstage, behind the drums and adjacent to Keith's enormous (and painfully loud) guitar amp rig. But more notably, it was in front of the horn players offstage waiting area, which was essentially a small tent. As soon as the horn players entered their "tent," the surrounding area acquired a smokey haze and a pungent order. I don't believe I had experienced anything like that since the early 1970s! The wonderful, crazy, and sadly, late Bobby Keys was the ringleader of the horns, and like everyone else in the Stones community, was friendly, accommodating, and simply delightful.

With the exception of one backup singer vocal line to the remote truck that decided to stop working mid show (and was quickly remedied), the recording went smoothly. The load out was as organized as the load in but at hyper speed. It was smooth, easy, and quite exhilarating to witness.

Right then, on to the next show!

THE ROLLING STONES AND MARTIN SCORSESE FILM
SHINE A LIGHT
THE BEACON THEATRE, NEW YORK, SEPTEMBER 29–OCTOBER 1,
2006, AND OCTOBER 29–NOVEMBER 1, 2006
BOB CLEARMOUNTAIN RETURNS.

We had worked on many film and video shoots with the Rolling Stones over the years, but this was the pinnacle for us New York–centric remote recorders. Mick had long owned a residence in the city, as did other band members. Scorsese is synonymous with New York and I had lived and worked here for many years. The Beacon Theater was right down the street when I lived in town and we recorded many shows here, so it was kind of like a homecoming. Bob Clearmountain knew all the Stones and their management from his earlier recording with them. He also worked with the film producers and postproduction staff, so everything went quite smoothly. Bob always had that relaxed sense of confidence and belief in what he was doing. It helped the entire crew feel confident in the mission.

DARYL BORNSTEIN REMEMBERS WORKING ON THESE SHOWS, WITH HIS USUAL SHARP OBSERVATIONS

"More camera men than I've ever seen in one theater." Reducing the Stones' arena show to fit in Madison Square Garden was nothing compared to squeezing the show onto the Beacon Theater's minuscule stage. Even with extending the existing stage to more than twice the size of the original, with all of the Stones' backline gear, lighting, sound and numerous camera jibs and dollies, there was barely room to move.

The available space for the remote recording truck mic splitters was against the back wall of the stage on top of some of the Stones' audio racks. It was a precarious position, with large lighting and power cables passing over, behind, and under. And it was directly behind Keith and Darryl's (bass) amplifiers. That said, it was a congenial location, with Darryl being particularly welcoming.

Bob Clearmountain would be the recording engineer for the film. His long experience with previous Stones recordings made for a good reunion with everyone involved. Bob brought along some new mic pre-amps designed and made by his wife's company, Apogee Electronics.

The first moment I entered the stage, I noticed that there were large jibs on both sides of the stage along with a dolly upstage of the guitar amps and drum kit. I wondered to myself if Marty Scorsese had thought this through. It seemed to me that the only thing certain was that each of those cameras would always have another camera in its shot. It was clear the next day that he did think about it, and the stage left jib had been removed!

There are no shortage of opinions about the Rolling Stones. Some feel they are nothing more than a tired bar band who should have hung up their instruments decades ago. Others will say, that after witnessing their extensive rehearsals during the week leading up to shooting, working on the same songs they have been playing for nearly 50 years, that I have never witnessed a harder working band, nor any as dedicated to perfection as Mick, Keith, Charlie, and Ronnie. The rehearsals were a master class in music and performance.

As many fans know, Charlie is particular. Some might call it OCD. He repeats the same actions—exactly—every time he steps up to the drum riser. There is a hanger for his jacket or sweater and a small tray for his watch. He steps up onto the riser using the same foot first each time and exits similarly. Charlie is famously private, and Mike, his longtime drum tech, is his dedicated gatekeeper. That made it that much more unexpected when Mike asked me to stand guard by the riser, and Charlie's jacket and watch, when he had to step away for a minute.

We were guests on the Stones' stage. It was our job to respect their authority and to try to be invisible. They have a routine they follow, and it was our responsibility, as guests, not to disrupt their routine in anyway. To be asked to participate in a small part of that routine, especially when it concerns members of the band, was a great honor. I have run into Mike, working with another band while the Stones were off the road, and he was just as professional and equally a pleasure to work with.

In the middle of the filming at the Beacon, the Stones had another date. It might have been a private party. This meant that they would need to load out all of the band gear and some of their sound equip-ment. Under the best of circumstances this would be a nightmare in the middle of recording. How we would get everything back exactly as it was when they returned was nightmarish. It was made that much more difficult given the lack of space and the density of equipment and cable on the stage. I worked with the Stones' "special forces" stage sound tech to disconnect our equipment from his, and then to my utter astonishment, he accepted my offer to help with getting his equipment off the stage. To be welcomed into such a tight knit rock-and-roll production family was a treat and another honor for which I am deeply grateful.

My position behind Jones's bass rig allowed for interaction with him. Having the same name, though spelled differently provided some common ground but wasn't really necessary. He is one of the friendliest, most down-to-earth superstar musicians I have ever met. Like everyone else, he made me feel at home.

Close by was the small space between Keith's amplifiers and Charlie's drum riser. There was a large plexiglass sheet on the side of the drum riser with the set list written with a white china marker. I suspect, however, the plexi was there to block some of the sound coming from Keith's guitar amplifiers.

I noticed that Keith, Charlie, and some of the crew hung out by the small passageway and had interesting conversations. I sought out the film's location audio mixer to see if he would like us to place a mic there to capture some of the conversations. Though he said no, I put the mic there anyway, and some of those conversations made it into the film!

Shine a Light was the second collaboration between Scorsese and the Stones. There were a lot of elements to this film, including a number of guest artists and a fully independent documentary crew. Adding to the insanity, one of the performances was a fundraiser for an organization associated with President Bill Clinton. Like we needed the Secret Service on top of everything else. It did provide some memories for me: Keith and Mick being introduced to Hillary Clinton's mother on stage during a meet-and-greet, Hillary and Chelsea "dancing" in the front of the balcony during the show, while Bill appeared to be sleeping.

The guest artists were Christina Aguilera, Buddy Guy, and Jack White. The rehearsals with Buddy and Jack went smoothly. The band worships Buddy, and Jack was appropriately reverential to the band.

Christina, in the midst of her difficult years (I had many encounters with her during that period), shot herself in the foot by acknowledging only Mick when she entered the stage to rehearse and clearly didn't know the words or the music for her duet with Mick.

After the rehearsal, Keith was in a state and made it clear he wanted her cut from the show. The movie brass wanted her because she was a big name at the time. Word must have gotten back to Christina because not only did she acknowledge the entire band when she performed for the audience the next night, but she also absolutely nailed her performance. It was a singular moment.

Drama abounds with the Rolling Stones. As a remote recording service, hired by the band, our job was to create absolutely no additional drama. Regardless of the chaos around us, like Marty not getting a set list before the band started playing, questions about whether Mick would be harmed making his entrance into the audience because of the heat the back lights in the lobby generated, or any personal issues that arise in a close-knit family.

We were visitors, on our best behavior, hoping to be invited back.

—Daryl Bornstein
Engineer, Producer, Designer

PS

One tragic but somehow fated event marred the last show. Ahmet Ertegun, the Atlantic Records executive, so prominent in the Rolling Stones' career, fell backstage and later died of his head injuries. It is often the wish of the cowboy to die with his boots on. Ahmet never stopped working, right to the end.

Ahmet Ertegun, RIP, July 31, 1923–November 14, 2006

Recommended Recordings

Rolling Stones *No Security*
Virgin Records

Chuck Berry, Keith Richards film, *Hail, Hail Rock 'n' Roll*
Rolling Stones *Steel Wheels Live at the Tokyo Dome*
The Rolling Stones *Shine a Light*
Paramount Classics

The Concert for New York City

SECRET ROLLING STONES REHEARSALS 2012
WILL THEY RETURN?

In April 2012 I was informed of a super-secret booking at John Hanti's SST Rehearsal Studios in Weehawken, New Jersey. Their IIWII Recording Studio would be used to record the rehearsals and I would be the recording engineer, being as I had a long history of live recordings with them. It was, of course, the Rolling Stones, who had not played live together as a band for some years but were seriously going to give it a go!

I had recorded a few jazz sessions in the excellent control room and spacious rehearsal hall designed by Sam Berkow. The vintage Focusrite console plus a large collection of microphones and outboard gear made it a perfect fit. The setting was an anonymous looking 1930s' industrial area that was just what Stones' security required.

The band's veteran road crew had stayed in shape with individual members projects and all the touring gear was set up perfectly. Keith Richards and Charlie Watts came in for a look at the control room and seemed pleased. They joined Mick and the rest of the band on stage and gradually started to warm up. When they finally started playing, it was like they never stopped! It was really great to see the grins as they played a set they had agreed on. No question, the Stones were still rolling.

That would be my last Rolling Stones recording, but they would go on to celebrate their 50th-Year Reunion Tour that stared in October 2012.

On October 29, 2012, Hurricane Sandy flooded the IIWII Studio with 13-foot waves of contaminated saltwater, decimating the infrastructure and equipment. I was stranded out in San Francisco at the AES Convention, watching the hurricane on television because all the flights were canceled. My BMW had been swimming in the floodwaters with thousands of other cars along the coast. Over the next several years I helped owner John Hanti rebuild the studio with another vintage Focusrite console before I retired in 2014.

I sometimes have to just grin and shake my head when I remember all those adventures. My thanks to the Rolling Stones for the many great performances that I was privileged to record.

(15)

THE WHO

Quadrophenia Tour and the Not Exactly "Last Tour" in 1982 with Glyn Johns

My Record Plant remote crew got the chance to record The Who's 1973 *Quadrophenia* Tour for the *King Biscuit Flower Hour* radio show. We had gotten off to a great start with *King Biscuit* earlier in 1973 by recording their first show with Bruce Springsteen and the Mahavishnu Orchestra. This would be a major show for them with a British superstar band just ending their US tour. It had been technically challenging for the band and crew, with a new Quad sound system and having to use prerecorded tape playback for complex songs, like "Baba O'Riley," that featured early multi-tracked synthesizers. It was the dawn of digital music folks—1973!

There were stories of Pete Townshend tantrums and Keith Moon melting down on the drum kit, but by the time they got to the next-to-last gig at the Spectrum in Philadelphia, we hoped it was all sorted out. As we interfaced with the new Heil sound system on stage, I was going to upgrade the drum overhead mics for the recording with some nice Neumann U-87s. Not having seen The Who play live before, sound mixer Bob Pridden came up and suggested "you don't wanna' do that, mate." I took his advice and was thankful when we watched drummer Keith Moon totally destroy his drum kit, along with the PA's sacrificial cheap mics.

The final show of the US *Quadrophenia* Tour was at the Capitol Center Arena, just outside of Washington, DC, on December 6, 1973. The show was a sellout with mobs of fans crushing each other against the stage, despite the band's pleas to move back. They did get through the show, despite their end-of-tour fatigue and promised the cheering fans they would return again to the United States. I believe *King Biscuit* actually used the Philadelphia show for their radio broadcast, which did receive great reviews.

The following week, we would return to the Spectrum Arena to record a live album for another great British Band—Emerson, Lake, & Palmer—for Manticore Records.

WHO'S LAST?

It would take nine years, but we met The Who again, right back at the Capitol Center Arena in Washington, DC, to start a tour recording of 15 live shows that would become the live album *Who's Last*. It would also end in a live satellite broadcast and video recording.

In 1982, I met with Glyn Johns, who had engineered and produced many of The Who's great albums and would take charge of recording what was supposed to be their last tour. Glyn is one of the truly original characters I've had the pleasure to meet in this business. We had a long lunch at the Irish Bar around the corner from Record Plant and by the end we had our plan.

Each show we would set up Glyn's favorite "Big Red" monitors in front of the Black Truck API console: classic Atec 604E speakers with custom crossovers, powered by our Bryston 4B power amps. This time we would set up the expensive mics around the drum kit (Keith Moon passed away in 1978), and we agreed to source a nice bottle of red wine for Glyn when he arrived at show time. We then proceeded to roll across the United States, recording more than 20 sold-out shows, from New York to Florida, LA to Seattle, and everywhere in between. There were big recording budgets back in the days of big record sales, not to mention stadium ticket sales high as 98,000.

Our ever-observant tech, David DB Brown, relates this story of The Who crew mischief:

> When we got to Orlando, Florida, to record the November 27th, 1982, show at the Tangerine Bowl; the band and crew discovered that several high school girls field hockey teams were in town to participate in the National Hockey Festival.
>
> Because field hockey has long been a popular sport in Great Britain, some of the band and crew decided to challenge the girls to a match. A young Bob Kinkel [who would later find fame with the Trans-Siberian Orchestra] was on the gig with us, getting his first taste of remote recording crew experience [which would later serve him well making many live recordings of Trans-

Siberian Orchestra]. When Bob and I learned about the match, we went over to the field to witness the fun. The sight of Roger Daltrey and Bobby Pridden, both in full drag wearing wigs and dresses, along with several other members of the road crew running up and down the field while being thoroughly trounced by a group of high school girls was one of the more hysterically entertaining side adventures we ever had out on the road.

We finally arrived in Canada for The Who's "final" concert at Toronto's Maple Leaf Gardens. This would be a worldwide live television and radio broadcast with fans of The Who celebrating the end of two decades of classic rock. The band and Glyn Johns delivered an outstanding "Last Show"; the classics "My Generation," "I Can't Explain," and "Baba O'Riley" still resonated in 1982, as the roaring sold-out crowd testified.

Of course, we now know, they found it too hard to quit. Look up the *Who's Last* recording and see if it still resonates for you in today's world. I think "Won't Get Fooled Again" still qualifies.

THE MUSIC OF PETE TOWNSHEND AND THE WHO AT CARNEGIE HALL

What better place for a musician to celebrate their 50th birthday than Carnegie Hall? Roger Daltrey's *The Music of Pete Townshend and The Who* was that and more. They immediately sold out two shows on February 23 and 24, 1994.

Michael Kamen, the Julliard-trained musician, who is at home on this stage, as well as rock stages around the world, wrote the orchestra scores for, who else, *The Julliard Orchestra*. John Entwistle, the original Who bassist, rejoined the band along with guest stars Lou Reed, Alice Cooper, Eddie Vedder, and others.

The uninvited guest was a record blizzard that snowed in New York City, making it impossible to get the audio and video recording trucks in place, until after the snow was cleared. We finally got parked and powered just in time to record the first night's show. Fortunately, master producer Bob Ezrin and my old friend, Record Plant veteran engineer, Thom Panunzio, were there to finesse all of the stars into playing with the big orchestra. There were many musical issues to resolve and the stories of what Thom and Bob went through to mix the CD and DVD were hair raising.

Michael Kamen's overture brought a grand opening medley for the return of the British rock gods to New York, with the Julliard Orchestra enjoying a youthful change of music. The whole orchestra clapped in time (sort of) for the acoustic guitar intro to Pete Townshend's "Who Are You," and then the full orchestra rocked along; it was great fun!

Show highlights included playing "Baba O'Riley," with the classic Irish band The Chieftains and Sinead O'Connor singing with Daltrey—a perfect song for her. Look for the video; there is a joyful Irish stepdance, turning into the grand finale. The shows were a huge success, and they did go out on tour for a few successful concerts, but production costs were prohibitively high and they reluctantly had to cease. But you can still watch the video!

THE WHO AT THE CONCERT FOR NEW YORK CITY ON OCTOBER 20, 2001

We would record The Who again, reunited at The Concert for New York City, the marathon live benefit show for victims of the 9/11 terrorist attacks. This would be bassist John Entwistle's last US performance with The Who; he would have a fatal heart attack a few months later. The band appeared as the hours' long show was flagging a bit and they charged on stage with a powerful set that brought the crowd roaring to their feet, playing "Who Are You?" There were great Townshend "windmill" guitar solos and lyrics that bite even today. "Baba O'Riley" 1960s' sequencer still played a great "solo" and the crowd screamed along with the choruses of "Teenage Wasteland." They finished their set with a newly relevant "We Won't Get Fooled Again," played full volume to a raving audience.

Roger Daltrey ended the set by thanking the first responders and said, "We could never follow what you did," to great cheers and applause. Many later reviews thought they were the highlight of the entire concert.

PS
TECH ALERT

In August 1971 I was working at Regent Sound in Philadelphia when a client brought in the newly released record, *Who's Next*. We spent the next week playing it on the big JBL studio monitors, marveling at Glyn Johns's recording and the band's creativity. That and how the hell did they do the synthesizer on "Baba O'Riley?" It still gets applause today.

Here is David DB Brown's explanation. "The stereo backing tracks for the songs 'Who Are You,' 'Baba O' Riley,' and 'Won't Get Fooled Again' were played back from a pair (main and backup) of 1/2-inch 4-track machines, located at Bobby Pridden's stage left monitor mix location. A third cue/click track went to a pair of Koss headphones on drummer Kenny Jones, driven by a 100-watt BGW amplifier.

"Having been bumped around on the road across the world for over a decade the tape machines would sometimes refuse to work, and we would get the call over the intercom to the truck 'Could DB please come down to the stage and try to fix the tape machine?'"

"Fortunately, being fairly familiar with Scully tape decks, I was always able to get at least one of them running again, so the show could go on as planned."

Recommended Recordings

1973 *Quadrophenia* Tour

King Biscuit Flower Hour

Who's Last
MCA Records

Roger Daltrey: A Celebration

The Music of Pete Townshend and The Who at Carnegie Hall
Continuum CD and DVD

The Concert for New York City
The Who's performance
Sony CD and DVD

16

THE ARTIST
FOREVER KNOWN AS PRINCE

Tales Pre—and Post—the *Purple Rain* Tour

I was not really familiar with Prince when Record Plant New York was booked to record four shows at the magnificent Masonic Temple in Detroit from November 30 to December 3, 1982. I had to leave the Black Truck on the *Who's Last* Tour and join the White Truck in Detroit.

It didn't take long to realize he was a major star. By the following August he would have his film deal and I would be seeing a lot of him.

I had just finished recording the Australian band, Men at Work, in Washington, DC, when we turned the Black Truck toward Prince's hometown First Avenue Club. Those shows on August 2–3, 1983, would yield the ultimate recording of the *Purple Rain* theme for the film and endless recordings to come. It was a live stereo mix on the Black Truck's API console that would become the master. Prince felt that was what he wanted and never remixed it. He often made decisions like that; at this point he was the undisputed master, and no one questioned him.

By 1984 I had left Record Plant to concentrate on my own company. My first gig was to provide remote trucks for Prince's *Purple Rain* Tour. Still on good terms with Record Plant, I hired the Black Truck for the first few shows. We immediately recorded shows back in St. Paul, the Cap Center in DC, the Spectrum in Philadelphia, and then a mixing session at Sync Sound's Studio in New York. David Tickle, Prince's British PA mixer, was really a studio engineer and did all those mixes.

Prince started rehearsals for the 1985 tour just before Christmas at the St. Paul arena. He hired a real performance venue so that Showco could set up their complete touring sound system and tune it for the *Purple Rain* Tour.

On Christmas Eve, Prince called a wrap, but his road manager came out to the remote truck and announced, "PRN [pronounced "Prin" aka Prince Rogers Nelson] wants the truck out to his house." I felt bad for my crew, but we are on the client's clock. So, we saddled up and brought it out to Prince's original, rather modest, ranch house.

We were let into the house, and even though there had been a studio there, the console had been removed and obviously we would work in the remote truck. I became the default electrician, looking downstairs for the main electrical panel to power up the truck. I figured it was probably not the red room with the heart-shaped bed and all the mirrors. The laundry room had an Ampex MM-1100 16-track recorded sitting there, covered in clothes. I prefer the later MM-1200s myself, but there was a 200-amp service to hook up the remote truck.

Prince's assistant engineer, Susan Rogers, knew what was expected and already had the 24 track tapes of a Sheila E. album that Prince was producing. She had that cued up as Prince made his grand entrance, nodded to the crew, and immediately plugged in his bass to overdub it on a few tracks. He seemed quite amused, played around with a guitar, and joked with Susan while he did most of the engineering.

In what seemed like the shortest session I've ever attended, Prince happily thanked us all and went in the house. We just looked at each other and pronounced it a "Merry Christmas." That's a wrap!

I think maybe the man just wanted some company on Christmas Eve.

This would become routine later on along the *Purple Rain* Tour. Prince would decide to record certain shows and then work on the Sheila E tapes in the remote truck after he finished! That made for some very long days. That may have been the *In Romance 1600* album, but I don't recall.

The Purple Rain Tour launched in January and was an outrageous success. Prince's showmanship had set a new high bar with boundless energy and showmanship.

PRN brought the pro wrestler Hulk Hogan in as his bodyguard, which instantly revived his career. What sight that made, Hogan towering over his master, both of them loving the crowd's reaction.

There were many more recordings to do; Prince appeared on the *American Music Awards*, the *Grammy Awards*, the *Academy Awards*, and many other live shows. It was a hectic schedule that had these big television award shows interspersed with the *Purple Rain* Tour bookings. I also had to use several different remote trucks when my Black Truck was booked elsewhere. The tour recordings started in Atlanta; went to Houston, Birmingham, Cincinnati, and Memphis; all recorded on the Mobile Audio truck. I flew to LA for Prince's appearance on the *American Music Awards*, where Record Plant LA's remote truck was already there for all the bands. It was a great crew, a great truck, and a great session. Check out the photo. Prince blew everyone away with his "Purple Rain" performance.

I linked up with the tour in Austin, Texas, then on to the New Orleans Superdome, using my Black Truck again. Then I flew back to LA for Prince's appearance at the *Grammys* with the Record Plant LA remote truck and crew. I loved these guys—brilliance with humor! Prince received a Grammy as a songwriter for "I Feel for You" and performed by Chaka Khan—what an incredible pairing.

The next Prince gig wasn't for a month, but we were booked pretty solid until then. Everything from great jazz, *One Night with Blue Note*, to the giant *Night of 100 Stars* at Radio City Music Hall and then *Tosca* at the Metropolitan Opera.

We caught up with the tour on March 28, 1985, at the Carrier Dome in Syracuse, New York, and then the Orange Bowl in Miami, Florida. This would be the end of the *Purple Rain* Tour, and it was sold out well in advance and even had serious turnstile jumpers. The Orange Bowl holds 60,000, and it was rockin' for an Easter Sunday in Miami. The last show of the tour was possibly the best; certainly the audience reaction won the vote. Everything was Prince perfect, especially the 20-minute "Purple Rain" encore. He was an astounding musician.

I feel fortunate to have experienced his boundless talents.

17

THE MONSTER SHOWS

Live Aid, Bob Dylan's 30th Anniversary,
Atlantic Records 40th Anniversary, Woodstock
'94 and '99, Night of 100 Stars I and II

PINK FLOYD
BRINGING THE GALAXY INTO THE THEATER

Listening to "experimental" music in the late 1960s inevitably lead to this band and the deep space of the psychedelic experience. Despite the early fade out of founder Syd Barrett, Pink Floyd continued to create an expanding universe of sound and philosophy that spoke to a generation that included me.

After all the years of waiting, my opportunity finally came to record Pink Floyd. Bob Ezrin had been coproducing Pink Floyd's albums since *The Wall* and had just finished *A Momentary Lapse of Reason*. I knew Ezrin from my days as the director of remote recording at Record Plant New York, where he worked with Alice Cooper, Kiss, and some Pink Floyd sessions. Bob is an incredible producer, musician, and a colorful character!

I was hired to record shows on Pink Floyd's 1987–1988 tour supporting the album *A Momentary Lapse of Reason*. It was a huge production and had specific recording requirements, as per Ezrin and their Live FOH engineer, Buford Jones, who would also be mixing my finished recordings. Buford was an original Showco mixer, one of the best in the business; we had worked together on Bowie and Prince tours.

These were busy times for my company, Remote Recording Services, so to cover all the bookings I occasionally had to hire other remote trucks.

This was the case for the Pink Floyd dates in Atlanta on November 4 and 5, 1987. We had been on tour with U2, recording for the film and album *Rattle and Hum*, and my Black Truck would be traveling between gigs on those dates. I had to find another truck fast! I knew Gary Hedden as an engineer and that he had built a new remote truck capable of meeting Pink Floyd's requirements: recording to a pair of Mitsubishi X-850 32-track digital tape machines along with two 24-track analog machines for the drum tracks. We recorded two shows with the GHL Truck. That allowed me to work out all the interface issues with Buford and learn all the cues, and the recordings came out fine. Unfortunately, after reviewing the shows, the band was not happy with their performances and they were not used on the live album or film, although later a bootleg turned up, ironically called *Would You Buy a Ticket to This Show?*

The next Pink Floyd record dates were to be at the Nassau Coliseum, Long Island, on August 19–22, 1988. I faced the same booking conflict because my Black Truck was scheduled to be at Tanglewood in Lenox, Massachusetts, for a gala celebration of the famed composer/conductor Leonard Bernstein's 70th birthday. The Boston Symphony Orchestra with guest stars ranging from Lauren Bacall to Yo-Yo Ma would be recorded for a PBS *Great Performances* television special. I wasn't concerned about arriving late because the legendary engineer/producer John McClure was on board for the show. Although John was known primarily for his classical work, he had recorded string arrangements for Pink Floyd's *The Wall*. Bernstein's longtime tour manager Daryl Bornstein, would be taking care of the live sound design. I couldn't ask for a better team!

I booked Randy Ezratty's Effanel company to record the New York Pink Floyd shows. Randy had recently purchased the Mobile Audio remote truck out of Atlanta, and I had used it to record Prince on some of the *Purple Rain* Tour, so I was confident with the package. In those days, equipment rental companies provided the hyper expensive digital tape recorders. The Mitsubishi X-850s were probably sourced from Audio Force or Jim Flynn Rentals at around $1,000/day times two, plus cartage! Effanel already had two Otari MTR-90 24-track tape recorders.

Thanks to Randy and his crew, with the assistance of Ringo Hyrcyn from Bob Ezrin's production company, we managed to get it all on tape with no one seriously injured. The shows were great, and David Gilmour approved the performances.

Buford flew to London where he had booked Abbey Road Studios to mix the record that would become *Delicate Sound of Thunder*. It was released on vinyl, CDs, and video and went triple Platinum in the United States, with many more sold worldwide. It also became the first rock album played in space when Soviet cosmonauts carried it aboard the *Soyuz 7* on a cassette. The record had been released in the Soviet Union on the Melodiya label—Kremlin approved!

I recently bought the new 180 g vinyl of *Delicate Sound of Thunder*, remastered by James Guthrie, Joel Plante, and Bernie Grundman from the original analog tapes. You can't beat that team! Aside from a few different takes, it seems to be the same mixes. I've stayed in touch with Buford over the years, so I called him up to see what he thought; same mixes as far as he knew. We had a great conversation about his adventures mixing the original 1988 record while Abbey Road was rebuilding the studio as he worked! That's a whole 'nother story!

MUSIC FOR UNICEF CONCERT 1979 AND JOC CONCERTS
APRIL 15–23, 1981, KENNEDY CENTER, UN GENERAL ASSEMBLY

NO NUKES: THE MUSE CONCERTS FOR A NON-NUCLEAR FUTURE IN 1979
SEPTEMBER 19–23, 1979

When I first heard of this concept for a large-scale series of concerts protesting nuclear issues, it did remind me of George Harrison's Concert for Bangladesh and how that started a movement of musicians making their voices heard. Graham Nash and Jackson Browne had often expressed their environmental concerns in song, and now they were moving them to a larger stage, namely Madison Square Garden in New York City. This would be five days of concerts by many of their like-minded musician friends, a massive project requiring lots of moving parts and people.

MUSE stands for Musicians United for Safe Energy, although the shows and subsequent record albums and film were known as *No Nukes*. This was such a huge effort by hundreds of musicians and production professionals to promote a public cause. It presaged many live benefit shows to come, such as Amnesty International, We Are the World, and Live Aid.

The event was produced by Jackson Browne, Graham Nash, John Hall, and Bonnie Raitt. Obviously, these artists know a thing or two about putting on a show. But this was five consecutive days of stars like Crosby, Stills & Nash, James Taylor with Carly Simon, the Doobie Brothers, Tom Petty,

Peter Tosh, and of course, Bruce Springsteen . . . not to mention, the monster finale, or, as we usually refer to big finales, celebrity train wrecks. This, thankfully, would be a good one.

Madison Square Garden is a difficult venue for remote trucks. The arena is about five stories above street level. There is a spiral concrete ramp that winds up to the backstage area. The Record Plant White Truck could clear all the overhead obstacles and drive right up. The Black Truck, however, was a different story. Even though I designed it to clear the Lincoln Tunnel going into New York, it had trouble clearing some of the lighting fixtures hung above the Madison Square Garden ramp. We dumped the air-ride suspension and even bled some air out of the rear tires, but it was still scraping the lights! Finally, we had stagehands standing on the fuel tanks with long poles pushing the light fixtures up out of the way. Madison Square Garden is a giant arena with many floors of support activity for shows to work around. One of those things were some leftover circus animals, including caged lions and other creatures, that provided a strong stench usually reserved for political conventions. Thankfully they were gone by showtime.

The good news was that this production was run by the artists and musicians who were performing in it. We really enjoyed all the camaraderie and reunion-like atmosphere of the five-day concert. I was the chief recording engineer, but I had a lot of help from the artist's engineers as well. Stanley Johnston, Greg Ladanyi and Joe Chiccarelli, among them, made it a pleasure. Record Plant engineers Shelly Yakus and Jimmy Iovine were there for Bruce Springsteen, as they had been in the studio for years.

I can describe what we went through to produce the audio and video recordings that made up the *No Nukes* vinyl records, CDs and the many video formats, but the only thing that counts is the music. There are some great photos here in the book, but you really need to look up the music to understand and enjoy the spirit of that powerful protest.

The concert sets played in this order, starting with the musicians that worked so hard to produce it:

Graham Nash, Jackson Browne, Bonnie Raitt, and John Hall, September 19, 1979

Doobie Brothers, James Taylor, John Hall, and Bonnie Raitt, September 20, 1979

Bruce Springsteen, Jesse Collin Young, Jackson Browne, Sweet Honey in the Rock, and Ry Cooder, September 21, 1979

Bonnie Raitt, Tom Petty, and Bruce Springsteen, September 22, 1979

Crosby, Stills & Nash; Gil Scott-Heron, Peter Tosh, Poco, Raydio, CSN, Review Finale, September 23, 1979

Bruce Springsteen and the E Street Band sets

I have to admit my bias here because at the time Bruce was a long term client of Record Plant New York and also of the remote recording trucks that I managed.

We had two days of shows before Bruce would play, so things were pretty well sorted by the time we got to his first set on September 21. He played a 12-song set, which included the premiere of "The River" and my favorite, "Stay," with Jackson Browne and Rosemary Butler. During that show, we had a bit of a scare. When Bruce's fans started rockin', the whole floor of the arena started to move up and down! It got so bad that we had to hold on to the Ampex 1200 24-tracks because they were rolling around on their castors! I've recorded a number of shows in Madison Square Garden but never felt it move like that. Later, I found out from Madison Square Garden producer Marc Bauman, that yeah, 19,000 hockey fans will do that, too.

Bruce's second show on September 22 was just as wild and made for a great recording. This was the infamous set where Bruce drug Lynn Goldsmith up on stage, after he spots her taking photos, which he thought she agreed not to do. He introduced her as his ex-girlfriend and has her escorted offstage. I don't think that made the album!

DAVID DB BROWN'S *NO NUKES* STORIES DB WAS MY LONGTIME TECH ON THE RECORD PLANT BLACK TRUCK

The great EQ swap, aka "Kids, don't try this at your home (studio)."

One of the major challenges in recording a several-day, multistar festival with just one remote truck was how to save the big-name engineer (Shelly Yakus, Jimmy Iovine, Greg Ladanyi, etc.) equalization settings they found during the sound checks for the various acts for that evening's performance (this was in the days before consoles had computer-assisted memory and instant reset of parameters.)

On the *No Nukes* gig we tried a risky procedure on a scale never before attempted: "hot swapping" the (what are now known as 500 series modules) EQ units. Hot swapping is the rather dangerous move of replacing a small unit of a larger system with a spare while the power is still turned on; pretty much the electronics equivalent of changing a wheel on your car while it's driving down the highway.

At the end of each afternoon's sound checks we would end up with several carefully labeled stacks of anywhere from four to eight API 550 and 560 equalizers (preset for important channels like bass DI, kick, snare, lead vocal, etc.) sitting on top of the console's meter bridge, ready to be hastily swapped into the correct channels during the band set changes onstage. Fortunately, we were able to borrow enough spare EQs from the studio to make this possible.

It's a real tribute to the design and manufacturing prowess of API that in the well more than 100 "hot swaps" we did that week that we didn't blow up a single EQ module.

THE DANCING TAPE MACHINES

Springsteen hadn't played NYC in a while before his headlining appearances at *No Nukes*, so about 15 minutes before he and the E Street Band were to take the stage, the filled-to-capacity fans started chanting "Bruce, Bruce" and stomping their feet. They managed to do so in such a rhythmic cadence that the large concrete slabs that make up the large arena on the fifth floor of Madison Square Garden started to move up and down almost two inches. The slab in the backstage loading area where the Black Truck was parked was swaying so much, we at first though it must be an earthquake. This led to our two 400+ pound Ampex 1200-multitrack tape machines (which were on casters) dancing across the floor in the back of the truck, which led to the comical image of Paul Prestopino having to use his body as a wedge to keep them in place.

Film crews captured the whole event from both out in the hall, backstage in the dressing rooms (where in one shot Bonnie Raitt says "Too bad the guy's name wasn't Melvin or something"), and a wonderful shot of the levels going up and down with the chanting on our API console's VU meters; all of which were included in the feature film.

However, the "Roll 'em, roll 'em" shot near the beginning of the film of two fingers of my right hand rolling one of the 2-inch tape machines to record was actually done as a staged pickup shot, filmed after the show one evening because there hadn't been enough light in the back of the truck to get the shot during the show. Just part of the film magic of shooting a feature length concert movie.

Thanks DB for your magnetic memory.

PS

My local nuclear power plant at Three Mile Island has shut down, 40 years after its melt down March 28, 1979, which helped prompt the MUSE concert. This happened not far from my home and family in Pennsylvania.

JACKSON BROWNE: *RUNNING ON EMPTY*

When asked to name a live rock record we did they might recognize, this is the one.

The album cover features a lone drum kit on stage with a mountain road disappearing into the clouds. A perfect logo for life on the road. Jackson brilliantly produced this 1977 tour, saying he could finally afford to hire *The Section,* LA's premier session musicians, and the best production crew, to play and record the music he wanted, not the usual hit list! The audience agreed, even though they had never heard the songs.

The live show performances were recorded on a Studer 24 track, set up backstage, by Jack Maxson's Showco crew. My Record Plant NY Remote crew recorded Jackson and the band working out songs in hotel rooms, backstage and even in the tour bus, driving down the road. Greg Ladanyi Engineered and mixed the original record and many outstanding remixes. There is even a remastered DVD on Elektra/Rhino, plus an excellent video on YouTube.

The *Running on Empty* song lyrics say it all: "Lookin' out at the road rushing under my wheels . . . running on empty, running wild," "Don't know how to tell you just how crazy this life feels." "I'd love to stick around, but I'm running behind."

The second song, *The Road*, was recorded in motel room 301, with a beautiful acoustic lament intro, "Highways and dance halls, a good song takes you far...." "You forget about the losses, you exaggerate the wins..." then fades into the live amplified stage recording, ". . . When you stop to let 'em know you got it down, it's just another town along the road. . . ."

As I always add to the story, you have to *listen to all the music*, this whole album *is* like the road. If you don't have it, it is still available online.

Last time I checked, it had gone seven times Platinum.

NIGHT OF 100 STARS (1ST OF TWO)
RADIO CITY MUSIC HALL, FEBRUARY 10–14, 1982
RADIO CITY MUSIC HALL, FEBRUARY 13–17, 1985

When I named this chapter The Monster Shows, these two shows were what I had in mind. What made them different from the big award shows like the Oscars, is primarily that it's Broadway, Baby!, and that only happens in New York City. It's a different world, with traditions that originate in classic theater, vaudeville, and burlesque, not to mention strict union rules and hierarchy. To survive in this world, you have to learn the rules.

I had the good fortune to be brought into this new world by Bob Liftin, an engineer and owner of Regent Sound, who had deep experience in theater and television. In chapter 11, I describe working on the major television award shows, the *Tony Awards* among them, which Bob Liftin engineered for many years.

Engineer Joel Spector worked for Bob on many of these shows and will give you an idea of the complexity of these incredible shows.

NIGHT OF 100 STARS
BY JOEL SPECTOR, MUSIC PLAYBACK ENGINEER

So, you want to salute the 100th anniversary of the Actor's Fund of America? This effective charitable organization had been assisting all members of the theatrical profession since 1882. Broadway producer Alexander H. Cohen was engaged to create a television special event to be staged in Radio City Music Hall on February 14, 1982, featuring more than 200 showbusiness personalities. The five-hour stage show would be edited down to fit into a three-hour time slot (including commercials), which would be seen, in Cohen's words, "at eight o'clock in the evening of March 8th on every inhabited continent on the planet." The first celebrity to sign on was Princess Grace of Monaco.

Let's take a look at just two aspects of this project which typify the logistical planning that was required.

All of the performers, whether as individuals or as members of ensembles, had to be transported to and from New York by more than 50 limousines from seven companies, housed in hotels, fitted for costumes, and then assigned dressing rooms at the Music Hall. This last task was the province of four stage managers and several talent coordinators. Working backward from the time an individual was required to set foot on the stage, the staff had to calculate the exact number of minutes for the journey from the nether regions of the multistory building—in some cases, at least 20 minutes. Once the talent arrived at their stand-by location, the audio staff would be sure that they received the necessary wired or wireless microphones. At the conclusion of their appearance, the gear was recovered and the reverse journey, also precisely timed, was made back to the dressing room. Therefore, a constellation of talent was in continuous motion.

The event was also a major fundraiser for The Fund, which was building its care and retirement home in Englewood, New Jersey. To that end, Cohen had commissioned 10 silk-screened posters that were located at the back of the audience area. Performers were encouraged to sign them and then each poster would be auctioned off for a minimum bid of $10,000—another task for the talent handlers to manage.

Musical director Elliot Lawrence and his orchestra were located on the music hall's "band cart," which could be placed in front of the stage or lowered to be moved all the way upstage and reappear as if by magic. The basic unit of cabling was 50-pair snakes. Some of the music performances and introductory music was prerecorded by senior audio engineer Bob Liftin at his Regent Sound over the course of eight days. At least one 11-minute number had to be recorded with the orchestra and background vocals; 100 musical play-ons had to be recorded, mixed, and loaded into individual audio tape cartridges for playback during the show; and each decade of the Actor's Fund received a three-minute salute from a star. The music for these, each a variation on "Before the Parade Passes By," was arranged by Torrie Zito and then recorded at Regent. These sessions were tightly scheduled, right down to pre-striping the 16-track tapes and choreographing the reel changes: 30 minutes of music for 34 players had to be scored, parts copied out, and then managed at the studio.

Once the event had been recorded, the first broadcast version was created at Windsor Video. The show had been staged in a sequence that would allow the scenery and performers to flow on and off the vast stage. There were many "tape stops" while the stage was reset in full view of the audience of entertainment industry professionals. These were eliminated during editing. Two more versions of the show were made, and for each one, Bob Liftin had to conform his 16-track master audio tapes to the reference 3/4-inch video tapes. The final layback to 1-inch video tape for version 3 was completed over the night of February 28. The video master had to be copied and flown to Vero Beach, Florida, on March 1 so it could be captioned in 10 different languages in time for the air date of March 8.

Thanks to Joel Spector for his detailed coverage, we could see none of this action from our own monitors in the remote recording truck. One of the most complicated shows we have ever recorded.

LIVE AID
THE PHILADELPHIA CONCERTS
JFK STADIUM PHILADELPHIA, PENNSYLVANIA
JULY 10–13, 1985

The original 1985 Live Aid concerts were held in Philadelphia and London. I was responsible for hiring and organizing the remote trucks for the Philadelphia shows. Promoters Bill Graham and Larry Magid put together an incredible lineup of stars, including a reunion of Led Zeppelin, Bob Dylan, and most of the Rolling Stones. It was like a small city-state of concerned musicians playing music to benefit Ethiopian famine victims, raising more than $150 million. The telecast reached an estimated 1.9 million viewers.

Here is what I wrote for my Audio-Technica blog in 2019:

The Live Aid Worldwide Broadcast from Philadelphia and London
July 13, 1985.

The Philadelphia Show

Many thousands of words have been written about this world-changing event. My blog is a brief account of the incredible people who made the Philadelphia show possible and broadcast it to the world. We will dwell on just the audio story here.

It was the legendary rock promoter Bill Graham and his longtime production manager Michael Ahern who organized the hugely complicated show. I can still see Bill Graham "Herding" the stars on stage to keep the show momentum going!

Clair Brothers provided the massive sound reinforcement and monitor systems. They were also augmented by See Factor equipment and crews. Many of the Live Aid artists already used Clair on tour and were familiar with their systems and crews, as were all of us live recording engineers.

My company, Remote Recording Services, was brought in to organize the audio facilities for the broadcast music mixes. Because of the huge number of acts playing on a massive rotating stage, with smaller satellite stages and guest speakers, we needed multiple audio remote trucks and crews, plus all the special audio gear requested by the individual engineers and producers!

The bands on the main rotating A/B stages would be mixed by engineers in two primary trucks: Record Plant NY's Black Truck and Guy Charbonneau's Le Mobile Truck. Record Plant would also supply their White Truck for mixing the auxiliary stages. I had been using the Mobile Audio trailer for some of Prince's *Purple Rain* Tour recordings, and it would function as a production office and also mix some of the auxiliary stage bands.

The special request audio gear (reverbs, delays, EQs, mics, etc.) were supplied by the late, great Jim Flynn's Rental Company—above and beyond the call of duty!

Because the live broadcast ran for so many hours, we needed relief mixing engineers to keep up with the changing acts. Many of the star performers wanted their own engineers to mix or at least be in the remote truck to supervise. Unfortunately, my production files are long gone, along with their names, but here are the names I do have:

Record Plant Black Truck: Bob Liftin, David DB Brown, Fritz Lang, and Steve Barish

Record Plant White Truck: Kooster McAllister, Eddie Ciletti

Le Mobile: Guy Charbonneau, Bob Clearmountain

Mobile Audio trailer: David Hewitt, sorry I can't find the original owner's information. Randy Ezratty later bought the trailer for his company Effanel.

All of the music mixes would be fed to the production audio mixers in the video trucks. Those mixes were of course dictated by the video directors, who had to integrate all the talking heads, guest stars, and world feeds into the live satellite feed.

Engineers in ABC's Phase 8 Audio Booth:

Don Scholtes, Jonathan Lory, and Harry Yarmark and the legendary Ed Greene was in his own truck.

Of course, all of these overworked people needed a break too! The Mobile Audio trailer had a separate back room with a couch that became a lifesaver nap pad for exhausted directors and mixers.

In preproduction meetings, the US television producers decided that no multitrack tape would be recorded, unlike the British Live Aid show, which recorded most of their shows on tape. To make matters worse, many of the live video tapes that were recorded were erased, discarded, or lost. Some MTV and radio station recordings survived, but all were of reduced audio quality and many only in mono. So, if you heard any of the Philadelphia Live Aid music after the original broadcast, that's why it sounds so poor! It could not be remixed like the London shows were.

For years after the live broadcast, I would receive calls from various producers, looking for the nonexistent multitrack tape masters of the bands. My answer would be "Here's the ABC television's phone number."

ATLANTIC RECORDS 40TH ANNIVERSARY
MADISON SQUARE GARDEN, NEW YORK, MAY 11–14, 1988

Atlantic Records commemorated their 40 years of music with a grand 13-hour marathon concert at Madison Square Garden. They were known for their jazz and blues records long before they became the bastion of rock stars in the 1960s. Some of my early Atlantic remotes were with the Gil Evans Orchestra, Donny Hathaway, Stevie Wonder, and Aretha Franklin. Atlantic would go on to sign some of the biggest names in rock: Crosby, Stills & Nash; Led Zeppelin; Yes; and Hall & Oates. They would join many other Atlantic artists on stage at this gigantic reunion celebration.

I was booked to record the show on the Black Truck, now owned by my company, Remote Recording Services. Thankfully we would have Atlantic producer Arif Mardin to help us through complex and changing script of the show. Arif was responsible for so much of Atlantic's success he arranged and produced their artists in the studio.

I was able to bring in engineer Stanley Johnston to alternate mixing bands with me. Stanley was Crosby, Stills & Nash's studio and live engineer for years. Veteran live engineer Ed Greene would mix our feed and many other elements for the live television broadcast.

Mixing a live TV broadcast while sorting out mispatched stage inputs and getting it all on tape was difficult. Like the title of this chapter, it was a monster show but what great music. From early R&B star Lavern Baker to soulful Wilson Pickett, rock stars Crosby, Stills & Nash and British bands Yes and Led Zeppelin—it was a night to remember.

The artists spanned the Atlantic history from Lavern Baker and Ruth Brown through Iron Butterfly; Yes; Genesis; Foreigner; and Crosby, Stills & Nash. Wilson Pickett, The Coasters, The Spinners, and many other stars of that era performed as well. The Blues Brothers brought the humor while Roberta Flack, Manhattan Transfer, and the Bee Gees brought the harmony. There were many others, but of course the crowd was waiting for the reunion of the legendary British band Led Zeppelin. Original members Jimmy Page and Robert Plant were joined by John Paul Jones and Jason Bonham to play the monster hits: "Kashmir" on through to "Stairway to Heaven."

It was an extraordinary lineup of stars that will never be duplicated. The recordings don't have all 13 hours of the show, but I guarantee it will keep you going for a couple of listening sessions.

My favorite memory of Atlantic Records president and cofounder Ahmet Ertegun is of him approaching the security guard at the entrance to the dressing rooms. With a grin, he waved an oversized laminate with the words "I Am My Back Stage Pass" in bold letters. No one questioned his imperial bearing. He was the son of a Turkish diplomat stationed in Washington, DC. He and brother Nesuhi learned their jazz and blues music in the clubs and never looked back.

BOB DYLAN'S 30TH ANNIVERSARY CONCERT
MADISON SQUARE GARDEN, NEW YORK, OCTOBER 14–16, 1992

Columbia Records has long been the grand wizard of record labels in New York and a great client for the live recording business. Longtime A&R producer Don DeVito had a long history with Bob Dylan, having brought him to the label and produced records with him. Don was instrumental in making this concert a joyful celebration of Dylan's music played by fellow musicians, all of whom earned the right to play it.

The backing band was Booker T. & the M.G.s with Donald "Duck" Dunn on bass, Steve Cropper on guitar, and Anton Fig on drums. Band leader G. E. Smith was perfect for this show, having worked *Saturday Night Live* for years.

This is still one of my all-time favorite recordings, and here is where I demand that if you read this far, you must go find this recording, preferably with video to watch the joy of these musicians playing for Bob Dylan's 30th anniversary! Or as Neil Young dubbed it "Bob Fest."

Here are some performances I always go back to:

"The Times They Are A-Changin'"
Tracy Chapman

"It Ain't Me Babe"
Johnny Cash

"What Was It You Wanted"
Willie Nelson

"Just Like A Woman"
Richie Havens

"You Ain't Goin' Nowhere"
Shawn Colvin, Mary Chapin Carpenter, and Rosanne Cash

"All Along the Watchtower"
Neil Young

"Absolutely Sweet Marie"
George Harrison

"Mr. Tambourine Man"
Roger McGuinn and Tom Petty & the Heartbreakers

"My Back Pages"
Bob Dylan, Roger McGuinn, Tom Petty, Neil Young, and George Harrison

"Knockin' On Heaven's Door"
Finale with everybody

Bob himself ending the show with "Girl From the North Country."

This has to be the greatest peer salute ever in rock music, played with love,
admiration, and big grins. Do look it up and listen!

OTHER MONSTER SHOWS INCLUDED:

Woodstock '94, or as we called it, "Mud-Stock"
Saugerties, New York, August 9–15, 1994

I did not attend the original Woodstock in 1969, because I was still involved in sports car racing and there was a conflict. My brother Lynn did attend and had lots of stories, among those the mud baths. He remembers Jimi Hendrix; I am sorry I missed him.

Woodstock '94 commemorated the 25th anniversary of the original concert. There were similarities with the crowd problems, security, substance abuse, and of course, mud. They estimated more than 500,000 folks made it up to Saugerties, New York. We made it up with a bunch of remote trucks to record the shows. I had my Silver Truck and Kooster McCallister had the Record Plant remote truck, a highly modified version of the 1970 truck I use to use at Record Plant. We were on the South Stage with engineers Ed Cherney, Elliot Scheiner, and Dave Theoner. The North Stage had the Effanel remote truck and several other vehicles. They were fortunate to have Bob Clearmountain as chief engineer and Mitch Maketanski as producer recording those bands. Record Plant founder Chris Stone was managing all the recorded master tapes and production elements. What a great team to work with; Chris always brought great enthusiasm and cheer to every show.

The first day was a little hectic, with Ravestock, but I do remember the second day with The Band and guests including Roger McGuinn (of the Byrds) and Bob Weir. The band Primus was outrageous as usual, playing "Pull the Tapeworm out of My Ass." Youssou N'Dour brought his magnificent songs for balance. The rain and mud were coming fast and the crowd figured out you could rip up the sod and throw it at the bands you didn't like. There is a great video shot of Green Day guitarist catching a mud clod right on his guitar, but he never lost a beat, a real trooper.

Even though the North Stage featured most of the headliner bands, we did get to record rare appearances by Gil Scott-Heron and Country Joe McDonald (minus the Fish). The Neville Brothers and Jimmy Cliff's All Star Reggae Jam made up for that.

I had gone to great effort bringing the two Studer D-827 48-track digital recorders ($175,000.00 each) to record this show. They were new at the time and I felt they made superior sounding tapes. There was a bit of panic when Chris Stone played the tapes back on Sony machines that didn't recognize a sync flag. Several heart attacks later, it was a nonissue. The recordings were eventually mixed for video and CD release.

I had enjoyed the company of our great collection of engineers and producers, but you can keep the crowds.

Woodstock '99, or as we called it "Riot-Stock"
Rome, New York, July 22–25, 1999

I was rather surprised when the promotors were able to mount another Woodstock concert after the last experience, but "parts is parts" as they say in the fast food business.

This concert would be staged in two separate areas in the deactivated Griffiss Air Force Base, a former strategic air command site. There was still a B-52 Stratofortress Bomber on pylons to greet us at the gate. Growing up in the Air Force and being a Vet, I know what used to be stationed here, but I didn't bring my Geiger counter.

Given the last two Woodstocks had been overrun by the crowds, they went to great lengths to tighten up the fences and security. It didn't work.

I know most of the production companies and the people that tried their best to make a safe environment for their crews and the fans. They could not control what the 400,000-strong audience would do when fired up by the likes of Limp Bizkit. All I can tell you is that the mob and some of the acts caused a riot. They tore down the plywood walls, set them on fire, destroyed concession stands and anything else they could. There were rapes and beatings to go with it. We were scared; police reinforcements came too late and too little. Fortunately, there was a back road out of the base, and all the production trucks, including our remote trucks and crews made it out in one piece.

Yes, there were some great performances made by the bands and artists that came, but frankly I'm still outraged by how far our "civilization" has sunk and I do not want to relive this "Riot-Stock." You can look it up online if you are curious.

Super Bowls 1996, 1997, and 2009

All of these recordings were made for *NFL Films*. Jerry Mahler, their director of audio engineering, would bring a complete digital production package from his studio, a new state-of-the-art production facility. He and his crew would record and edit live interviews with football team members and stars for use on broadcasts leading up to the Super Bowl games. We used our compact vocal isolation booth in the rear of the Silver Studio trailer for vocal isolation. It was a great easy gig for us; Jerry and his crew did all the work. They were lightning fast after years of practice.

The Eric Clapton Crossroads Guitar Festivals certainly deserve the Monster Show moniker, but you can read about them in chapter 4.

(18)

THOSE MAGNIFICENT ORCHESTRAS

Film Scores, Live from Lincoln Center, the Met Opera, the Three Tenors and the Three Sopranos

> History is not what happened, but what survives the shipwrecks of judgment and chance.
>
> —Maria Popova

I never imagined when starting my recording career that I would work with some the finest orchestras and classical musicians in the world. Operating some of the best remote recording studios in the country gave me that opportunity, especially in New York, which was one of the culture capitols of the world.

My first opportunity to be the mixing engineer on a live classical music performance came by surprise, as they often did in those days. Record Plant New York had an RCA Red Seal Records booking to record the eminent Cuban pianist Jorge Bolet at Carnegie Hall in February 1974. At the last minute, the designated engineer was not available, so it looked like I was in the hot seat! I had recently assisted on RCA remote recordings at Carnegie Hall for the British songstress Cleo Laine and for the grand début of Carnegie's new giant electronic Rogers pipe organ, played with the equally giant talent of Virgil Fox. That session is a whole story in itself! It blew up before the show!

Fortunately for me, executive producer Jack Pfeiffer would be there to guide me through the piano score. Jack was not only the legendary producer of classical artists like Vladimir Horowitz and Arthur Rubinstein, but he also designed electronics and composed music. I would build a long relationship with Jack over the years, as he produced many great artists for records and television, including early *Live From the Metropolitan Opera* broadcasts. He was among the last of the gentlemen producers, always immaculately dressed, and he had a calm, benevolent authority, whom the artists trusted implicitly.

I remember that we used the RCA Studio's Neumann U-67 tube microphones for the piano, although I owned four of those U-67s from my Regent Sound days. Perhaps I used those for distant stage mics. I loved the sound of the tubes, even though the transistor U-87 microphones had superseded them. The U-87s were much more reliable for live recording, and they became the standard. Carnegie Hall had cables hung for ambience mics, but I have no record of the microphone types.

With Jack reading the solo piano scores and cuing me on Bolet's huge dynamic range, there was quite a lot of fader movement. Fortunately, the DeMedio recording console had quite a bit of headroom! It was built in1965 for the Johnny Cash TV show, quite a change in musical styles!

The program was almost all Chopin preludes, with just a little Bach to open and Wagner to close! I felt exhausted after a long day and that intense program! What incredible power and artistry Bolet has; the reviews to this day say that this performance and recording propelled his career to new heights. Of course, I didn't know that at the time, for me it was just on to the next gig, recording a great vocal group, the Bee Gees playing at Lincoln Center. Some 40-odd years later I happened to find a nice copy of the double album *Jorge Bolet At Carnegie Hall* at a local flea market. I was really amazed at how great it sounded!

Wikipedia quote:

> "Only in 1974 did he come to national prominence, with a stupendous recital in that year at Carnegie Hall, which sealed his reputation." Listen and see if you don't agree. Jorge Bolet—Carnegie Hall Recital, 1974 part 1—YouTube

On February 8, 1996, Jack Pfeiffer passed away of a heart attack at his executive desk, listening to a recording with his headphones on. I'm sure he would have loved that image, playing his own exit music.

I am so glad to have known you, Jack; thank you for all the great music you shared.

MY EARLY ORCHESTRA LESSONS

Like most US kids coming of age in the 1950s, I mainly listened to the popular hits on the AM radio. Orchestras were only heard on the movie soundtracks and scratchy old 78 records, belonging to our parents.

In the late 1950s, my Air Force family was stationed in San Antonio, Texas. There were still a number of active military bases and a large enough civilian population to support a symphony orchestra. My mom made sure that we brats attended a few concerts!

Some 30-odd years later, I found myself recording that very same San Antonio Symphony Orchestra in the beautifully restored Majestic Theater, where I had once watched the classic "B" horror and sci-fi movies as a kid: *The Blob* and *The Day the Earth Stood Still!!*

I had been contracted to record the Western music singer and historian, Michael Martin Murphey, for his new album, *The Sagebrush Symphony*. MMM (as his fans know him) has a long history of great songs, including his Platinum hit "Wildfire." We had recorded him playing that song at the famous Cellar Door Club in Washington, DC, circa 1973, but this was different! Veteran producer Jim Ed Norman was there to record for Warner Brothers Records with his engineer Eric Prestidge mixing.

In addition to MMM's own songs and narration, he brought some classic guests; 83-year-old singer/actor Herb Jeffries, "The Bronze Buckaroo," the incredible harmonies of the *Sons of the San Joaquin* and Native American Robert Mirabal, playing hauntingly beautiful music and poetry. All of these artists were accompanied by the San Antonio Symphony Orchestra playing original arrangements. The final concert on October 9, 1994, played to a full house of fans, grateful to attend this rare performance.

It was a great trip for me to revisit one of our many homes from my dad's Air Force years. I also did my own Air Force basic training there at Lackland in 1966.

I felt so fortunate to have heard all of these wonderful performances and historical tales. Do look up this recording online; it is a great piece of Americana! *Michael Martin Murphey Sagebrush Symphony*

NEW YORK ORCHESTRAS AND THEIR THEATERS

Not only is New York City home to the New York Philharmonic Orchestra, originally founded in 1842, but it is also home to the Metropolitan Opera, whose orchestra is considered one of the world's finest. New York also

attracts orchestras and classical stars from around the world, eager to appear in the city's famous venues.

Perhaps the busiest is Lincoln Center for the Performing Arts, founded
in 1966. It encompasses three major venues and several important smaller
ones.

Avery Fisher Hall, now David Geffen Hall, is where I recorded many
Live from Lincoln Center shows for PBS television with line producer
Mark Bauman. One of my favorite gigs was simply bringing my early Sony
1610 digital stereo system to record archival tapes for their broadcasts.
That meant no remote truck to manage, just hanging out with Mark and my
friends at Live from Lincoln Center while listening to great classical music.
It was a real education, with performances by the Chamber Music Society,
the Mostly Mozart Festival and many a guest star like opera diva Beverly
Sills and world-renowned violinist Isaac Stern.

The larger *Live from Lincoln Center* shows would require a remote truck
to handle all the inputs. There were many that included a full orchestra,
guest singers, and hosts, like the prestigious Richard Tucker Galas, honoring operatic talent. The *Classic Music Awards* had their own show and
there would be visiting performers from around the world, like the Osaka
Philharmonic Orchestra that required multitrack recording.

The State Theater, now the David H. Koch Theater, is primarily used for
ballet and theatrical arts. I had made a few recordings there for the New
York City Ballet and Orchestra, but the most memorable was the ballet
premiere of Peter Martins's *A Fool for You*, dedicated to Ray Charles, who
performed live with his eight-piece band, the Raylettes, and the New York
City Ballet Orchestra on May 16, 1988. I brought in my portable Studer
consoles to augment *Live from Lincoln Center*'s normal console, which
mixed the orchestra. Having worked with Ray Charles before, I mixed his
vocal, the band, and the Raylettes. It didn't matter that Ray couldn't see the
dancers, he could feel it and loved playing for them. You've never heard a
ballet audience cheer like this one!

The largest theater at Lincoln Center is the Metropolitan Opera House,
where we recorded the audio for all of the televised operas and galas from
the early 1980s until they built their own digital multitrack recording studio in 2011. All of the final mixes were by the master producer himself,
Jay David Sacks. Jay always mixed a live stereo of the opera and used our
multitrack recordings for post-production. The Met Opera Orchestra under
James Levine was widely regarded as one of the world's best. He was the
music director from 1976 to 2016.

Met Opera Beverly Sills Gala, October 27, 1980, Black Truck

I cherish those 30 years of recording the classic operas for *Live from the Metropolitan Opera*, later changed to *The Metropolitan Opera Presents*, as they were now taped performances.

Among the many performances we recorded were Puccini's *Madama Butterfly*, Mozart's *Le Nozze di Figaro*, Wagner's *Ring Cycle*, and so many more. Not to mention hearing the incredible talents of singers Kathleen Battle, Renée Fleming, Luciano Pavarotti, and Plácido Domingo.

If you add José Carreras to those last two names, you have the Three Tenors. I was fortunate to record their live broadcasts from Giants Stadium in New Jersey and Dodger Stadium in Los Angeles. An estimated 1.3 billion viewers worldwide witnessed the live Dodger Stadium show. Good thing I had music producer Louise Del Fuentes and a score with me for that live mix!

WNET/13 THE FLAGSHIP PBS FOR THE NEW YORK CITY AREA

WNET/13 *Great Performances* is a major producer of live television for the arts, not only in their native New York City, but also other US cities and other countries as well. They have one of the most experienced and talented production teams in television. Executive producer David Horn, line producer Mitch Owgang, and technologist Mark Schubin always made for a great show. They also brought in many great individual music producers like John McClure, Daryl Bornstein, and Andrew Kazdin.

Many of their larger music productions required remote audio trucks. There were Broadway Shows like *Fosse, Broadway Sings Jule Styne, Grapes of Wrath, Black & Blue on Broadway*, Hammerstein Gala, *South Pacific*, the play, *Black & Blue* on Broadway, A Shakespeare in the Park production of *King Lear*, a classic Gilbert and Sullivan opera, *The Pirates of Penzance* staring Angela Lansbury and Linda Ronstadt, The Natalie Cole Christmas Special, Houston Grand Opera La Cenerentola, San Francisco Opera, America in Healing after 9/11, and Jessye Norman.

Then there were the music specials like *Let's Dance*, with the legendary Big Band leader and clarinetist Benny Goodman, in one of his last performances.

The late jazz icon, Charles Mingus's monumental *Epitaph*, played for the first time in its original form, conducted by Gunther Schuller with the Julliard Orchestra.

Miles Ahead: The Music of Miles Davis, included my recording of his band at 1986 New Orleans Jazz Festival.

Opera Super Star Luciano Pavarotti sang live at Madison Square Garden, like a previous generation of stars had sung at the previous Madison Square Garden. They tore that one down, just like they tore down Grand Central Station to put this one up! A sold-out audience didn't seem to care; it was a great show, broadcast live on WNET/13 television.

Piano Grand was the Smithsonian Museum's celebration of the piano's 300th anniversary, hosted by Billy Joel, with many exceptional artists, including my hero, Dave Brubeck, along with Diana Krall and a still-rocking Jerry Lee Lewis!

The Italian Opera Star Andrea Bocelli was to perform live at New Jersey's Liberty State Park, on July 4, 2000, to celebrate the national holiday. The view of the Statue of Liberty made for great television shots. The rehearsal recording went fine, which was fortuitous, because by showtime, a powerful windstorm threatened to blow the outdoor stage rigging on to the exposed orchestra! WNET/13 wisely broadcast the taped performance rather than chance any injuries to cast and crew.

The most famous conductor, composer, and educator in the United States, Leonard Bernstein, would celebrate his 70th birthday at Tanglewood, the summer home of the Boston Symphony.

And WNET/13 helped produce the Eric Clapton Crossroads Guitar Festivals!

Carnegie Hall is on every artist's list of dream performances. I have been fortunate to record many great international stars appearing there to claim that honor.

Every year Carnegie Hall opens the season with a gala performance featuring a guest symphony orchestra and star performers. New York's WNET/13 broadcasts the event live over PBS. There to produce and mix the audio in my remote truck would be classical recording legends like RCA's Jack Pfeiffer, Columbia's John McClure, and the Met Opera's Jay Sacks. These are the giants I learned from.

There were so many great guest orchestras, such as the Berliner Philharmoniker conducted by Claudio Abbado, the Philadelphia Orchestra conducted by Christoph Eschenbach with soprano Renee Fleming and Yo-Yo Ma on cello.

One gala I definitely remember featured the Cleveland Orchestra and a last-minute crisis when a star singer became ill. Carnegie Hall management scrambled to find an appropriate sub. Jay Sacks, who was also the music producer for the Met Opera, remembered that the German soprano Dorothea Roschmann was in town at a Mozart rehearsal. She bravely agreed to fill in, but then the wrong music score was sent! A last-minute cross-town sprint brought the correct piece and Carnegie Hall's 116th season opened without a hitch. After all, the show is called *Great Performances!*

You can see these online on YouTube.

Great Performances on PBS: Live classical performance recordings by the San Francisco Opera, Houston Grand Opera's *La Cenerentola*, Lyric Opera of Chicago's *Anthony and Cleopatra*, and many more.

ORCHESTRAS FOR FILMS AND VIDEOS

Film scores were another interesting part of our client base. We recorded a number of them; among my favorites were composer Michael Kamen's scores for *Diehard with a Vengeance* and *Mr. Holland's Opus*, both with the Seattle Symphony. Those were recorded in a former Catholic seminary chapel with great acoustics.

I first met the multitalented Kamen playing keyboards for David Bowie at his 1974 *David Live* recording. Michael was a Julliard trained classical oboe player who rocked! I loved hearing his scores when recording Roger Daltrey's *The Music of Pete Townshend and The Who* at Carnegie Hall. He also wrote scores for Eric Clapton and many other stars. One score was on Babyface's *MTV Unplugged* with Eric playing.

The last time I saw him was at the 2002 Winter Olympics as we recorded some of his scores with the Utah Symphony. There was a classic bit of Kamen humor with the Mormon Tabernacle Choir. For one recording they had to sing choruses of "Amen," so Michael got them to sing "Kamen" instead. There were choruses of laughter once they figured it out!

Sadly, Michael died of a heart attack in 2003. There were many dedications to him, including David Gilmour's album *On an Island*.

The Harrison Ford Russian submarine thriller, *K-19: The Widowmaker*, was based on the real story of a nuclear submarine having a reactor meltdown with horrible results. I did go see it, mainly because we recorded the film score, but it was fascinating Cold War history. How they got all the Russian cooperation was a mystery to me, and it turns out the conductor is good friends with Vladmir Putin!

The film had a magnificent score by Klaus Badelt, known for many blockbusters like *Pirates of the Caribbean*, but this one was dark and mysterious.

It was performed by the Kirov Ballet Orchestra conducted by Valery Gergiev. The sessions were exciting, every aspect was high pressure, from the explosive conductor Gergiev, to the overworked Kirov Orchestra, who were playing concerts at the Kennedy Center in between score recordings. Imagine moving the whole symphony orchestra in between concerts over to the Daughters of the American Revolution Hall, which is really designed for speaking. Fortunately, the veteran film score engineer Alan Meyerson was on the case and had theatrical drapery hung to help control the acoustics. His sound design guaranteed all the right microphones and placements with help from our crew.

Then there was the Pro Tools recorder brought in from LA that would not stay in record beyond a fixed time. This was still 2002, and complex digital recorders sometimes disagreed with foreign sync sources. I used my pair of Studer D-827 digital tape recorders. The ones they had said "don't bother bringing those."

It all came out great: An incredible orchestra, perfectly dark, rich, appropriately mournful score for the disaster that the submarine crew endured. Alan Meyerson did a phenomenal mix; I recommend listening on a real stereo system with bass!

Recommended Listening

Blu-ray *K-19: The Widowmaker*

THE BIG BAND ORCHESTRAS

Orchestra categories often overlooked in the modern age are those who played with popular singers and jazz stars of the day. As a young rock and modern jazz fan in the 1960s, I thought Big Bands were a relic of my parent's generation and not to be taken seriously. Hearing the Buddy Rich Big Band live at the 1969 Newport Jazz Festival certainly opened my ears to the larger ensembles! Assignment at Otis Air Force Base in 1971 allowed me to go back to the Newport Jazz Festival to see and later record the Gil Evans Orchestra at the 1973 Newport Jazz Festival in New York, which became his album *Svengali*.

Then Frank Sinatra came to Carnegie Hall on April 8 to start his 1974 tour. I was there with the Record Plant remote truck to start recording for a live album. It was a difficult gig, with contract and union problems delaying our setup. We barely made our microphone connections by show time. My log shows Lee Hirschberg and Record Plant's Shelly Yakus as engineers. They were amazingly calm as they mastered those microphones into a mix, especially because Shelly had ripped his tuxedo climbing into the remote truck, after a cop had removed the ladder, thinking it a pedestrian hazard!

Frankly, all I remember of the concert was the saying "Old Blue Eyes is back"!

In September 1974, chief engineer of MGM Studios, Ed Greene, booked the Record Plant New York remote truck to record more of Sinatra's concert tour. We started recording in Boston with a sold-out show at the famous Boston Garden, an old wooden hockey and basketball venue. The next show was almost canceled due to a blizzard in Buffalo, but the fans showed up anyway. The next show was Philadelphia, then Pittsburgh, and finally, the grand finale at Madison Square Garden.

This show would feature Woody Herman's Big Band, the "Young Thundering Herd," joined by a lush string section. Bill Miller magnificently conducted the Don Costa arrangements.

Ed had requested his preferred orchestra microphones and Record Plant kindly obliged, much to the distress of the other engineers, when I absconded with most of the studio's Neumann U-87s! That caused a bit of a disaster in between Sinatra's shows. We had a previous booking to record the rock band Blue Oyster Cult at the Palladium in New York. In the scramble to wrap after that show, a box with all the U-87 shock mounts disappeared! You can't mic an orchestra without them, so we had to scramble to replace those expensive parts from Germany. Oh yeah, they also stole the rental tuxedos for the Sinatra stage crew!

The day before loading into Madison Square Garden, I went with Ed to check out the ABC television studios where the live mix would be uplinked via satellite. This was also going to be a stereo simulcast over FM radio stations. We had ABC engineer Doug Nelson to help map all the audio paths, which were via telephone lines in those days. Because of union jurisdiction, Doug would mix the live broadcast stereo while Ed took care of the recording, as he had been doing on the tour.

We did record the rehearsals at Madison Square Garden, which helped us prepare for the live show. The first show on October 12 went well and some songs were used on the live album, but of course the show on the 13 was *The Main Event*. The sold-out show was packed with celebrities and sports stars, and the legendary Howard Cosell introduced the live broadcast like a championship fight.

This was a big adventure in 1974; broadcasting live television over satellite and feeding local radio stations a stereo mix so home audiences could enjoy quality sound, instead of the tiny mono speaker on the TV.

The broadcast was a huge success, thanks to Ed Greene's meticulous production and recording, and the live album went on to be a landmark for Sinatra's return to live touring.

That was the first of so many adventures with Ed Greene over the years. He constantly advanced the level of audio for television with his technical innovations, mixing prowess, and a personality that could deal with the most difficult producers and stars, as well as the diverse technical crews. Everyone in the business knew and respected Ed Greene.

Applause, applause, applause . . . Credit roll, fade to black. We miss you, Ed.

"HAPPY BIRTHDAY, LENNY," PBS
TANGLEWOOD, LENOX, MASSACHUSETTS
AUGUST 26–28, 1988

A REMEMBRANCE BY DARYL BORNSTEIN OF THIS EVENT

In celebration of the 70th birthday of Leonard Bernstein, conductor, composer, teacher, and beloved "son" of the Boston Symphony, a worldwide live telecast with a cast of a who's who in the music business was planned by PBS and the Boston Symphony Orchestra for August 25, 1988.

It was a huge undertaking and quite ambitious given the limited technical facilities and offstage space in the Koussevitzky Shed, the summer home of the Boston Symphony.

John McClure, longtime audio producer for Bernstein, asked me to design a new sound system for the shed and to act as sound designer and live sound mixer for the event. This seemed appropriate since I had served as personal assistant to Bernstein only a few years prior. Additionally, I had mixed sound, earlier in the year for a Broadway production of *Gospel at Colonus* that David Hewitt had designed.

Remote Recording Services was the audio truck for the event.

The birthday bash included stars of classical music, jazz, and pop, all of whom had a personal relationship with Bernstein. The show was complicated, especially trying to pull off heavily amplified pop/rock performances in a hall designed for an acoustic orchestra. But as always, everything was falling together nicely—with the possible exception of some power issues between the generator and the Remote Recording Services truck.

The truck was measuring a significant voltage potential between ground and cold—70 volts to be precise. It turns out the ground stake from the generator was not actually ground to anything. It took a while to find the problem, and no time at all to rectify it.

There was a dress rehearsal the afternoon before the actual show. The house mix position was in front of a pillar, which had a camera platform on it. The camera man, Ron Washburn, was one of the best live performance cameramen in the business and a nice fellow. About 30 seconds before the rehearsal began, Ronnie kicked the largest container of Coca-Cola (regular, not sugar free) off the platform over my head, onto me by mistake and into the Yamaha PM3000 I had rented for the event. To this day, I don't know how my comixer, Bob Etter, didn't get any on him. (Bob had been the monitor engineer for *Gospel at Colonus*, and then replaced me as the front of house mixer.) Needless to say, there was no time to change or swap out desks. The rehearsal was starting.

We mopped up what we could off the surface of the desk, and to our utter surprise, the desk worked flawlessly. Nine months later, the rental shop found a substantial amount of sticky, dried soda in the pan of the desk. Why it took them nine months to find it, I'll never know.

After that, I expected everything to go smoothly. I mean, what else could happen?

One of the first performers on the night of the live broadcast was pianist and comedian, Victor Borge. Victor entered the stage with a wireless, handheld microphone. When he started to speak, the mic was dead. How could an actor enter the stage with a dead mic?

I called Bob Aldridge, the A2, on the intercom and asked what was up. He said that the mic worked perfectly when he handed it to Victor.

A bit of history for those of you who don't know Bob. At the time he was one of the best audio engineers in the business. Since then, he has proven himself, time and again, one of the best television production mixers in the world.

I, on the other hand, was relatively new to the business and building a reputation as hot head. That two liters of Coke from the previous day didn't have much of an effect on me, it seems.

I said something to Bobby over the intercom which cannot be printed. And imagine my surprise and embarrassment to learn, after the fact, that it was all part of Victor's act. He did it explicitly so that the A2 would have to come on stage and bring him a new mic.

Although that episode did not engender any fond feelings at the time between Bobby and me, eventually, we would become good friends. In fact, I owe much of my success in television to Bobby, who gave me my first opportunities in television, working on a wide variety of shows with him.

By the way, the show included the Boston Symphony Orchestra, Seiji Ozawa, Mitislav Rostropovich (Slava), Michael Tilson Thomas, John Mauceri, Lauren Bacall, Beverly Sills, Hildegard Behrens, Frederica von State, pianist-comedian Victor Borge, Patti Austin, Roddy McDowall, Yo-Yo Ma, Betty Comden, Adolph Green, Bobby McFerrin, and Bernstein's kids—Nina, Jamie, and Alex.

There are other stories of recording orchestras that fit better in the chapters where they played, like the Oscars in chapter 11 and Barbra Streisand in chapter 19. However, there are some that don't quite fit any chapter.

For example, Grand Funk Railroad, the power trio rock band of the 1960s and 1970s, with a symphony orchestra!

It was a well-intentioned fundraiser for the country Bosnia and Herzegovina after the terrible civil wars there. It was quite a unique performance, with guest appearances by Peter Frampton, Alto Reed (of Bob Seger's Silver Bullet Band), and Paul Shaffer (*Late Night with David Letterman*) conducting the Michigan Symphony Orchestra. Paul, best known for his *World's Most Dangerous Band* on the David Letterman show, brought his great humor and skill to make it all work.

If you were of age in Grand Funk Railroad's prime years (1960s–1970s), you can imagine them singing "We're an American Band and I'm Your Captain" with a full symphony orchestra. It was an amazing performance, not to be missed if you are a die-hard fan.

This was issued as *Grand Funk Railroad Bosnia* on Capitol Records

We had also recorded Grand Funk Railroad's 1975 live album, *Caught in the Act*.

FRANK ZAPPA WITH A CHAMBER ORCHESTRA
PERFORMING ERIK SATIE'S *SOCRATE*
THE RITZ, NOVEMBER 5–7, 1991

I was a fan of Frank Zappa's satirical lyrics and manic guitar playing back in the 1960s. One day I happened to be listening to a classical music radio station while the host was discussing the music of Edgard Verese with a guest. I thought he sounded familiar, and it turned out to be Frank Zappa! I had no idea how deep his musical knowledge went, but I would find out over the years of listening to his compositions and getting to record some of his live performances. Several of those became live albums, *Frank Zappa Philly '76* and *Zappa in New York*, also 1976.

Frank's son Dweezil and orchestra director Joel Thome planned a 50th birthday celebration for him at the Ritz Theater in New York on November 5–7, 1991. We all knew that Frank had advanced prostate cancer but were still jolted by the last-minute announcement that he was too ill to travel.

Dweezil had been touring with the band for years and would be playing Frank's parts, but sadly he had to come on stage and explain to the sold-out crowd that Frank couldn't make it. He explained that Frank and Joel Thome had arranged the show to include Erik Satie's classic composition *Socrate*. The *Orchestra of Our Time* would play for the operatic mezzo-soprano and tenor singers. There was an animated set piece designed for Satie by the mobile artist Alexander Calder. This was a major artistic and political statement by Frank. Socrates, as we know him, was the Greek philosopher who was tried for corrupting the youth and disregarding the gods. He was sentenced to suicide by poison. Frank thought that was still relevant then, just as it is today.

Dweezil had to sternly dictate to the crowd: "Frank wants you to listen to this, it's important!" The audience tried, but toward the end I heard an almost child-like groan in the audience mics, "We-e-e wa-a-a-nt Frank!" *Socrate* was a beautiful operatic piece from 1918, a period when Satie was involved with musicians like Claude Debussy and Igor Stravinsky. Maybe a few of them will come to appreciate it as Frank did. My favorite Satie composition is still "Trois Gymnopedies (No. 1)."

The CD of *Zappa's Universe* is available on Verve, unfortunately, I can't find that recording of *Socrate* anywhere.

THE THREE TENORS IN CONCERT 1994
DODGER STADIUM, LOS ANGELES, CALIFORNIA, JULY 16,1994

THE THREE TENORS IN CONCERT 1996
GIANTS STADIUM, EAST RUTHERFORD, NEW JERSEY, JULY 26, 1996

José Carreras, Plácido Domingo, and especially Luciano Pavarotti had been opera super stars for years, and as their worldwide reputations grew, the producer Tibor Rudas promoted even larger concert events. International television broadcasts and recordings became huge successes. Having recorded them at the New York Metropolitan Opera and other live events, we were contracted to mix and record the shows from the United States. I would be the engineer mixing the live broadcast and recordings for later productions. I was fortunate to work with producer Louise Del Fuentes reading the scores. We had worked on many shows over the years at Lincoln Center. The sound design was excellent, with the highest quality microphones, which were almost all Schoeps and Neumanns. I was using Millennia preamps on stage feeding the Neve VRM console and recording on Studer D-827 48-track digital tape recorders. At the time, they sounded better and were much more reliable than the computer-based recording systems.

ARLO GUTHRIE AND THE METROPOLITAN SYMPHONY ORCHESTRA
KENNEDY CENTER, WASHINGTON, DC, AND GORDON CENTER, OWINGS MILLS, MARYLAND
NOVEMBER 19 AND 21, 2001

Arlo Guthrie is, of course, the son of the legendary folk singer and political activist, Woody Guthrie, most famous for his song "This Land Is Your Land."

Arlo performed this show during a Thanksgiving week of American Music at the Kennedy Center in Washington, DC. He did, of course, sing his classic folk songs "The City of New Orleans" and his father's "This Land Is Your Land," but most of the evening was devoted to US orchestral music conducted by John Nardolillo, with the Metropolitan Symphony Orchestra. They performed many favorites like Leonard Bernstein's *Candide* overture and Aaron Copland's *Appalachian Spring*. Having recorded Bernstein conducting these pieces with his orchestra in New York, I thought Nardolillo was excellent; he and Arlo produced a wonderful variety of US musical history.

Arlo opened with the sobering "Nobody Seems to Care When a Soldier Makes It Home." It is still relevant today as it is in all wars. The orchestra played beautifully in "The Patriot's Dream," as he sang the emotional lyrics. Guthrie had the audience clapping along with "This Land Is Your Land," interrupted by a humorous story. The last song, "Key to the Highway," was my favorite, of course.

Thanks, Arlo, for your unique music and social wisdom.

PS (POST SHOW)

One of those random bits of serendipity on the road: I had to have a car service drive up to the next venue for Arlo's recording. The driver thankfully had a jazz station on the radio for the trip and the DJ was playing every version of "Stardust," the classic 1928 Hoagy Carmichael tune, that he could find. It lasted the whole trip and provided me and the jazz-loving driver with great conversation. Of course, we had heard that song all our lives, from our parents' 78 rpm records and endless radio, TV, and films. The Glenn Miller Orchestra, Nat King Cole, and of course, Frank Sinatra; for my generation, it was Dave Brubeck's and John Coltrane's versions, but I had never heard guitarist Larry Coryell or the British Band The Shadows play it! The DJ offered in-depth history, including the fact that songwriter Carmichael finally admitted that "Stardust" was originally written about cocaine. I wonder if Eric Clapton ever recorded "Stardust"?

"A REQUIEM FOR SEPTEMBER 11," PBS
LIBERTY STATE PARK, NEW JERSEY
SEPTEMBER 10–11, 2002
A REMEMBRANCE BY DARYL BORNSTEIN
FOR THE FIRST ANNIVERSARY OF 9/11, PBS SHOT A LIVE
PERFORMANCE OF THE VERDI'S REQUIEM IN LIBERTY STATE
PARK IN NEW JERSEY

The stage was placed so that Lower Manhattan and the site of the twin towers were the background, behind the orchestra and chorus (there was no back wall or curtains behind the stage). In fact, the only thing that, in anyway, blocked the view of Manhattan and the Hudson River were the chorus mics that were flown on a cable above the chorus, with large black wind screens, a necessity due to the wind off the river.

Unlike the concert at Riverside Church the previous year, there had been ample time to plan everything about this concert. No one, however, had anticipated what Mother Nature would throw at us on the day and night of the show.

Load in was uneventful. The rehearsal, on September 10, the day before the live broadcast, with no one in the massive audience area, went smoothly. The orchestra, chorus, and soloists performed as though the audience were full. Even the trumpets on the satellite stage were in fine form and played in time with the conductor who was a considerable distance away from them.

Cameras found their shots, the director called the show, and the TD cut it live. It was a relaxed evening, with clear skies, and virtually no wind until the sun went down. Even then, the winds were not a concern.

The following morning, Jay David Sacks, audio producer, took the multitracks to Sync Sound and remixed the rehearsal, just in case.

On site, we worked through a list of technical notes and decided to land the large flown line arrays because the wind was beginning to gust at an uncomfortable and unsafe level. As the wind speed increased throughout the day, the bungee cords holding the roof skin to the roof truss started to come undone and became intimidating projectiles. Many were hitting the stage, missing, thankfully, people working on and around the stage. In between bungee assaults, we recorded a number of public service announcements during the afternoon, on stage!

By 6:00 pm, the winds were gusting as high as 60 miles per hour, knocking over anything on stage that wasn't weighted down. I was concerned that music stands would crash into any one of the many Schoeps microphones on stage.

After voicing our concerns to production management, we were told that they were not going to cancel the show due to weather. It should be noted that the string section of the New Jersey Symphony Orchestra, the orchestra for the concert, were playing on a set of

The great comic Don Novello as I recorded his *Father Guido Sarducci Live at St. Douglas Convent* album. Blessing the API.

Photo courtesy of author and Thomas Taxi Briell

Crosby, Stills, Nash & Young 1974 World Tour on stage at the Nassau Coliseum, Uniondale, NY.

Crosby, Stills, Nash
& Young 1974
World tour. One
of many CSN&Y
shows we would
record.

Crosby, Stills, Nash
& Young 1974
World tour. I love
this shot of Neil
Young after a killer
encore.

Neil Young's 1978
*Rust Never Sleeps
Tour*, still one of
my favorite rock
recordings, on the
brand new Black
Remote Truck.
Photo courtesy of David
DB Brown

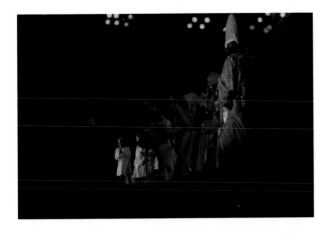

Neil Young's 1978 *Rust Never Sleeps Tour*, a great shot of the "Road-Eyes" and the giant RCA Mic. As Neil sang, Rock 'n Roll will never die.
Photo courtesy of David DB Brown

Crosby, Stills & Nash at a MUSE (Musicians United for Safe Energy) Concert. They staged five star studded concerts protesting nuclear dangers, shortly after the Three Mile Island power station meltdown in 1979. Right down the road from where I lived!
Photo courtesy of David DB Brown

Crosby, Stills & Nash at a MUSE Concert. Graham Nash was instrumental in organizing the massive effort, along with many like-minded musicians.
Photo courtesy of David DB Brown

**Blues legend
Muddy Waters
plays at Henry
Hope's Club
outside Chicago.**
Photo courtesy of David
DB Brown

**Muddy Waters is
joined by Texas
blues man Johnny
Winter for a rare
set. The album
was called** *Muddy
"Mississippi" Waters
- Live.*
Photo courtesy of David
DB Brown

**Bruce Springsteen
and the E Street
Band at the
fabulous Fox
Theater in Atlanta,
GA in 1978, still in
the Jimmy Iovine/
Shelly Yakas
Record Plant days.
Bruce lived there
in the studio those
days.**
Photo courtesy of David
DB Brown

Bruce Springsteen and the E Street Band at the fabulous Fox Theater in Atlanta, GA. An incredible example of the 1930s opulence, it is one of the few survivors of that era. Loved recording there.
Photo courtesy of David DB Brown

Jackson Browne at a MUSE Concert. Jackson was also a driving force behind these shows and always a brilliant performer.
Photo courtesy of David DB Brown

James Taylor and Carly Simon at one of the MUSE Concerts. They were at their prime singing "Mockingbird" and joined other artists during the five shows.
Photo courtesy of David DB Brown

Bonnie Raitt at a MUSE Concert singing her soulful version of "Angel from Montgomery." Do look for her live album Road Tested with a great performance of it as well.
Photo courtesy of David DB Brown

The Doobie
Brothers at a
MUSE Concert.
Now that's a
Big Band! I still
remember them
delivering their
hit "Takin' it to
the Streets" with
James Taylor.
Photo courtesy of David
  DB Brown

Bob Weir of the
Grateful Dead
at the Capitol
Theater concert on
stage.
Photo courtesy of David
  DB Brown

Jerry Garcia and
Bob Weir of the
Grateful Dead
at the Capitol
Theater on stage
with Keith and
Donna Godchaux.
Photo courtesy of David
  DB Brown

Ian McDonald of the band Foreigner on stage.
Photo courtesy of David DB Brown

Van Morrison on stage at The Bottom Line Theater.
Photo courtesy of David DB Brown

J. Geils Band and Danny Klein on stage at the Bowery Theater.
Photo courtesy of David DB Brown

Richie Havens on stage celebrating the 10th anniversary of Woodstock.
Photo courtesy of David DB Brown

Music For UNI-CEF Concert, on stage at the UN: Barry Gibb, Rita Coolidge, John Denver, and Olivia Newton John.
Photo courtesy of David DB Brown

Music For UNICEF Concert, on stage at the UN: Jim Cregan, Rod Stewart, and Phil Chen.
Photo courtesy of David DB Brown

Stradivarius violins (rare and *extremely* expensive), which were on loan to the orchestra.

Around 6:30 p.m., the orchestra management was center stage, looking over the set up, and noticing the wind. They were standing next to the concert master's stand, which had a sandbag on it.

I happened to be on stage at the same time and asked them what they thought of the weather, and before they answered, I removed the sandbag from the music stand, which, immediately, crashed to the stage with a gust of wind.

The concert was immediately canceled.

The broadcast that evening was the performance from the previous evening. The experience of watching the orchestra play to an empty house seemed an appropriately eerie comment on the first anniversary of 9/11.

As we started our load out, at 8:00 p.m., the time the concert had been scheduled to begin, the winds stopped. Completely, without a whiff of wind the rest of the evening.

Coincidence or the work of a higher power?

—Daryl Bornstein
Engineer, Producer, Designer

⑲

HELL FREEZES OVER

The Eagles Fly Again,
LA, New York, Florida, and Australia

After a 14-year "vacation," band founders Don Henley and Glenn Frey had lunch and decided the Eagles could thaw out. Henley's famous quote, after the band's 1980 breakup, was they would play together again "When Hell freezes over."

A major live *MTV Unplugged* special and a tour brought them together again in 1994. Master engineer and producer Elliot Scheiner, who had recorded *Glenn Frey Live in Dublin* and other studio albums like *Soul Searchin'*, was in charge of the live sessions for MTV at the Warner Brothers Studio in Burbank, California. Elliot and Rob Jacobs would produce the *Hell Freezes Over* live album.

I had recorded many of MTV's *Unplugged* shows for artists Mariah Carey, Nirvana, and others, but our Silver Truck was not available for this one. The Eagles dates overlapped with a Dolly Parton recording at Dollywood, in Pigeon Forge, Tennessee, but thankfully, Guy Charbonneau's Le Mobile was available. Elliott asked me to come out as a consultant because I had recorded on that truck and was friends with Guy. It was a rare opportunity for me to enjoy time on stage, visit with the monitor and FOH mixers, and the video truck audio mixer as well.

It was amazing to see the band back in perfect sync again and note perfect recall of their hits and a few new soon-to-be hits. The extensive rehearsals and discussions gave me new appreciation of Elliot's calm, confident genius for guiding the musicians through the minefield of reuniting these megastars. I discreetly left the truck when those discussions occurred; it got a little crowded.

Because of my previous booking, I had to leave before the show. Elliot was in good hands with Guy Charbonneau, designer and owner of Le Mobile. I did get to hear the final mixes when they were released as a DTS CD and DVD.

I knew Elliott's studio mixes were great and now he had set a new standard for mixing live recordings! The resulting DVD and CD, *Hell Freezes Over*, each went on to sell nine times Platinum, plus many more worldwide, last time I checked.

THE EAGLES FAREWELL I TOUR
MELBOURNE, AUSTRALIA, NOVEMBER 14–17, 2004

We did record several other shows in the United States, but the ones I really loved were in Melbourne, Australia, during their 2004 tour. Elliot Scheiner would again produce, record and mix the live DVD and CD. He is known for his pursuit of perfection, so my assignment was to find recording gear in Australia to meet his needs. Fortunately, I knew the renowned audio guru Bruce Jackson, who had just returned to his native home in Sydney, Australia. We had worked on Bruce Springsteen and Barbra Streisand concerts, where he had designed and mixed the live sound. Bruce had also founded Apogee Electronics, who were always ahead on digital designs, and he helped connect me to the right engineers and studios that would rent us the gear Elliott required. Simon Leadly and Track Down Studios helped procure and operate the Pro Tools digital recording systems.

The rest of the recording chain would be analog. Vintage Neve pre-amps were Elliot's preference. A retired Australian Broadcasting Corporation remote truck with a vintage analog Neve console was a good start. We set up a control room to house the racks of Neve pre-amps and outboard gear for Elliott to mix the live feed on a Yamaha DM-2000 console.

We located quite a few vintage Neve pre-amps from generous studio owners and musicians around Australia and New Zealand. We did have to nurse a few of them back to health. It was a crazy technical adventure that almost blew up but triumphed in the end.

The band, effects, and ambience microphone inputs had to be routed through the Neve console and many different individual Neve pre-amps, then into the 96 Pro Tools channels. Running at the high sampling rate on that number of tracks for that length of time was really pushing the limits of reliability. I have seen many a digital disaster as the technology evolved, so there we were, more than 10,000 miles from home, working on various vintage analog gear into a maxed out rental Pro Tools rig. What could go wrong?

After much help from touring sound system Clair Brothers Audio and mixer JD Brill, we came up with enough cable and interfaces to get all 96 inputs into the Pro Tools and out to the Yamaha DM-2000 digital console for mixing the live feed. Elliott was an early adapter of the DM-2000 and was adept at mixing on them. Unfortunately, the rental console had been set up in such a way that after the rehearsal, the console lost Elliott's mix and would not recall it! Just what you want before a live broadcast.

After a few choice words, Elliot just played back the rehearsal recording and remixed it. Faders love Elliott; they just do as he thinks, and the live broadcast went out perfectly.

Yet another Platinum record for the Eagles and 30 Platinum, last time I looked.

Recommended Recordings

Eagles Hell Freezes Over
Geffen Eagles Recording Co.

Eagles Farewell 1 Tour: Live from Melbourne 2004 Warner Vision

Here is another great recording Elliot Scheiner made on the Silver Truck with me.
Donald Fagen, NY Rock & Soul Revue, Beacon Theater, NYC
Giant Records

PS

As I started writing this chapter, I decided to look on YouTube for any songs from the Eagles Melbourne show to play. Naturally they had the intergalactic hit, "Hotel California." How many times have I heard that song in every imaginable environment?

I use an Apogee Duet DA converter into my trusty old Bryston 2B pre-amp and Bryston 4B amplifier feeding into original 1980 B&W 801 speakers. I'm familiar with them and how poor most YouTube recordings sound, so I was pleased with how well the Eagles video mix came through. Elliot Scheiner had such a clear vision of what live music sounds like; he gets every detail right, and his mixes always come through, no matter what electronic abuse it suffered getting there! Thanks Els!

⑳

THE DIVAS

The Met Opera to Aretha,
Whitney, Gloria, Madonna, and Barbra

THE NEW YORK METROPOLITAN OPERA

The opera stage is where the term "diva" originated. We recorded many of
the greatest divas at the New York Metropolitan Opera, Live From Lincoln
Center, the San Francisco Opera, the Chicago Lyric Opera, and the Houston Opera, and not to mention guest appearances on other television shows.
We even did a TV talk show staring the star soprano Beverly Sills, who also
went on to become general manager of the New York City Opera and later
the chairwoman of the Metropolitan Opera. She was affectionately known
as "Bubbles," which suited her wonderful sense of humor.

As I tried to explain almost 30 years of recording the multitrack audio tapes
for the Met Opera's television shows, I realized that it's a whole separate
book. There are hundreds of years' worth of opera stories to tell. I'm hoping
that Jay David Sacks, the longtime audio producer for the Met, and broadcast
ops director Bill King will rise to the occasion and write that book! I recommend watching the *Nightly Met Opera Streams* via metopes.org.

ARETHA FRANKLIN: THE DIVA OF SOUL
RADIO CITY MUSIC HALL, NOVEMBER 1, 1974

Aretha Franklin certainly ranks as the Diva of Soul, and she was really out
to prove it on this show. Just a few days previously we had recorded and

broadcast Frank Sinatra's epic *The Main Event*, right down the street at Madison Square Garden. It was almost like Franklin showing them who was boss! She put on a spectacular show with a Big Band and flaunted her gorgeous costume changes. We recorded her for Atlantic Records, where they really understood how to let her sing like Aretha!

Over the years I have recorded her at many venues, including at her father's church in Detroit, where she grew up singing gospel.

One of those recordings was my worst nightmare when her microphone went dead to the remote truck while she was singing "Nessun Dorma," from the Puccini opera *Turandot* at a live Music Cares benefit show. Producer Phil Ramone had to overdub Aretha singing it again in the studio. Take a bullet for the boss; excuses need not apply.

It gets even stranger. Two days later on February 25, 1998, the *40th Grammy Awards* were aired live from Radio City Music Hall in New York. The opera superstar Luciano Pavarotti was to perform, you guessed it, "Nessun Dorma," for which he is world renowned. The live TV broadcast had already begun when Pavarotti became ill and could not sing. Well, Aretha was to appear later singing *Blues Brothers* songs with Dan Aykroyd, John Goodman, and Jim Belushi. Executive producer Ken Ehrlich knew about her performance at the Music Cares benefit, so he ran to her dressing room to plead his case. After hearing Pavarotti's rehearsal tape, she agreed to sing, with the iron confidence she was famous for. If you did not see the broadcast, you must find it on YouTube; it is one of the most incredible live performances you will ever see!

I did see a replay of that Grammy broadcast, but I was actually out in LA at the Shrine Auditorium, working on the *60th Academy Awards* broadcast. All of us that work in live television agreed that it was a heroic performance by Aretha, and one we will never forget.

Remembering Aretha, from my Audio-Technica blog in 2018:

Remembering Aretha

Like so many of us around the world, I felt a deep loss with the news of Aretha's passing. She was such a formative part of my musical life, starting in the 1960s.

My family was stationed in Europe with my Air Force pilot father. I remember sitting in a German bar listening to the jukebox playing Aretha and the guy sitting next to me was singing along, almost in tune. He had on jeans and a leather jacket; I assumed he was a US soldier, so I made some remark about the song. He grinned and said he didn't speak English but could sing the lyrics! The Beatles recorded some early records in German, but I don't think Aretha did.

Later when I returned Stateside and became involved in live music recording, I would have many opportunities to hear her perform. Her power and charisma delivered on stage is just astounding!

Working for Record Plant New York, I became a specialist in live recording. One of my first gigs (as an assistant engineer) was dashing around New York recording the Newport Jazz Festival shows, spread all over the city in different theaters! I know we recorded Aretha, because she's on the album . . . but frankly I don't remember it in the blur of multiple artists' shows.

I do remember recording a later 1974 show at the magnificent Radio City Music Hall for Atlantic Records. This time she played a full set and brought the house down, I became a lifelong believer.

Funny the things you remember; in rehearsal I had run out of cigarettes (yeah, we all still smoked in the control room then), so Nesuhi Ertegun, the Atlantic Records producer, went out and bought me a fresh pack!

My most cherished memory of Aretha was recording her 1987 return to gospel albums with *One Lord, One Faith, One Baptism*. As it says on the album sleeve, Aretha had "Sole Creative Judgment" for Clive Davis's Arista label. As her engineer, I could speak with her directly on all aspects of the recording.

I flew out to Detroit to advance the recording location, which was her late father's New Bethel Baptist Church on CL Franklin Blvd. It was disheartening to drive through areas of Detroit that were still ravaged by the riots of 1967. Many wounds were not yet healed. As I was introduced to the church officials and was given the church tour to plan our recording, I was aware that I was the only white person there. It was a relief to be warmly greeted by the musicians and choir, who figured I must be there to help. I witnessed a joyous service with a great performance by the band and choir, and I flew home inspired and eager to help Aretha make her record.

When I returned on July 26, 1987, with the Record Plant Black Truck, we quickly set up to record the next three days of performances. After introductions by Rev. Cecil Franklin, Aretha was joined by the Franklin Sisters, Clara Ward, and a soulful five-piece band. I can't begin to describe the power of their combined spiritual joy.

Later, Aretha would be joined by Mavis Staples and Edwin Hawkins for classics like "Oh Happy Day." The entire congregation became one with the choir and the VU meters were dancing on my API analog console and Ampex 1200 tape machines.

There were politics as well, Rev. Jesse Jackson was speechifying (he would later run for president) and Aretha was always heavily involved in many causes. Appropriately, she sang "Higher Ground" with Rev. Jaspar Williams to a fully supportive audience.

Aretha closed the three days of performances with Mavis Staples and Joe Ligon of the Mighty Clouds of Joy and with the Franklin Sisters. The song was "Packing Up, Getting Ready to Go." Reluctantly, we did; it had been a singular experience we would not soon forget.

I had made cassettes for Aretha every night, and she was happy with the recording, but early on I had her singing on a modern mic that I currently favored for powerful vocalists. She called me up and asked if she could go back to her standard Shure SM-58! Well, of course, the artist is always right, and it was her signature sound. Lesson learned . . .

If you have a chance, look up "One Lord, One Faith, One Baptism." It is available again on CD and for download, if you can't find an original vinyl record.

Thank you, Aretha, for a lifetime of soulful Music.

David W. Hewitt

BARBRA STREISAND

Barbra Streisand certainly deserves the title of diva, and she wears it like a crown.

Barbra Streisand in Concert
Las Vegas, December 26–31, 1993, and New York June 19–27, 1994

Being married to a Jewish Princess and having lived on the upper West Side of New York City, I was fully indoctrinated into the "Babs" mystique. Barbra Streisand went from being a Brooklyn movie theater usher to the most successful female recording artist in history, garnering endless honors as a movie star, writer, producer, and of course, music composer.

Barbra's many studio and Broadway musical recordings were not in my purview until 1993 when she started her first real tour as a singing star, with 26 shows across the United States and England. We recorded the Las Vegas shows at the MGM Grand starting December 26 through New Year's Eve in 1993. One of the true perks in this business was getting to work with some of the greatest engineers and producers in music. Shawn Murphy is one of the finest film score recordists ever and had worked with Streisand many times in the studio. His calm, confident manner and incredible mixing abilities made these high-pressure shows a pleasure. For this tour and the 1999 tour, I was glad to see my friend Bruce Jackson as the sound designer and live concert mixer for Streisand. Bruce had worked with everyone from Elvis Presley to Bruce Springsteen in the rock genre but was equally skilled at dealing with large orchestras. Another bright star with the orchestra was Marvin Hamlisch. He was arranging and conducting for Streisand, as he had for many years, going back to her *Funny Girl* days. Marvin was her music director for all these tours and would add another Emmy Award to his collection with this recording.

Back in the days of the pager (pre-cell phone) Barbra wanted her key concert heads to wear one, so she could reach them at will. On our first rehearsal day, a flustered assistant came running into the remote recording truck with a bag and a list. "Shawn Murphy?" she shouted, digging into the bag. With a bemused smile, Shawn raised his hand and the assistant thrust a pager at him. "What's that?" he asked, and she replied that Barbra wanted him to carry this pager at all times. "No," was his reply. But, but Barbra . . . "No." Seeing her panic, I offered to keep it on the remote truck, but that didn't work, and she went running out to meet her fate. Bruce Jackson told me of her calling him at 1:00 a.m. complaining about the cassette tape of the rehearsal sounding terrible. He went over to her hotel and put the Dolby switch on.

All of us were there to give her millions of fans the best possible rendition of her incredible performance. It reminded me of what an outsized influence she has been on our lives over the years, on stage, records, radio, films, television, and finally the live concerts. As always, words fail me; just listen to the music or look up the video.

Marvin Hamlisch's "Overture," accompanied by a giant screen video of her career, set the stage for Barbra singing "As if We Never Said Goodbye." The seemingly endless stream of her favorites included, of course, "People," "The Man Who Got Away," and "On a Clear Day." Act 2 started with "The Way We Were" on through "Ordinary Miracles" and finished with "For All We Know."

For once in a casino, everyone won.

The Concert
Madison Square Garden, June 20–30 and July 10–12, 1994

Timeless: Live in Concert, from the millennial 2000 New Year's Eve show at the MGM Grand, was HBO's highest rated musical event in their history. The live album and video both went three times Platinum. Just add that to the more than 150 million records she has already sold worldwide.

Thankfully, the dreaded Y2K bug did not crash our computers.

LIZA MINNELLI
AVERY FISHER HALL, NOVEMBER 12, 1978
CARNEGIE HALL, SEPTEMBER 3–6, 1979, AND MARCH 5, 1980
BEACON THEATER, JUNE 7–8, 2002

Liza Minnelli was born theatrical royalty to Judy Garland and Vincent Minnelli, but she earned her own Tonys, Oscars, and Emmys. I was privileged to record two *Live at Carnegie Hall* albums and one of her later 2002 performances, *Liza's Back*. She was also a regular at the *Tony Awards*, back when we provided audio for the live broadcast.

You won't often hear this from an audio guy, but you absolutely need to *see* Liza perform while she is singing to appreciate her many talents. Watch the movies.

A sign of the times: at one of those Carnegie Hall shows, a gentleman who shall remain nameless, was changing into his white sport coat for the show. Reaching into his side pocket, he was startled to come up with an envelope of white powder! With a grin he mused, "I haven't worn this coat since that tour last year. I hope it's still good!"

WHITNEY HOUSTON
CISSY HOUSTON'S NEWARK CHURCH TO THE ACADEMY
AWARDS MISFIRE

In early April 1987, I got a call from Bob Liftin at Regent Sound to record a last-minute PBS TV shoot over in Newark, New Jersey. My interest picked up to learn it was for Cissy Houston's New Hope Baptist Church Choir. In addition to her well-known gospel and solo work, Cissy has sung on many great recordings, including Jimi Hendrix's "Electric Ladyland." Now she was adding her daughter, Whitney Houston, to the performance. I don't have to tell you that hearing Whitney sing live with the gospel choir was a real thrill. Now I understand where those hit records came from—what a family!

It wasn't long until her second album *Whitney* was charting number one on worldwide charts, breaking records everywhere. In September 1987, we traveled to Saratoga, New York, to record a live video shoot for MTV and the promotion for the release for the 1988 Summer Olympics album, *One Moment in Time*. She delivered an amazing show with her already long list of hits, backed by A-list musicians, singers, and dancers, everything MTV needed. By the end of the tour, she sold 20 million copies of the *Whitney* album! She would soon be earning Grammys, American Music Awards, and endless accolades. They would all pale in comparison to her blossoming career as a Hollywood movie star.

THE BOBBY BROWN CONNECTION, A MOST UNPLEASANT TRIP

Whitney's soon-to-be husband, the singer/rapper Bobby Brown, was on tour supporting his latest album and video for *Don't Be Cruel*, and I was booked to record the shows down in Baton Rouge, Louisiana, on February 11 and 12, 1989.

Unfortunately, the week before the show, we had a disastrous crash on winter ice that destroyed my Black Remote Truck. My seatbelt had let go and I was thrown around the cab, but thankfully not through the windshield, and knocked unconscious and pretty beat up. It's a long story, but driver Phil Gitomer and I survived, and I was able to rent the Midcom Remote Truck out of Dallas, Texas, to cover the Bobby Brown recording. I flew down to Louisiana, drove to Baton Rouge, and made it all work. What didn't work was the two band crews getting into a fight and shooting at each other. One guy did not make it. I managed to get home in one piece.

By the time I was called for another Whitney recording (she was now a single name superstar), we had spent a year designing and building the new Silver Truck, a ground-up, custom, state-of-the-art tractor-trailer. It matched my Porsche 911 because German race cars were typically painted silver. They made a nice couple.

Whitney was now a superstar actress as well; having won all the other awards there are, she could now look forward to an Oscar. *The Bodyguard* film with Kevin Costner produced her "I Will Always Love You," a lifetime anthem and not to mention Grammy record of the year and the biggest selling film soundtrack ever. World tours and White House dinners honoring Nelson Mandela and her charitable works abounded. The movie *Waiting to Exhale* repeated her successes and she shared the soundtrack with Aretha Franklin, Patti LaBelle, and other black singers. That album went seven times Platinum.

Whitney's next film, *The Preacher's Wife*, brought my new Silver Truck to a sound stage in Atlanta, Georgia, to record orchestra and choir music for the soundtrack. Veteran engineer Joseph Magee was the sound designer and had elaborate isolation booths for the drums and percussion, along with acoustic treatments to control reflections. The recordings with the full orchestra, band, and the Georgia Mass Choir were so rich and powerful, it was worth all the effort.

Unfortunately, there was a financial dispute where my terms were not honored. We did not continue working on the film.

Whitney at the Academy Awards 2000

The *72nd Academy Awards* were held at the Shrine Auditorium in Los Angeles on March 26, 2000. I had been providing the audio remote truck for the broadcast since 1993, so I was looking forward to hearing Whitney sing live again. She was originally slated to appear with Garth Brooks, Queen Latifah, Isaac Hayes, and Ray Charles in a tribute medley during the live ABC broadcast. The rehearsals did not go well for her. Several times she was erratic and missed cues. At her last rehearsal, the orchestra played the intro to "Over the Rainbow," but Whitney started singing a different song and then stopped. The sound of the orchestra falling out of tune into silence and Whitney leaving the stage was heartbreaking. The production intercom erupted with colorful language and heads were heard banging. Finally, the legendary songsmith and music director, Burt Bacharach had to ask Whitney to bow out. After a frantic scramble, they were saved by country star Faith Hill, who stepped in with little time to rehearse and delivered a great performance on the live broadcast.

Everyone felt the pain of seeing a wonderful talent like Whitney fail in public, but at least it wasn't during the live broadcast. The press and management spun it as a sore throat and fatigue, which may have been true, but the years of substance abuse and marital problems could not be hidden. Whitney recovered and came back with a $100 million Arista contract! That is one incredible constitution. Too bad it had not been strong enough to save her from the other demons. I'm sure there are at least 100 million fans who mourned her passing in 2012, and I'm one of them.

MADONNA
FROM HER NEW YORK CITY START TO THE OSCARS

Without a doubt, Madonna invented a new category of divas in the 1980s' dance era of MTV and the New York Club scene. She was impossible to miss and as her popularity grew, so did her live show tours. The 1985 *Like a Virgin* Tour was where we recorded her for Warner Music Video and Sire Records. The venue was Cobo Hall, the famous Detroit Sports and Rock Arena, where I had recorded Bob Seger and other Motor City stars.

Madonna is from the Detroit area so this was a perfect "homecoming" setting, with her extended family and friends packing the audience. I remember her giving a shout out to her mom, before performing a rather risqué version of a song about her box. Sorry, Mom!

This successful *Like a Virgin* Tour and video proved her performance and production prowess. There would be no stopping her now.

In 1990 Madonna starred in Warren Beatty's *Dick Tracy* film, as the blond bombshell, Breathless Mahoney. They were both nominated for Academy Awards and would appear on the live 1991 telecast of the *63rd Annual Academy Awards*. Madonna would perform the song "Sooner or Later" from the film, backed by the live Bill Conti Orchestra. If you happened to see the show, the proscenium curtain rises with Madonna upstage in the spotlight, with the orchestra playing the stripper intro. She sashayed downstage in a most seductive strut.

Now I pause to set this potential live TV disaster scene. I'm in my audio remote truck with engineer Tommy Vicari mixing the live orchestra and what will be Madonna's live vocal. That is, if the sleeping stagehand wakes up and hands her the microphone on cue! On the intercom, we hear the audio director start to yell "WTF, where is that microphone? She's almost to her intro!!"

In a brilliantly choreographed move, one of the real pro-stage A2s grabs a backup radio mic, yells at the video director to cut to an audience shot, streaks across the stage, handing off the mic to Madonna, who never loses her cool, and makes it off camera just as the director cuts back to a close up of Madonna belting out her big number! Perfect save, the television audience never saw a thing, and Madonna gave a powerful adrenaline-fueled performance. I've seen lesser talents freak out under that kind of stress.

Sometimes the most entertaining part of the show is offstage.

MARIAH CAREY

Tommy Mottola, who was then head of CBS Records, discovered Mariah Carey almost by chance, via a cassette demo tape. He quickly recognized her talent and signed her to a recording contract with CBS and a management contract as well.

I first met Tommy in 1972 when he signed Daryl Hall and John Oates to Chappell Publishing and formed his own Champion Management company. Daryl, John, and I had all been working in Philadelphia Studios. They were working on writing the first records and I ended up working at Regent Sound. Tommy had been through the rock-and-roll recording trip as a singer and was now on to much bigger things.

In October 1990, Tommy arranged a showcase for Mariah Carey at the Tattoo Club in New York. Rumor had it that a 747 full of Sony Music executives had flown in from Japan to hear Tommy's new superstar! I can vouch for her success; as the recording engineer I was impressed with her five-octave range and soulful melisma. Of course, it didn't hurt that all the A-list New York session players were backing her up! Even though the house piano was poor, Richard Tee made it sing for Mariah. Sony Worldwide was sold.

Her stream of hit singles like "Vision of Love" and the first album, simply titled *Mariah Carey*, going nine times Platinum proved the point! Her records were wildly successful, but she wasn't touring to promote them, and critics accused her of being a "Studio Act." She was still young and had little road experience.

MTV had started a new series of live videos titled *Unplugged*, and Tommy Mottola correctly figured that would work for Mariah. We were booked to record her session and also a separate one for the band Pearl Jam. This would take place at the legendary 1920 film stages of Kaufman Astoria Studios, over in Queens, New York. Never mind that the first Sherlock Holmes sound film was shot there, and the *Sesame Street* TV series my kids grew up with were still produced there! I was a hero at home.

Mariah's producer, Walter Afanasieff, assembled a great orchestra, did the arrangements, and played keys as well. The players were all A-list New York session vets, including ten background singers. Mariah was nervous but still approachable, as long as Tommy was by her side. She defiantly rose to the occasion, as you will hear when you listen to the show. Words don't do her justice.

The *Unplugged* album went four times Platinum in the United States and did equally as well worldwide. The video release, which in those days was on

VHS tape, went Platinum as well. The critics finally agreed that, yes indeed she could deliver her amazing songs live! Not only did this show boost her worldwide popularity, but it did the same for the *MTV Unplugged* series. Many critics say Mariah's show made the *MTV Unplugged* franchise a hit. I can vouch for that, we recorded quite a few of those shows after Mariah: Pearl Jam, Babyface, Brian Adams, K.D. Lang, Nirvana, Stone Temple Pilots, The Wallflowers, Jewel, and Neil Young with the Stray Gators.

Here Is Mariah Carey
Thanksgiving NBC TV Special, July 13–16, 1993

The Proctors Theatre in Schenectady, New York, is a beautifully restored 1926 vaudeville-era theater. With a magnificent proscenium arch stage and a domed ceiling designed for acoustic orchestras, it was perfect for producer Walter Afanasieff's expanded orchestra. We had the luxury of a rehearsal day to sort it all out. The performance was designed to showcase Mariah's new *Music Box* recording and, of course, the upcoming tour. There were new songs like "Dream Lover" and "Hero," along with the hits "Vision of Love" and "I'll Be There," which was joined by the Albany Police Athletic League. Never tell your constable he's out of tune. It was a great show in a beautiful setting.

The music video went Platinum, and many individual songs were released separately.

Christmas Special, St. John the Devine, December 7–8, 1994
Mariah Christmas
The Cathedral of Saint John the Devine

We have recorded many a Christmas-themed performance over the years, Bruce Springsteen's version of "Santa Clause Is Coming to Town" rings a bell, but Mariah's concert at the largest Gothic cathedral in the country really tops them all. It is an incredible acoustic space, originally designed for the massive choirs and grand pipe organ. Musicians like the alto sax player Paul Winter and many other small vocal groups have found success recording there as well.

Mariah Carey with a full band is another story. With the long reverberation and reflection times, it called for lots of tight mixing and direct feeds. That said, I thought that judicious use of the ambient microphones added to the holiday feel.

Mariah's *Merry Christmas* studio album had just been released in late October 1994 and the singles, especially "All I Want for Christmas Is You," went multi-Platinum, along with the album. The video of *Mariah's Christmas*, played out in the magnificent Cathedral of Saint John the Devine, set the stage for all her fans to celebrate with her. There are deluxe anniversary editions that include many of the music performances recorded at Saint John's Cathedral. Maybe I'll finally get to hear them this Christmas!

Sometimes the drama happens in the remote recording truck. We had just finished recording a rehearsal when Mariah was escorted in to meet Mottola. It was Sony Studios protocol that everyone not attached to Mariah must leave the room. Tommy graciously gestured that I may stay. After some conversation, Tommy presented a little black box to Mariah, and she gasped aloud to see two large diamond earrings. It is Christmas after all, and though I didn't speak, I was smiling and looking at Mariah as she tried on the earrings. She looked up, happened to meet my gaze, and froze for a second before turning to whisper to Tommy. He kind of looked at the ceiling and gave me the exit stage left sign.

As it turned out, that would be my last live recording with Mariah.

Mariah Live from Madison Square Garden
The one I couldn't do—competing divas, 1996

It was one of those damned if you do, damned if you don't situations. I got a rather late call from Sony Music for a live Mariah Carey broadcast from Madison Square Garden. Big production, international satellite feed, etc. Unfortunately, I had a long-standing New York Metropolitan Opera recording on those dates, and they book a year in advance for their hugely complicated productions. The only other remote truck acceptable to the Met as a substitute was not available. That's when the phone calls started; he-who-shall-not-be named was upset that I wouldn't abandon the Met Opera for Mariah!

I offered to find another remote truck for her, but it had become an emotional sovereignty issue. Sadly, after all those great shows we recorded for her, that was the end of the calls for me.

But a call did come years later in 2018 from the British company ITV Studios, producers of television and film shows worldwide. They were producing a film called *Mariah: The Diva, the Demons, the Drama*. They had seen my credits on some of her live videos and wanted to interview me on camera. After talking to the producers, I realized they had all the diva stories but wanted a real look at Mariah's live shows that we recorded over the years. I did remember some interesting stories that I didn't have time for here, and there were other interesting interviews with lots of film footage.

Frankly, I had forgotten what a long, tumultuous career she has had and how many recordings and videos she has produced. A total of 200 million records and counting, last I looked. I would recommend the film, if you are a real fan, but otherwise just listen to the music. She is an amazing talent.

Recommended Recordings

Live from the Metropolitan Opera from 1977
IMDB
Try a Die Fledermaus

Mariah MTV Unplugged and *The Live Debut*
1990 Columbia Records

PS
HIGHLY RECOMMENDED *BRITISH DIVA*

Cleo Laine Live at Carnegie Hall, 1973
Cleo Laine Return to Carnegie Hall, 1976

21

WORLD TRADE CENTER 9/11/01

The Concert for New York City

Having spent almost five decades in the New York music business orbit, I was devastated by the terrorist attack on the World Trade Center. By then I was living in the Pennsylvania countryside, far from the chaos of the tragedy, but many of my loved ones and music comrades lived in New York City. It was a fearful time waiting to hear from everyone dear.

PREAMBLE

Before I relate the stories of the post–9/11 memorial concerts, there is a most unusual remote recording to present. In June1978 I was asked to record the filming of a rock band on a helicopter-landing pad. The only problem was that the pad was located on the South Tower of the World Trade Center!

After a site survey I didn't see why not, so my Record Plant remote crew unloaded the contents of the White Truck and rode the elevators up 110 floors to a storage room below the landing pad. We built a control room using the trusty DeMedio console and a pair of MCI JH-24 recorders from Record Plant. I tapped into the local electrical mains and ran hundreds of feet of cable up to the roof. The film crew were all situated up on the roof. Thankfully the June weather stayed warm and dry.

The band, Year One, had been recording at Record Plant, so it was a relatively simple session recorded at night to avoid disturbing the business tenants. They were a loud rocking band; I hope the rest of Manhattan appreciated the live concert! Down in the remote recording control room, I could hear their great performances, but with only one black-and-white spy camera on stage, I couldn't see their lively show. This show was to be part of an ambitious film that already had footage of the band playing in the Grand Canyon and planned on the Great Wall of China for the next concert. I did recently see a video someone posted online of that World Trade Center show, and it was quite good. Sorry we didn't go to China.

Needless to say, when the airplanes struck the towers on 9/11, I shuddered to think of those unfortunate victims trapped on the upper floors and roof as the tower collapsed. I will remember them always. When it became possible, I went down to the remains of the towers to pay my respects. It was a horrendous sight: the twisted remains of the huge towers, reduced to rubble covering the remains of so many victims.

AMERICA IN HEALING WNET/13
RIVERSIDE CHURCH, NEW YORK CITY, SEPTEMBER 16, 2001
A REMEMBRANCE BY DARYL BORNSTEIN

There were numerous concerts and memorial services after 9/11. The ones that occurred immediately after the Twin Towers fell were extremely emotional, and logistically challenging, to say the least.

Several days after 9/11, I received a call from Julie Shapiro, a producer at Channel 13, a PBS affiliate, about putting together a last-minute concert for September 16, at Riverside Church in Manhattan. I needed to find a crew, design, and order a sound system, coordinate with Remote Recording, and act as audio producer.

Finding a crew, designing the sound system, coordinating with the truck, and even getting delivery of the sound system was much easier than I thought it would be given that access to Manhattan, especially by trucks, was extremely limited and the rules in constant flux.

The hard part was finding an available generator because every available one was currently at Ground Zero, supporting the recovery efforts.

Miraculously, and I mean that literally, everything came together, and we loaded in and set up the morning of September 16, 2011, in preparation for what I think was a mid-afternoon live concert.

The main sanctuary at Riverside Church is enormous. The dais is also quite large. And the event would use all of the available performance spaces.

The concert would include numerous clergy speaking from a variety of positions, the Riverside Church chorus, the Riverside Church organ, a dancer from the Alvin Ailey Dance Company, and a cavalcade of music luminaries including violinist Josh Bell, sopranos Susan Graham and Dawn Upshaw, baritone Thomas Hampson, musical theater star Mandy Patinkin, among many other performers who somehow managed to make their way to Riverside Drive and West 120th Street, and found the strength to perform under extreme emotional distress.

If I recall correctly, we had little, if any, rehearsal. Thankfully, we had the best in the business, Skip Kent, onstage to set and remove microphones, Bob Aldridge masterfully mixing a woefully inadequate PA for such a large, reverberant room, and joining me in the Silver Truck, the longtime and first-rate crew of David Hewitt, Phil Gitomer, and Sean McClintock.

Mixing a live event for a live broadcast is challenging under the best of circumstances. Mixing a show less than a week after we watched the two towers fall and, without any substantial rehearsal, requires an iron constitution.

Thankfully, the entire audio crew had worked together for years on every imaginable project and had processes in place for challenges like this, and the show was a complete success.

But what I took away from the day was gratitude to have participated in an important and necessary service in the acknowledgment and remembrance of those who not only lost their lives during the attack, but also the countless heroes who were selflessly digging through the incomprehensible pile of rubble at the other end of Manhattan. I was thankful that my dear friends were available to join me and contribute to the event in ways that are incalculable.

In the world in which we work, the entertainment world, it is easy to get caught up in the drama and the glamour of an awards show or a major rock concert. "America in Healing" was a day of serving the performers who were serving those needing an opportunity to mourn.

Nearly 20 years later, I can still see, hear, and feel what I did in the Silver Truck, watching, and listening, to a heartfelt show unfold, live, for an audience of millions. It is as relevant today, as it was then.

—Daryl Bornstein
Engineer/Producer

THE CONCERT FOR NEW YORK CITY: MADISON SQUARE GARDEN
OCTOBER 20, 2001

This concert was certainly the most powerful musical event I have ever witnessed. It was dedicated to the first responders of New York's Fire and Police departments, who lost their lives trying to save the victims of 9/11. Many survivors and rescue workers, along with families of the fallen, attended.

The concert was originally organized by Paul McCartney and featured many British stars, The Who, Mick Jagger and Keith Richards, and Eric Clapton. US stars Billy Joel, James Taylor, Jay-Z, and Jon Bon Jovi joined actors Harrison Ford, Robert De Niro, and many others to honor their heroes. The Robin Hood Relief Fund was organized to benefit New Yorkers victimized by the 9/11 attack. The 5½ hour concert was broadcast live on VH1 and would also be recorded and rebroadcast later.

More than $35 million was raised that night. A DVD and CD were also produced with Sony Music's net proceeds going to the fund.

I was there as chief engineer on the Silver Truck and Mark Repp did likewise for the MTV truck. We alternated mixes as the acts changed. These are some of the highlights of the concert.

As the opening applause died down, a lone spotlight shone on David Bowie, sitting cross-legged on the lip of the stage. He started playing a simple intro on a little keyboard, and then started singing Simon & Garfunkel's song "America," which was such a brilliant, understated, perfect statement, coming from an immigrant. It brought the house down. He followed that up with a powerful version of his own song "Heroes," with his full band, again a fitting salute to the first responders.

The other mega performance was delivered by Billy Joel, which is detailed in chapter 9.

Eric Clapton is always there for deserving concerts and this time he played "I'm Your Hoochie Coochie Man" with Blues master Buddy Guy. Telling the world don't you mess with us!

The Rolling Stones' Mick Jagger and Keith Richards played a heartfelt version of "Miss You," which the audience gladly helped sing choruses of "Ooh Ooh" and "Aah Aah." Mick gave the lesson to the world, "You Don't Fuck with New York!" They both sang a version of "Salt of the Earth," which was strangely relabeled "Swords of the Earth" on the CD.

It's hard for me to go back and listen to the whole concert, but I have played the Bowie performance of "America" and "Heroes" for friends and family. When words fail me, the music conveys the love and the pain.

Never forget those we lost and those who tried to save them.

THE LAST GIG

George Strait: *The Cowboy Rides Away*

I had actually been retired for a while when my former company, Remote Recording, got a call from famed Nashville engineer and producer Chuck Ainlay. One of Chuck's longtime clients, country superstar George Strait, had decided to retire from touring and wanted to record the last grand finale show. There would be many guest artists joining him on stage for a big country farewell to the road.

Chuck has always worked with the best analog recording studios for George's records, and he wanted a proper analog remote truck for this important show. There are few analog trucks in operation those days because almost all have digital consoles, as do all the video trucks. I had long admired Chuck's recordings and after discussing the complexities of the large-scale concert, we agreed to go all analog with the Millennia and API preamps on stage, using no digital converters until the recorders. Those would be Apogee converters feeding Nuendo recorders. Chuck was also a Nuendo fan and used that system for his many Grammy-winning albums for Mark Knopfler and Dire Straits.

Bringing my old Silver Truck back to full operation would take some doing. Neither the Silver Truck nor I had worked since coming out for Eric Clapton's 4th Crossroads Guitar Festival on April 11–13, 2013, in New York. I had worked on all of those festivals up to that point.

I spent almost a week going over every detail of the 96 channels of Neve and Studer modules, all the outboard gear, patch bays, etc. Analog equipment does not like to sit around unused. Switches, buttons, and relays can oxidize and cause intermittent audio. Maybe I was a bit rusty too and needed some exercise.

The concert at the new AT&T Stadium in Dallas set attendance and gross receipt records for a single show with 110,000 screaming fans. There were so many stars coming out to pay tribute to George, everyone from Martina McBride and Faith Hill to Alan Jackson and Vince Gill.

It was a great show and I thought appropriately titled for both George and me. This would be my last recording with the Silver Studio as I retired from a life on the road. The name of the show was *The Cowboy Rides Away*.

Back in my Record Plant Studio days, producer Jimmy Iovine use to call me "The Long Ranger," a pun on the endless miles we traveled to shows. Youngsters will have to look up *The Lone Ranger*, a classic 1930s' radio hero and later 1950s' television show, to get the cowboy joke. A mighty white stallion, a hearty "Hi-Yo Silver, Away!" To the sound of Rossini's "William Tell Overture!" After having recorded the New York Metropolitan Opera Orchestra play that refrain many times, I guess I can get away with retiring too.

Happy Trails to you all

Recommended Recordings

George Strait
The Cowboy Rides Away: Live from AT&T Stadium
MCA Records Nashville
The William Tell Overture New York Philharmonic Orchestra, Leonard
    Bernstein on YouTube

CODA

I hope you all have enjoyed reading the stories in this book, *On the Road: Recording the Stars in a Golden Era of Live Music*. It's not just a title. When I started accumulating the material for the book, I was amazed at the sheer number of shows we had recorded and the incredible diversity of the music! There were so many more shows than I had room for here. Such a brief period of time, but so much great music! The 1960s through the 1990s, even early 2000s, were indeed, a Golden Era of music, never to occur again.

This has been a priceless musical education for me, I hope you all will look for and enjoy listening to this wide spectrum of classic performances. There are recommended recordings listed with each chapter and many are available in high resolution on the internet.

Please support the live musicians playing in your area as well; gold is for the ears of the listener, not just the gold records hanging on the wall!

Cheers!

David W. Hewitt

INDEX